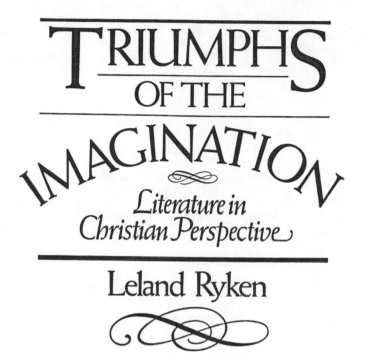

TRIUMPHS OF THE IMAGINATION

Literature in Christian Perspective

Leland Ryken

InterVarsity Press
Downers Grove, Illinois
60515

InterVarsity Press is the book-publishing division
of Inter-Varsity Christian Fellowship, a
student movement active on campus at hundreds of
universities, colleges and schools of
nursing. For information about local and regional
activities, write IVCF, 233 Langdon St.,
Madison, WI 53703.

Distributed in Canada through InterVarsity Press, 1875
Leslie St., Unit 10, Don Mills, Ontario M3B 2M5, Canada.

Acknowledgments

To Pantheon Books, a division of Random House, Inc.,
for permission to quote from Dr. Zhivago,
by Boris Pasternak, trans. Max Hayward and Manya
Harari, copyright 1958.

To Farrar, Straus & Giroux, Inc., for permission
to quote selections from Mystery and Manners by Flannery
O'Connor, selected and edited by Sally and Robert
Fitzgerald. Copyright © 1957, 1961, 1963,
1964, 1966, 1967, 1969 by the Estate of Mary Flannery
O'Connor. Copyright © 1962 by Flannery O'Connor.
Copyright © 1961 by Farrar, Straus and Cudahy (now
Farrar, Straus & Giroux, Inc.). Used by permission
of Farrar, Straus & Giroux, Inc.

To Little, Brown and Company for permission to quote from
poem #341 in The Complete Poems of Emily
Dickinson, edited by Thomas H. Johnson, by permission
of Little, Brown and Company. Copyright 1929 by Martha
Dickinson Bianchi. Copyright © 1957 by Mary L. Hampson.
To Liveright Publishing Corporation for permission to
quote "in Just–" from Tulips and Chimneys
by E. E. Cummings, with the permission of Liveright
Publishing Corporation. Copyright 1923, 1925 and
renewed 1951, 1953 by E. E. Cummings. Copyright © 1973,
1976 by Nancy T. Andrews. Copyright © 1973,
1976 by George James Firmage.

Biblical quotations, except where otherwise noted, are from
the Revised Standard Version of the Bible, copyrighted
1946, 1952, © 1971, 1973.

ISBN 0-87784-583-2
Library of Congress Catalog Card Number: 79-2381

Printed in the United States of America

For Philip,
Margaret
and Nancy

Preface

For the glory of God and for fun. This is the reason a writer of religious drama gave for writing plays. It also summarizes what I have tried to say in this book.

I have written about the nature of literature and its study. Because I write as a Christian, the book covers issues that may be of more interest to Christian readers of literature than to others. I have, however, tried to avoid something that troubles me in most of the books and articles that I have read on the same subject, namely, concentrating on what Christian readers do differently from other readers to the neglect of what Christians share with all readers of literature.

I have also tried to strike a balance between theory and practice. On the one hand I have covered the perennial topics and problems that come up in discussions of how literature relates to religion. Along with this theory I have mingled many illustrations from works of literature.

The last two or three decades have produced a flowering of literary scholarship that has interpreted literature from a religious viewpoint. I have provided a brief survey and critique of Christian literary criticism in the last chapter of the book. Although I have learned much at every turn from other writers on the subject, my immersion in this scholarship as I prepared for this book left me increasingly discontent with some of the trends that I discovered.

There is, for example, a prevailing indifference to the Bible as a guide to answering the question of what constitutes a Christian approach to literature and literary criticism. Surely it is time to insist on a point so obvious that it is easy to ignore—that Christianity is a revealed religion based ultimately on the Bible, not on people's opinions. I am also unfavorably impressed by the way in which religious literary criticism has been preoccupied with (1) contemporary literature to the exclusion of the whole Western tradition and (2) the ideas or content of literature to the neglect of literary form. By reading the existing criticism in the field one would find it hard not to get the impression that a religious approach to literature consists of conducting theological analyses of the plot summaries of modern literature.

In writing this book, therefore, I have asked questions such as the following. Can a Christian read literature for sheer enjoyment and in delight over the beauty of created things? Does a religious approach to literature leave room for analyzing the form of a sonnet or epic? Must the Christian critic of literature always keep his nose to the theological grindstone? Can a Christian reader/critic devote his or her best energies to Homer and Shakespeare and Wordsworth as well as the literature of the last several decades? This book constitutes my answers to these questions.

A critic once wrote an essay objecting to the obscurity of modern literature and concluded the essay with the laconic statement, "I hope I have made myself clear." I have a similar hope about my book. I have been disappointed by the esoteric, obscure and specialized nature of much of the writing on the subject. Most of the books dealing with the relationship between literature and the Christian faith are in no danger of being intelligible to the educated reading public, including college students. My goal in this book is to clarify the world of imaginative literature for anyone who loves to read it.

The answers to the questions that arise when we relate our reading of literature to the Christian faith are, of course, not cut and dried. Different people answer the questions in different ways. If I have answered the questions with what appears to be a too-confident conviction, it is not because I do not respect the right of people to come to conclusions different from my own. It is, rather, because the "party line" has singlemindedly excluded what are to me some of the basics of a Christian approach to literature. I trust that on points where my readers disagree with my conclusions I will have served them well by asking the right questions.

My writing of this book was aided by a grant from the Wheaton College Alumni Association. For permission to reprint material that I had earlier published elsewhere I am grateful to *Christianity Today*.

1 The Necessity of Literature

Literature and Christianity: The Perennial Conflict
The Church as a body has never made up her mind about the
Arts. □ Dorothy L. Sayers, *"Towards a Christian Aesthetic"*
The year was 797. An influential Christian leader named
Alcuin was worried about worldliness in the church. One
of the things that troubled him was the monks' fondness for
fictional stories about heroes such as Beowulf and Ingeld.
Alcuin stated his concern in a letter to a bishop named Higbald. In it he laid down this rule: "Let the words of God be
read aloud at table in your refectory. The reader should be
heard there, not the flute-player; the Fathers of the Church,
not the songs of the heathen." To clinch his point, Alcuin
asked rhetorically, "What has Ingeld to do with Christ?"[1]
Alcuin was not the first person to be alarmed about the
effects of literature on Christians. Six centuries earlier Tertullian had raised the same issue by asking, "What indeed
has Athens to do with Jerusalem?"[2] The identical sentiment
is contained in Jerome's question, "How can Horace go
with the the psalter, Virgil with the gospels, Cicero with the
apostle?"[3] To understand how serious the charges against
literature are, we need to remember the original source of
these questions. The original text, echoed by Jerome, Tertullian and Alcuin, is Paul's call to Christian living in

2 Corinthians 6:14-15, where he asks rhetorically, "What partnership have righteousness and iniquity? Or what fellowship has light with darkness? What accord has Christ with Belial?" It is clear that the medieval objections to imaginative literature are deeply rooted in Christian conviction and feeling.

The tradition that has viewed literature and religion as antagonists has pre-Christian origins, having been initiated in Western thought by Plato. Since some of Plato's claims have been echoed by Christian writers, it will repay our attention to pause a moment over the Greek philosopher's disclaimers against literature.[4] Plato voices three objections to literature: (1) the poet, because he imitates the objects of the sensory world—objects that are themselves imperfect copies of transcendental Ideas—is not only "thrice removed from the truth" but by his fictional imitations "may deceive children or simple persons"[5]; (2) literature has a bad moral effect on its readers because, far from exalting reason, it "feeds and waters the passions instead of drying them up"[6]; (3) literature is not useful, being "only a kind of play or sport" and not to be accepted unless it can be shown that "there is a use in poetry as well as a delight."[7] These three objections—that literature is fictional and deficient in truth, that it leads to immorality and that it is not useful and therefore a waste of time—have never been absent from Western thought after Plato.

The specifically Christian tradition of opposition to literature begins with the Church Fathers. Tertullian, for example, was of the opinion that the arts were demonic in their very essence, having been contrived by the demons "to turn man from the Lord."[8] Tertullian also objects to the fictional nature of literature when he asserts that the Christian hymns are superior to secular drama because they "are not fables, but truths, not artful devices, but plain realities."[9] And like Plato, Tertullian suspects the imaginative pleasure that literature gives, asking simply, "What greater pleasure is there than distaste of pleasure itself, than contempt of all the world can give.... ?"[10] Tertullian's case against literature follows the same pattern as Plato's, centering on the immoral effects, fictional nature and pleasure-giving element of literature.

Augustine also resembles Plato in his attitude toward literature. He fears the emotional effect that drama has upon the viewer, taking the position that to be thus moved is "a miserable madness" and that the more a person is affected emotionally by dramatic actions, "the less free he is from such affections."[11] Augustine believed that literature is instructive in nature but suspect because it teaches vice rather than virtue, and he distrusted the fictional element in literature. Thus he commends Plato for having "absolutely excluded poets from his ideal state, whether they composed fictions with no regard to truth or set the worst possible examples before wretched men under the guise of divine actions."[12] Looking back at his own classical education, Augustine states that "we were forced to go astray in the footsteps of these poetic fictions."[13] The impractical nature of literature also troubled Augustine, for he asserts the superiority of "reading and writing" (that is, instruction in grammar as a tool) to "poetic fictions," and goes on to state that he "sinned" when, as a schoolboy, he disliked the sound of "one and one, two; two and two, four" but loved to hear "the burning of Troy" and "the wooden horse lined with armed men."[14] The usual complaints about literature's fictional character, bad moral influence and impracticality are all here.

The conflict between Christianity and literature continued in the Reformation era. One of the best indexes to this is found in Sir Philip Sidney's *Apology for Poetry* (circa 1580). In replying to Puritan charges, Sidney finds it necessary to defend imaginative literature (which is what he and others in the Renaissance often meant by "poetry") against four familiar charges:

First, that there being many other more fruitful knowledges, a man might better spend his time in than in this. Secondly, that it is the mother of lies. Thirdly, that it is the nurse of abuse, infecting us with many pestilent de-

sires. . . . And lastly, . . . that Plato banished [poets] out of his Commonwealth. [15]
There is plenty of evidence that Sidney was defending imaginative literature against real opponents. William Tyndale, who pioneered in translating the Bible into English, despised Thomas More's *Utopia* as "painted poetry." [16] Since *Utopia* was written in Latin prose, Tyndale could not have meant "poetry" in our definition of the term. What he really had in view with his phrase "painted poetry" was fictional literature. William Perkins denounced "ballads, books of love, and idle discourses" on the ground that they are "nothing but vain enticements and baits unto manifold sins." [17] On the American scene, we find Cotton Mather counseling young men preparing for the ministry that "the powers of darkness have a library among us, whereof the poets have been the most numerous as well as the most venemous authors. Most of the modern plays, as well as the romances, and novels and fictions, which are a sort of poems, do belong to the catalogue of this cursed library." [18]

The views of Richard Baxter can be regarded as a kind of touchstone of Puritan literary theory. Baxter believed that fictional literature "dangerously bewitcheth and corrupteth the minds of young and empty people" and takes "precious time in which much better work might be done." [19] Among the fifteen objections that Baxter lists against the plays of his day are the charges that they are sensual, a poor use of time and guilty of having morally harmed "thousands of young people." [20] Baxter disapproves of literature that falls into the category of "pastimes," which he equates with "time wasting." [21]

The early Puritan attitudes have been surveyed in detail by Lawrence A. Sasek and Russell Fraser. [22] Both surveys provide abundant evidence of the prevailing Puritan attitudes toward imaginative literature. They show that the Puritans were suspicious of fiction (which they equated with falsehood), were convinced that literature had a fearsome potential to be morally corrupting and disapproved of the purely recreational function of literature. The importance of the Puritan work ethic, which elevated useful work above any other human activity except religion, through several centuries of European and American history is too well known to require comment.

Christian resistance to literature has not departed from the scene in our day. Some Christians still oppose the fictional nature of literature, as well as its alleged immorality and uselessness. A decade or two ago one of the Christian giants of our century said in an address at a writer's conference that he thanked God that he had been delivered from the vice of reading novels because novels are fictional and therefore lies. The same sentiment is still occasionally expressed in denominational publications and by some Christian educational institutions. Several years ago in a letter to the editor of a Christian publication a well-known Christian philosopher objected to an article on the contemporary playwright Samuel Beckett, commenting, "The great Christian philosopher Augustine, who was more and more evangelical as he grew older, condemned the theater. The Puritans condemned the theater. . . . Then, tell me why you put such a repulsive article in your issue." A major Christian Sunday-school publishing house drew unexpected criticism when it serialized C. S. Lewis's fantasy story *The Lion, the Witch, and the Wardrobe* in one of its young people's publications. Christian students occasionally ask whether they can justify taking a course in writing poetry or fiction when the time might be spent on something allegedly more useful.

This brief survey of the historical tension between Christianity and imaginative literature makes one thing clear. The arguments against literature are long-standing, widely held and formidable. Nor can the charges be easily swept aside. Any Christian who takes a look at the contemporary paperback fiction displayed in department stores or the list of current movies in American cities can scarcely avoid sensing their incompatibility with the quest for personal holiness. The perennial Christian reservations about literature demand to be taken seriously by anyone who wishes to reconcile literature and the Christian faith and to establish a Christian basis for reading and studying literature.

The Contemporary Crisis
Now, what I want is Facts. Teach these boys and girls nothing but Facts. Facts alone are wanted in life. Plant nothing else, and root out everything else. □ *Thomas Gradgrind, in Charles Dickens's* Hard Times

Quite apart from the perennial Christian resistance to literature, there are contemporary forces that have undermined belief in the value of literature. One of the chief antagonists of literature has been the rise of modern science and the technological orientation of our culture. Technology has placed such a premium on practical results that the alleged nonusefulness of literature and the arts has been taken as an argument against their importance, or even their right to exist. To observe the impact of the technological spirit one need only observe the curriculum changes that have occurred in education during our century. Throughout the history of Western education, literature has held a position of prominence, and often of primacy, in educational programs. It has long since lost that position, and it, along with the other arts, is under increasing attack in our scientifically oriented society.

The bias in favor of the useful sciences is everywhere evident in our culture. It is evident in the allocation that society makes of its time, resources and wealth. It is summed up in the stereotype of the engineer who, if he reads anything besides technical journals, reads biography and history because they are at least true. Several years ago a woman who had majored in literature and had done brilliant academic work at Vassar stated during an interview that when her father and brothers, themselves scientists, heard that she planned to major in literature, they said that she might as well become a chorus girl. College teachers of literature who counsel students are con-

tinually reminded of parents' opposition to such a sup-
posedly impractical subject as literature. The utilitarian
impulse is evident when students whose main interest and
talent are in the area of literature are pressured to major in
science (so they can become nurses) or sociology (so they
can get jobs as social workers) or Christian education (so
they can get jobs at camps). "What can I *do* with a literature major?" is the question that dominates the scene. The
question that fails to get asked is, "What can literature do
with and for me as a person?"

During the past three centuries the human race has
directed enormous energies toward exploring and controlling the external physical world. We have exulted in facts
and statistics. Western culture has emphasized the person
as worker (the Reformation tradition and Marx) and the
person as thinker (Aquinas and Descartes). And the result,
in the words of Harvey Cox, is that "man's celebrative and
imaginative faculties have atrophied. . . . His shrunken
psyche is just as much a victim of industrialization as were
the bent bodies of those luckless children who were once
confined to English factories from dawn to dusk."[23]

In addition to the contemporary obsession with technological usefulness, the place of literature has been eroded
by a growing disregard for the written word. The truth is
that our civilization, with the most advanced means of
communication in the history of the world, and with the
most universal educational system ever available to a culture, is lapsing into relative illiteracy. The problem re-
ceives feature coverage in national magazines from time to
time. Marshall McLuhan, assessing the impact of the electronic media on contemporary society, has long claimed
that literary culture is dead. He writes, "We have moved
into the period of post-literacy."[24] The American poet Karl
Shapiro has written, "I wish to report to you my version of
the degeneration of the literary intelligence and its atten-
dant confusions everywhere in our lives. . . . What is really
distressing is that this generation cannot and does not
read. . . . We are experiencing a literary breakdown which

is unlike anything I know of in the history of letters."[25] Several years ago a Gallup poll found that fifty-eight per cent of Americans had never finished reading a book (other than a textbook or the Bible).[26]

What makes the breakdown of interest in literature particularly devastating for modern society is that we now have an unprecedented amount of leisure time. The subject has been expertly discussed from a Christian perspective by Robert Lee and Harold D. Lehman.[27] Lehman surveys a number of studies that show how difficult it has proven for people to spend their leisure time in creative and enriching ways. This is reinforced by Paul Elmen, who, while not concerned specifically with leisure, analyzes the cultural malaise that is perhaps most evident in many people's leisure life: boredom, the search for distraction, the fear of spending time by oneself, sensuality, escape into comedy, violence and the appeal of horror ("the fun of being frightened").[28] Robert Lee concludes,

Leisure is a part of man's ultimate concern. It is a crucial part of the very search for meaning in life, inasmuch as the social malaise of our time has been diagnosed as anxiety and boredom, alienation and meaninglessness. . . . It is in the realm of free time that these conditions will be brought into bold relief, bringing man to the depths of despair or to the heights of ecstasy and creativity. Increasingly it is in our leisure time that either the meaningfulness or the pointlessness of life will be revealed.[29]

Aristotle in his *Politics* claimed that the aim of education was the enlightened use of leisure time. He lived at a time when education was limited to the aristocracy, but his point is equally valid in a society that believes in universal education. The way in which people use leisure time continues to be one of the most reliable indexes to whether they are truly educated. At a time when the masses of people spend their leisure time in trivial and mindless ways, and sometimes depraved and vicious ways, we need to explore with new seriousness the question of what literature can do for an individual and a society. And by "literature" I mean the great works of the ages that awaken the imagination, enrich the mind and ennoble the spirit.

Such literature is different in quality and effect from the entertainment offered by the mass media. Someone has aptly said that such entertainment provides "a mass audience with a standardized fantasy life," with the result that "life is reduced to a series of shared clichés. People lose their sense of identity, become passive, empty, and conformist, feel safe with mediocrity and uniformity."[30] People who are content with mediocrity in their leisure pursuits will not think with the dignity nor feel with the intensity nor imagine with the greatness that people do when reading Shakespeare or Milton.

The Example of the Bible

The Bible belongs to literature; that is, it is a piece of art. Does it make any difference that the Book we look upon as holy comes to us in literary form rather than in the form of abstract doctrine or systematic theology? . . . The Bible is an imaginative book. ☐ Clyde S. Kilby, "Christian Imagination"

There is an initial consideration that should carry immediate impact for a Christian. Christianity is the most literary religion in the world. It is the religion in which the word has a special sanctity. The Christian tradition is full of stories, poems and hymns. The clearest evidence of the literary bent of Christianity is the Bible.

When we turn to the example of the Bible as the basis for integrating literature and the Christian faith, one generalization that we can make at once is that there is no antithesis between Christianity and literature per se. The tradition of opposing literature and religion is either pre-Christian (Platonic) or postbiblical (the patristic era and following). The Bible itself is emphatically not a part of any such tradition. There is no trace in the Bible of a negative attitude toward literature. It is worthy of note that Paul, writing in a context of Greek culture and consumed with a moral and spiritual vision much higher than paganism, does not share the Platonic antipathy to literature.

On the positive side, the Bible itself is in large part a work of literature. This means primarily two things. It means first that the Bible is experiential and concrete. It is not primarily an expository treatise on systematic theology, though it contains this too. Instead, it continually presents poems and stories about characters. Its stories are full of the usual ingredients of literary narrative—adventure, mystery, brave and wise heroes, beautiful and courageous heroines, villains who get their comeuppance, rescues, quests, suspense, romantic love and pageantry. The poems of the Bible, though they are theological in content, are also about the weather, trees, crops, lions, hunters, rocks of refuge and human emotions such as love and terror and trust and joy. The book of Job is theologically about the problem of why the righteous suffer, but on the experiential level it is about a man covered with sores sitting on an ash heap, about despair and anger, about snow, hail, mountain goats, the ostrich and the horse.

The second way in which the Bible is literary is in its preoccupation with literary form. This is something that needs emphasis, because Christians with a high regard for the Bible as God's Word are often so preoccupied with theological content that they are scarcely aware of the artistic features of the Bible. Yet the concern with literary form is so pervasive that it cannot be ignored without drastically distorting the Bible as a written document. The Bible is an anthology that contains numerous literary forms, including narrative or story, epic, tragedy, satire, lyric poetry, epithalamium, elegy, encomium, proverb, parable, pastoral, prophecy, gospel, epistle, oratory and apocalypse. It becomes clear that biblical example itself affirms the importance and necessity of literature for the Christian life, for Scripture itself *is* literature.

In addition to being literary, the Bible encourages acquaintance with fictional literature and poetry through the example of the New Testament writer Paul. In writing to Titus concerning the Cretans, Paul quotes from Epimenides, a native poet of Crete, following the quotation with the comment, "This testimony is true" (Tit. 1:12, 13). In 1 Corinthians 15:23 Paul quotes from a play entitled *Thais*, written by the Greek dramatist Menander. Most impressive of all is Paul's speech to the Areopagus in Acts 17. Paul's comment that God intends people to "feel after him and find him" may allude to Homer, where the verb "feel after" is used to describe the groping of the blinded Cyclops Polyphemus as he sought the entrance of his cave, and to Plato, who uses the word in the *Phaedo* to describe man's guesses at the truth.[31] Later in the speech (v. 28) Paul quotes from the works of the Greek poets Cleanthes, Aratus and Epimenides, drawing attention to the allusions with the comment, "As even some of your poets have said." Since Paul did not have a *Bartlett's Familiar Quotations* to aid him, we would have to conclude that he had a firsthand acquaintance with Greek literature, including fiction, and knew parts of it by heart. The principle that emerges is that the Bible affirms, in a variety of ways, the value of reading literature.

At a time when the value of the written word is steadily being undermined, the example of the Bible should assure the Christian of the continuing validity of the written word. Literature is, in a special sense, a necessity for the Christian faith, whose content cannot be fully conveyed apart from the word. But the application of the principle is much broader than this. The Bible, by virtue of being literature, must make a Christian reject any viewpoint that questions the importance of literature. There is power in the word. Even if literacy continues to decline in Western civilization as the electronic media progressively dominate culture, it is obvious that someone will control what the media say. The people with the mastery of words will continue to hold the greatest influence over the masses of people. If the right people do not possess the power of words, the wrong people will.

Is Literature Necessary?

Man is by his very nature a creature who not only works and thinks but who sings, dances, prays, tells stories, and celebrates. He is homo festivus. *. . . Man is also* homo fantasia, *the visionary dreamer and mythmaker.* □ Harvey Cox, The Feast of Fools

To ask whether literature is necessary is equivalent to asking what literature is and what functions it performs in society and the life of an individual. Once we are clear about how literature works and what it does, it will be evident that literature is not an option or a luxury but a necessity for human well-being.

So far as the content of literature is concerned, we can say unequivocally that the subject of literature is human experience. Literature as a whole gives its readers the entire range of human experience, not simply intellectual facts or fragments of information. The approach that literature takes to human experience, moreover, is not abstract but concrete. It does not discourse about virtue, for example, but tells a story of a virtuous character in action.

A brief comparison between expository writing and literature will illustrate what I mean by the concrete, experiential content of literature. A newspaper account of the death of a small girl might read something like this:

Lucy Brown, two-year-old daughter of Mr. and Mrs. Paul R. Brown of 1410 Evergreen Drive, passed away at the Good Samaritan Hospital last Tuesday, March 17. Death followed an attack of pneumonia. Interment was at Woodlawn Cemetery.

This account contains the information or objective facts *about* the event. The writer is totally objective, and no emotional meanings come through.

By contrast the following stanza from a poem by Emily Dickinson presents the same experience, death, in terms of how the living who remain actually experience the death of a loved one:

This is the Hour of Lead—
Remembered, if outlived,

As Freezing persons, recollect the Snow—
First—Chill—then Stupor—then the letting go—[32]

The following poem, also by Emily Dickinson, is very similar:

The Bustle in a House
The Morning after Death
Is solemnest of industries
Enacted upon Earth—

The Sweeping up the Heart
And putting Love away
We shall not want to use again
Until Eternity.[33]

We might say that the literary presentation includes all of the human responses to death and feelings of loss that the newspaper account leaves out. That is why Cleanth Brooks theorizes that the literary writer's "primary role in the human economy . . . is to give us an awareness of our world, not as an object viewed in clinical detachment . . . but . . . as it involves ourselves."[34]

The literary description of the world differs from the scientific description of it by being concrete and experiential instead of abstract and analytic. A scientific description of a cold winter night will be similar to this: "Last night's low temperature was recorded as ten degrees below zero. Two inches of snow was measured. The sky was overcast with a cloud cover." The virtue of expository writing is its precision; it refers unambiguously to the body of information about the weather. It gives the facts. What it omits is the qualitative reality of the actual human experience of a cold night. Here is John Keats's poetic rendition of a cold winter night in the opening stanza of his poem *The Eve of St. Agnes:*

St. Agnes' Eve—Ah, bitter chill it was!
The owl, for all his feathers, was a-cold;
The hare limped trembling through the frozen grass,
And silent was the flock in woolly fold:
Numb were the beadsman's fingers, while he told

His rosary, and while his frosted breath,
Like pious incense from a censer old,
Seemed taking flight for heaven.

One of the functions of literature, it is clear, is to hold up some aspect of human experience for the reader's contemplation. Nathan A. Scott has said that the writer's vocation "is to *stare*, to *look* at the created world, and to lure the rest of us into a similar act of contemplation," a viewpoint that Ralph Waldo Emerson expressed memorably when he wrote, "As the eyes of Lyncaeus were said to see through the earth, so the poet turns the world to glass, and shows us all things in their right series and procession."[35]

In addition to being experiential, literature is artistic. For one thing, the content of a work of literature is presented in the form of a novel, a play, a short story, a poem and so forth. Each literary kind, or genre, has additional elements of artistic form, such as unity, pattern or design, centrality, balance, contrast, recurrence, variation, intricacy or complexity, and progression or unified development. All of this is to say that when a writer sits down to write, he asks not only, What do I want to say? but also, How do I want to say it? What kind of literary artifact do I wish to make? Mastery of form is as essential to literature as is significance of content. C. S. Lewis, with his genius for aphorism, has written, "It is easy to forget that the man who writes a good love sonnet needs not only to be enamoured of a woman, but also to be enamoured of the Sonnet."[36]

Literature, then, does two things: it presents human experience for our contemplation, and it offers itself as an object of beauty for our artistic contemplation. The further question is, What value attaches to these functions? I would isolate five values that are available from the reading of imaginative literature.

The experience that a literary work embodies is either like an experience that the reader has had, or it is a new experience. The two kinds of literature have different rationales that commend them for reading. When literature presents an experience different from what we have ourselves known, it offers the possibility of enlarging our being. C. S. Lewis expresses it thus:

> We seek an enlargement of our being. We want to be more than ourselves. Each of us by nature sees the whole world from one point of view with a perspective and a selectiveness peculiar to himself.... We want to see with other eyes, to imagine with other imaginations, to feel with other hearts, as well as with our own.... We demand windows.... This, so far as I can see, is the specific value or good of literature...; it admits us to experiences other than our own.... My own eyes are not enough for me, I will see through those of others.[37]

Literature not only gives us new experiences but also has a recognized power to embody universal human experience. Much literature gives expression to experience that is common to everyone. It is a commonplace that the writer is our representative: he says what we want said, only he says it much better than we can. Emerson puts it well when he writes that "the poet is representative. He stands among partial men for the complete man, and apprises us not of his wealth, but of the common wealth.... For all men live by truth and stand in need of expression."[38] The writer speaks for us, giving form and expression to our feelings and values. This, too, is a value of literature. It allows us to celebrate experience and truth as we have known them. Literature serves this function whenever it leads us to say, "How like real life!"

A third value of literature is that it provides the materials and occasion for recreation or enjoyment. Imaginative literature gives us pleasure. One of its distinctives through the centuries has been that people read poems or listen to stories or watch plays because they want to, not because they have to. Literature carries its own reward and does not have to be a means to a utilitarian end. The pleasures of reading imaginative literature are perhaps more comprehensive than those of any other human activity. Literature gives intellectual pleasure, comparable to that which we feel whenever we encounter ideas that we enjoy. Literature goes beyond this, though, and gives emotional pleasure. It also provides imaginative pleasure because it activates the reader's own imagination and exists, in the final analysis, only in the reader's imagination. Finally, some literature, including the Bible, gives spiritual pleasure. To defend imaginative literature as being recreative, then, is not a trivial claim. Our recreation is one of our most crucial areas of choice, and one in which God expects a responsible exercise of stewardship. To choose enriching kinds of entertainment is not peripheral but essential to the Christian life.

Fourth, reading literature leads to an understanding of human experience. The writer's task is to "freeze" some aspect of human life so that the reader can contemplate it. A close look at anything usually yields a deeper understanding of it. This is what literature does for the thoughtful reader. Great literature offers a heightened and clarified vision of reality, so the reader can return to life with a better understanding of his own world and experience. Literature is a window to reality. And even when a work of literature fails to provide Christian answers to the problems of human experience, it clarifies the human issues to which the Christian faith speaks.

A final value of reading literature is that it is an activity that confirms the uniqueness of man. The ability to contemplate human experience—to stand back from it and ask, "What does it mean?"—is an ability differentiating people from animals and the rest of the visible creation. So, too, is the ability to make something beautiful and enjoy it. G. K. Chesterton has written that "art is the signature of man," that is, it identifies man as man. The statement comes in an essay entitled "The Man in the Cave," in which Chesterton discusses the lessons to be learned from the drawings of animals by early cavemen on the walls of their caves. Chesterton writes, "The simplest lesson to learn in the cavern of the coloured pictures . . . is the simple truth that man does differ from the brutes in kind and not in degree.... When all is said, the main fact that the record of the reindeer men attests... is that the reindeer man could draw and the reindeer could not.... This creature was truly different from all other creatures; because he was a creator as well as a creature."[39]

Are the functions and values of literature that I have cited important? The history of human civilization indicates that they are. There has never been a civilized culture that did not feel the need of producing and enjoying literature. Such universality indicates that literature springs from a basic human impulse and fulfills a basic human need. Literature is not an isolated and eccentric thing, but springs from the most fundamental interests of the human spirit. To put it into a Christian context, people have been created by God with an aesthetic faculty that demands cultivation.

The universality of the artistic impulse has been somewhat obscured by the distorted way in which moderns look at past history. The usual assumption is that human history is a history of technology, an attitude capsulized in Thomas Carlyle's description of man as a "tool-using animal." Yet as Lewis Mumford argues, "This overweighting of tools, weapons, physical apparatus, and machines has obscured the actual path of human development.... Esthetic invention played fully as large a part as practical needs in man's effort to build a meaningful world."[40] Harvey Cox, too, notes that "students of prehistoric man have often said more about man's tools than about his tales. Perhaps this derives from our present obsessive interest in technology. Perhaps it is because clubs and knives remain to be found, although myths disappear. Still, both were there very early.... "[41] The ancient Greeks applied the word "poet" or "maker" equally to the writer and the carpenter, while Genesis 4:20-22 attributes the advance of civilization not only to mastery of agriculture and "instruments of bronze and iron," but also to the playing of "the lyre and pipe."

The necessity of the arts has been articulated with great

conviction by Herbert Read. In one of his best essays, Read observes that "all the way down the long perspective of history it is impossible to conceive of a society without art... until we come to the modern epoch." After discussing the modern "insensitivity to the arts" and the corresponding "atrophy of sensibility," Read proceeds to argue thus:

> I believe that there is only one way of saving our civilization and that is by so reforming its constituent societies that... the concrete sensuous phenomena of art are once more spontaneously manifested in our daily lives. I have called this reform 'education through art.'... An education through art does not fit human beings for the mindless and mechanical actions of modern industry; it does not reconcile them to a leisure devoid of constructive purpose.... It aims to create 'stir and growth' everywhere, to substitute for conformity and imitation in each citizen an endowment of imaginative power.[42]

I would wish to place Read's thesis in a Christian context, but having done so I find myself in great agreement with what he has said. Surely the basic problem of modern civilization is its alienation from God, and surely the only thing that can save society is God's redemptive activity in Christ. To claim, as Read does, that "aesthetic education develops ethical virtue"[43] is to claim for the arts something that only the Holy Spirit does in regeneration and sanctification. But there are, in addition to the ultimate cause, secondary causes for our miserable plight in the twentieth century, and one of these is our culture's unwillingness to grant importance to the artistic enterprise. Our civilization has not seen beauty as a value, and as a result it has desecrated God's good earth, threatening the entire human race. Our civilization has not regarded the artistic imagination as a value, and as a result it has reduced people to cogs in a machine and has made them unthinking, passive robots. Our civilization has not regarded artistic enjoyment as a value, and as a result it has reduced human experience to a matter of practical efficiency, devoid of the kinds of imaginative and contemplative activity that people were created to experience.

What kind of knowledge is most worth having? That is really the question I am asking. The scientific or "thought" disciplines give us primarily knowledge about the external world of nature, society and persons. Literature gives primarily knowledge of human values. Literature is perhaps the most accurate repository of information about what people value, about what Northrop Frye calls "man's views of the world he wants to live in, of the world he does not want to live in, of his situation and destiny and heritage, of the world he is trying to make and of the world that resists his efforts."[44] Literature is the language of concern—a vision not simply of what exists in the world but a vision of reality as perceived by a valuing being. A nature poem, for example, is not about nature but about nature as valued by a person. Shakespeare's *Macbeth* is not about crime but about the human horror at the criminal capabilities of the human heart.

We need both kinds of knowledge. We must know about objective reality (including supernatural reality) in order to live well. But we also need to know about reality as perceived and valued and experienced by the human creature. And where do we find such a vision? Chiefly, it seems to me, in the record of what people have *imagined* —in their stories and poems and plays. It is here that we find the most articulately organized vision of human fears and longings, "of what man wants and does not want."[45] In most cases literature deals with the same subject matter (nature, society, God) as other disciplines do. What distinguishes literature is its attitude or approach to these realities. Literature presents reality, not as it objectively exists, but as it is of concern to people. Literature embodies "man's concern for his world."[46] The best expressions of this concern are the constructs of the human imagination, including poems and stories.

Is literature necessary? It is necessary as long as it remains important for people to understand human nature, human values, human fears and longings and the meaning of human life in this world. The literature of the imagination is an indispensable guide to all of these things. For a Christian, literature is necessary as an expression, in a clarified form, of the human situation to which the Christian faith speaks.

John Milton, in his treatise *Of Education*, defines the goal of education as regaining what was lost with the Fall and becoming like God. And what is God like? Among other things, he is the greatest Imaginer, the Creator and Maker and the Word. When God planted the first garden for the first people, he put into the garden not only every tree that is "good for food" but also every tree that is "pleasant to the sight" (Gen. 2:9). The requirements for human well-being have never changed from that moment. An education that helps a person to become like God and live well in God's world is both functional and artistic, a training of both the practical intellect and the artistic imagination.

Milton defines "a complete and generous education" as one that equips a person to perform "all the offices, both private and public," that a person might be called on to perform in life. Contemporary education is preoccupied with the public roles, and usually only one of them, the economic one of job or vocation. But what about the private roles? They include being a good spouse or roommate or parent or friend. And they include the most private world of all—the inner life of the mind and imagination. An education is complete and generous when—and only when—it equips people to spend a meaningful evening at home, or to fill their leisure time with enriching rather than mindless pursuits, or to adorn the mansion of their mind and imagination with noble furnishings. A love of great literature is one of the things that fulfills this ideal.

2 Literature and the Quest for Beauty

A Neglected Dimension of Literary Study
A universe having no other function than to be beautiful would be a glorious thing indeed. Those for whom that notion means nothing should not carp at others for dreaming about it and enjoying, in the beauty of works of art, a glimpse of it. □ *Etienne Gilson*, The Arts of the Beautiful

I have placed this chapter on beauty early in the book for an important reason: beauty is the dimension of literature that is always getting shortchanged in literary criticism. The people who talk about the pursuit of beauty are those interested in art rather than literature. This is not to say that literary critics have ignored literary form. Formalist literary criticism has long since established technique, and not simply ideas, as the domain of literary analysis. But what do these critics perceive as the function of literary technique? Not beauty, but vision, or meaning, or communication of content. The emphasis has been on form in the service of content. I do not question that literary form serves as a vehicle for presenting human experience and ideas and feelings. But I am equally convinced that one of the values of literature is its nurture of our sense of beauty. And by "beauty" I mean the whole broad range of artistic excellence, not the specific style that a given age has agreed to call beautiful.

The importance and nature of artistic beauty in literature will become clear when we compare literature with the other arts, such as music and painting. The neglect of beauty by literary scholars is in large part a result of their indifference to aesthetics in general.[1] But to ignore the correspondences between literature and the fine arts and to neglect the element of beauty in literature is to cut oneself off from the enjoyment of one of the important ingredients of literature and something that writers labor to build into their works.

What do aesthetic theorists mean by beauty, anyway? Observe the common emphasis in three well-known definitions of beauty:

Beauty is pleasure regarded as the quality of a thing. ... This pleasure must not be in the consequence of the utility of the object or event, but in its immediate perception.... Beauty is ... a positive value that is intrinsic; it is a pleasure.[2]

Any formal organization or pattern which is intrinsically satisfying may be said to possess beauty.[3]

The beautiful ... is *'id quod visum placet,'* that which, being seen, pleases.... Beauty consists of intuitive knowledge, and delight.[4]

These definitions agree that beauty consists of pleasure or enjoyment of an object in itself, not for any usefulness that the object may have beyond itself. If the object is a poem or story, its beauty is that part of it which pleases a reader by its sheer craftsmanship, quite apart from what the reader might find useful in its ideas or social importance. Artistic pleasure can be differentiated from other types of pleasure by its source, namely, a work of literature or art or music. In the words of Ernst Cassirer, "If art is enjoyment it is not the enjoyment of things but enjoyment of forms."[5] Artistic pleasure, in short, derives from artistic form, and literary pleasure, to make it specific, derives from literary form.

To insist on beauty as a legitimate domain of literature

will, I fear, seem to some readers to surround literature with a threatening cloud of mystery. Most people are comfortable with ideas and abstract thought, and they therefore approach literature solely in terms of its ideas and paraphrasable content. How, they wonder, does one approach literature in terms of literary form and beauty and technique?

The fear is quite unwarranted. The dimension of literature that I wish to clarify in this chapter is in fact something that most people respond to in literature, whether or not they are aware of it. One of the great fallacies that underlies most people's statements about literature is that the reason they read novels and poems or go to see plays is to get ideas and insights. Now it is no doubt true that *after* we have read a novel or seen a play we tend to reflect upon it in terms of its intellectual content or view of life. But it is, in my view, quite preposterous to claim that the reason why we read novels or attend plays or watch television dramas *in the first place* is to be instructed or to increase our knowledge.

The overwhelming majority of people go to literature for entertainment and enjoyment. They regard literature as a leisure time pursuit, which is, after all, what it is. People do not read a short story for the same reason that they attend a church service, or watch a television drama for the same reason that they attend a lecture, or go to a play to achieve the same thing that prompts them to read an informational book. People who say they read imaginative literature for improvement or for its ideas are not content with a list of the ideas in a work of literature but insist on the pleasures of the poem or story or play itself.

There has been a lot of misunderstanding and some hypocrisy on this point, and these should not be allowed to stand in the way of coming to understand and value literature as an object of beauty and a source of pleasure or enjoyment. People who do really go to see a play with the same didactic expectations they bring to a sermon or lecture do a double injustice to themselves: as individuals they regard even their recreation as a form of work, and as literary critics they must plead guilty to C. S. Lewis's observation that much bad criticism results from trying "to get a work-time result out of something that never aimed at producing more than pleasure."[6]

Beauty and Pleasure in Biblical Perspective

For as God is infinitely the greatest Being, so he is allowed to be infinitely the most beautiful and excellent: and all the beauty to be found throughout the whole creation, is but the reflection of the diffused beams of that Being who hath an infinite fulness of brightness and glory; God . . . is the foundation and fountain of all being and all beauty. □ *Jonathan Edwards,* The Nature of True Virtue

As image-bearer of God, man possesses the possibility both to create something beautiful, and to delight in it. □ *Abraham Kuyper, "Calvinism and Art"*

Why should a person feel it important to cultivate his capacity for literary beauty? Is there any world view or aesthetic theory that would make the pursuit of beauty a compelling motive in a person's life? It is my conviction that a Christian world view and Christian aesthetic make the pursuit of beauty an obligation, not an option.

A Christian aesthetic must be based on more than human opinion, helpful and even indispensable as some of these opinions are. The person who believes that God's revelation as embodied in the Bible and in Christ tells the truth about reality can rest assured that it will tell the truth about art and literature, too. There are two ways in which the Bible functions as the groundwork for a Christian philosophy of literature—through doctrine and example. A Christian aesthetic, then, rests partly on the answer to the question, "What does the Bible say about the pursuit of beauty and pleasure?"

The Bible teaches that beauty is an attribute or perfection of God and that he is the source of beauty, just as he is the source of truth. We must conclude this, it seems to me, even though the word translated "beauty" in English versions of the Bible encompasses a variety of Hebrew terms and includes the idea of spiritual as well as physical or artistic beauty. David "asked of the LORD ... to behold the beauty of the LORD" (Ps. 27:4), suggesting not only that beauty is an attribute of God but that beholding it is the desire of the believer. Similarly, the writer of Psalm 90:17 prayed, "Let the beauty of the LORD our God be upon us" (KJV). Zechariah exclaimed regarding God, "How great is his goodness, and how great is his beauty!" (Zech. 9:17 KJV).

In the prophecy of Ezekiel we read that God gave to his people the gift of his beauty, which was perfect until people in their sinfulness desecrated it: "And your renown went forth among the nations because of your beauty, for it was perfect through the splendor which I had bestowed upon you, says the Lord GOD. But you trusted in your own beauty.... You also took your fair jewels of my gold and of my silver, which I had given you, and made for yourself images of men" (Ezek. 16:14-15, 17). From such a passage we can infer that beauty is a quality or possession of God, that he bestows it as a gift, and that, as with all of God's gifts, people can either use beauty to God's glory or defile it by making it the object of religious devotion.

As an attribute of God, beauty is sometimes mentioned along with other divine qualities, suggesting that it is an inseparable part of God's nature and spiritual perfection. The command to "worship the LORD in the beauty of holiness" (KJV), or "the splendour of holiness" (NEB), occurs three times in the Old Testament (1 Chron. 16:29; Ps. 29:2; 96:9). Holiness and beauty are similarly joined in the statement that "our holy and our beautiful house, where our fathers praised thee, is burned up with fire" (Is. 64:11). Jehoshaphat is said to have appointed singers to "praise the beauty of holiness" (2 Chron. 20:21 KJV). A similar joining of holiness and beauty occurs in God's command to Moses to "make holy garments for Aaron your brother, for glory and for beauty" (Ex. 28:2).

Scripture also asserts that God created a beautiful universe and that the creation reflects his own nature. The creation account in Genesis tells us that "the earth was without form" (Gen. 1:2). The divine act of creation consisted of filling the earth with a host of beautiful forms—trees and mountains and flowers and animals and people. God's concern that people live in a world that is beautiful as well as functional is evident from the description of how in the Garden of Eden "the LORD God made to grow every tree that is pleasant to the sight and good for food" (Gen. 2:9). The beauty of God's created universe, even in its fallen condition, is regarded by biblical writers as a picture of God's beauty and craftsmanship. A biblical poet declared, "The heavens are telling the glory of God; and the firmament proclaims his handiwork" (Ps. 19:1). That God, in his role as Creator, is a craftsman with an awesome regard for beauty is equally clear from the descriptions of the new heaven and the new earth (Rev. 21), just as all the biblical descriptions of heaven portray it as a place of transcending beauty.

The Bible gives reason to believe that God not only creates but also takes pleasure in contemplating the beauty of his creation. We read in Genesis 1 that after each of the days of creation "God saw that it was good." And after the act of creation was completed, "God saw everything that he had made, and behold, it was very good" (Gen. 1:31). We can infer that God experienced delight and satisfaction in contemplating the perfection and beauty of what he had made. Abraham Kuyper has commented, "After the Creation, God saw that all things are good. Imagine that every human eye were closed and every human ear stopped up, even then the beautiful remains, and God sees it and hears it."[7]

The lesson to be learned from the Bible's portrait of God as Creator is that God values beauty as well as utility. He did not create a purely functional world. From a utilitarian point of view God did not have to create a world filled with colors and symmetrical forms. He could have made everything a drab gray color, or he could have created people colorblind. Surely God could have made trees whose leaves do not turn to beautiful colors in the fall of the year, or a world in which all flowers are brown in color or grass that is gray instead of green. The biblical picture of God is that he made provision for the quality of human life, not simply its survival. He is pictured as desiring that people will lead an enjoyable earthly life, not merely a utilitarian existence. We might say that the biblical view of creation encourages us to believe that artistic beauty needs no justification for its existence, any more than a happy marriage does, or a bird, or a flower, or a mountain or a sunset. These things have meaning because God made them. Artistic beauty has meaning in itself because God thought it good to give beauty to people, quite apart from any consideration of practical usefulness. Abraham Kuyper has written that "the beautiful... has an objective existence, being itself the expression of a Divine perfection.... We know this from the creation around us... for how could all this beauty exist, except created by One Who preconceived the beautiful in His own Being, and produced it from His own Divine perfection?"[8]

If the biblical doctrine of creation is the chief basis for a Christian theory of beauty, the related doctrine that calls for emphasis is that people are created in the image of God. When we first encounter this idea in Scripture (Gen. 1:26-27), God has not yet been portrayed as Redeemer or the God of providence or the covenant God or the God of moral truth. He has been portrayed only as Creator. In its immediate narrative context, therefore, the doctrine of the image of God in people emphasizes that people are, like God, makers. This biblical doctrine of the image of God in people is the religious or theological reason why people write literature and paint pictures and compose music. They create because they have been endowed with God's image. This, in turn, deflects the ultimate praise for literary achievement from people to God, as Christian writers have acknowledged and as pagan poets have perhaps hinted when they invoked the muses to inspire them.

The poet Chad Walsh has said that the writer "can honestly see himself as a kind of earthly assistant to God (so can the carpenter), carrying on the delegated work of creation, making the fullness of creation fuller."[9] To delight in the work of the human imagination is to value the image of God in people, and to write imaginative literature is to express that image.

A final repository of biblical teaching about artistic beauty is the various accounts of the Old Testament places of worship. These passages, too, portray God as the source of beauty. God is pictured as having a concern for more than functional practicality when we read that it was God himself "who put such a thing as this into the heart of the king, to beautify the house of the LORD" (Ezra 7:27). The Hebrew worshiper could declare regarding his God that "strength and beauty are in his sanctuary" (Ps. 96:6), and if we were to have asked whether the beauty that he sensed at the temple was a quality of the God whom he worshiped there or of the temple surroundings, he would probably have replied that both were a part of his total experience. In prophesying the restoration of Israel, God, speaking through Isaiah, is recorded as saying, "The glory of Lebanon shall come to you, the cypress, the plane, and the pine, to beautify the place of my sanctuary; and I will make the place of my feet glorious" (Is. 60:13).

The account of the building of the tabernacle reinforces the idea of God as the source of beauty and the dispenser of artistic talent to people. Commenting on the tabernacle, Moses stresses that it was God who had called Bezalel and "filled him with the Spirit of God, with ability, with intelligence, with knowledge, and with all craftsmanship, to devise artistic designs, to work in gold and silver and bronze, in cutting stones for setting, and in carving wood, for work in every skilled craft" (Ex. 35:31-33). Moses makes an identical claim for the other artisans who beautified the tabernacle (Ex. 35:35). And after pages describing the artistic beauty of the tabernacle, we read again that the making of this beautiful structure was nothing less than the outworking of God's creative imagination: "According to all that the LORD had commanded Moses, so the people of Israel had done all the work. And Moses saw all the work, and behold, they had done it; as the LORD had commanded, so had they done it" (Ex. 39:42, 43).

All of these Old Testament passages encourage us to believe that beauty is divine in its origin. We can infer the same thing from the broader principle stated in the New Testament that "every good endowment and every perfect gift is from above, coming down from the Father of lights" (Jas. 1:17). A little reflection will suggest, moreover, that if God is perfect in all his being, as the biblical writers portray him, it must follow that God is the source of beauty rather than ugliness.

In view of the biblical emphasis on beauty it is most unfortunate that an influential theorist in the Christian tradition should write that "beauty is not a biblical notion or term" and that "the Scriptures speak . . . very little or not at all of beauty."[10] Even worse is the statement of a Christian scholar who speaks of "the curse of beauty."[11] Such viewpoints do not accurately reflect the Bible's comments, direct and indirect, about artistic beauty, and they represent the kind of thinking that has hampered the formation of a truly Christian aesthetic.

Even the example of the Bible, as distinct from its doctrinal ideas, affirms the value of beauty. God could have revealed himself and communicated his truth to people in a book devoid of literary beauty. Instead, we have the Bible, a book that a famous antagonist of biblical religion called "unquestionably the most beautiful book in the world."[12] If the message were all that mattered in the Bible, we would be left wondering whether the biblical poets did not have something better to do with their time than putting their utterances into the form of poetic parallelism and inventing apt metaphors. Biblical example leads us to conclude that in God's economy they did not have something better to do than be artistic to the glory of God.

The Bible endorses pleasure as thoroughly as it approves

of beauty. Pleasure and its synonyms are, for example, one of the recurrent themes in the Psalms. The writer of Psalm 16 rejoices in the fact that "the lines have fallen for me in pleasant places" (v. 6) and asserts that at God's "right hand are pleasures for evermore" (v. 11). For another poet the "harp with the psaltery" is "pleasant" (Ps. 81:2 KJV). And another psalm declares about God's people, "They feast on the abundance of thy house, and thou givest them drink from the river of thy delights" (Ps. 36:8).

One of the unifying themes of the book of Ecclesiastes is the contrast between the false, purely humanistic pursuit of pleasure and the legitimate, God-oriented quest for pleasure. Two of the key assertions about the legitimacy of pleasure when it is placed in a context of faith in God are these:

> I know that there is nothing better for them than to be happy and enjoy themselves as long as they live; also that it is God's gift to man that every one should eat and drink and take pleasure in all his toil. (Eccles. 3:12, 13).

> Behold, what I have seen to be good and to be fitting is to eat and drink and find enjoyment in all the toil with which one toils under the sun the few days of his life which God has given him, for this is his lot. Every man also to whom God has given wealth and possessions and power to enjoy them, and to accept his lot and find enjoyment in his toil—this is the gift of God. (Eccles. 5:18, 19).

These same sentiments are reiterated in a classic New Testament passage in which Paul comments on wealthy people. Paul advises Timothy, "Charge them that are rich in this world, that they be not highminded, nor trust in uncertain riches, but in the living God, who giveth us richly all things to enjoy" (1 Tim. 6:17 KJV). This key verse establishes three important principles: (1) God is the giver of all good things, (2) he gives people these things to enjoy, and (3) the misuse of them consists not in enjoyment of them but in trusting them or making idols of them.

The biblical doctrine of heaven also exalts pleasure. If heaven is the place where there is no more pain (Rev. 21:4), C. S. Lewis can correctly assert that "all pleasure is in itself a good and pain in itself an evil; if not, then the whole Christian tradition about heaven and hell and the passion of our Lord seems to have no meaning."[13]

No one could have lived a busier life than Jesus did during the years of his public ministry. Yet he did not reduce life to continuous work or evangelism. He took time to enjoy the beauty of the lily and to meditate on the meaning of life. If we could arrange the Gospel accounts of Jesus' habitual activities into a series of portraits, one of them would be a picture of Jesus attending a dinner or party. We read about Jesus eating dinner with Matthew (Mt. 9:10), a Pharisee (Lk. 7:36), "a ruler who belonged to the Pharisees" (Lk. 14:1), Zacchaeus (Lk. 19:1-10), and Mary, Martha and Lazarus (Jn. 12:1, 2). He turned water into wine to keep a wedding party going (Jn. 2:1-10). By his example, Jesus consecrated pleasure and enjoyment, and gave a basis for our agreeing with John Calvin that "if we ponder to what end God created food, we shall find that he meant not only to provide for necessity but also for delight and good cheer."[14]

A person's attitude toward pleasure is actually a comment on his or her estimate of God. To assume that God dislikes pleasure and enjoyment is to charge him with being sadistic toward his creatures. The Bible, of course, does not allow such a conclusion. As Norman Geisler writes, "God is not a celestial Scrooge who hates to see his children enjoy themselves. Rather, he is the kind of Father who is ready to say, 'Let us eat and make merry; for this my son was dead and is alive again; he was lost and is found' (Lk. 15:24)."[15]

All that I have said about the Bible's approval of beauty and pleasure needs, of course, to be qualified. It would be easy to adduce dozens of biblical passages that make it clear that beauty and pleasure can be used in evil and destructive ways. These qualities are created or given by God and are good in principle. Like any of God's gifts, they can be perverted to a bad end by fallen people. That is why one of Dostoyevsky's literary characters can say that beauty is the battlefield where God and the devil fight for the human heart and why Aldous Huxley can write that "as a matter of plain historical fact, the beauties of holiness have often been matched and indeed surpassed by the beauties of unholiness."[16] What we are talking about, though, is the abuse of something, not its inherent nature.

What does the biblical affirmation of beauty and pleasure have to do with the reading of literature? Primarily it validates the enjoyment of the imaginative beauty of literary form as a Christian activity. Scripture tells us that people are created in the image of God. This means, among other things, that people possess the ability to make something beautiful and to delight in it. Given this biblical aesthetic, when we enjoy the beauty of a sonnet or the magnificent artistry of an epic or the fictional inventiveness of a novel, we are enjoying a quality of which God is the ultimate source and performing an act similar to God's enjoyment of the beauty of his own creation. To the question, "How do we read literature to the glory of God?" one good answer is, "By enthusiastically enjoying the artistic beauty of the literature that we read, recognizing God as the ultimate source of the beauty that we enjoy."

The way to show gratitude for a gift is to enjoy it. Any parent knows that the only real gratitude he or she desires from a child who has received a gift is simply the enthusiastic enjoyment of the gift. If artistic beauty is, as the Bible claims, a gift of God, we can scarcely demonstrate our gratitude for the gift any more adequately than by using and enjoying it. The task of literature is here identical to that of the other arts, namely, to enrich the human capacity for appreciating that which is beautiful. And in this the arts, as part of God's creation, help to awaken a person's lively sensitivity to beauty in all of creation, including the realm of nature.

If the act of enjoying something beautiful seems either

blameworthy or trivial, it is because we have fallen prey to an unbiblical attitude, whether it be derived from Platonism or asceticism or the Puritan work ethic (which holds that only hard work is a legitimate use of time) or scientific utilitarianism. It is a fallacy to suppose either that pleasure is wrong or that an activity must be directly useful, in a utilitarian sense, in order to be considered worthwhile. God has created people with the ability to enjoy, in a purely contemplative act, that which is beautiful, even as God does.

In view of the Bible's affirmation of pleasure and enjoyment I must confess my dismay at the published statements of aesthetic theorists, some of them Christians, who speak of artistic enjoyment in a derogatory manner. One prominent critic speaks slightingly of "mere aesthetic pleasure." Another talks about "the trivial notion that art is intended simply for pleasure and entertainment." And yet another states that "reading a work of fiction as an artistic accomplishment... is not relevant to ordinary human concerns." In the whole body of literary theory, ancient and modern, I have seen few writers who do not denigrate the specifically entertaining function of literature. But this is surely wrong, based on the unwarranted assumption that beauty and enjoyment are somehow ignoble.

C. S. Lewis has argued convincingly that the ability simply to enjoy literature is precisely what separates the Christian from at least some non-Christians. He writes,

> The Christian will take literature a little less seriously than the cultured Pagan: he will feel less uneasy with a purely hedonistic standard for at least many kinds of work. The unbeliever is always apt to make a kind of religion of his aesthetic experiences.... But the Christian knows from the outset that the salvation of a single soul is more important than the production of all the epics and tragedies in the world.... He has no objection to comedies that merely amuse and tales that merely refresh.... We can play, as we can eat, to the glory of God.[17]

If, in a Christian view of things, everything that God has created is not self-contained but points toward him, Ralph Waldo Emerson was not quite correct when he wrote that "Beauty is its own excuse for being."[18] But surely Emerson came much closer to the truth than many literary theorists and many Christians.

The Artistic Beauty of Poetry

But what then does this extra quality of verse . . . do for us? It gives us, certainly, an added delight; it is, when it is well done, more fun. Paradise Lost is much more fun written in blank verse than it would be in prose, or is so to anyone capable of enjoying that particular kind of fun. Let us have all the delights of which we are capable. □ Charles Williams, Reason and Beauty in the Poetic Mind

Artistic beauty consists of the elements of artistic form that literature and the other arts share. DeWitt H. Parker lists these as the elements of artistic form: (1) organic unity, or unity in variety (every part contributes to the whole); (2) theme (a central motif or pattern or idea that unifies the work); (3) thematic variation (elaboration of the central theme in different ways); (4) balance (consisting of contrast or symmetry or repetition); (5) evolution (the unified progression from beginning to end); (6) hierarchy (subordination of parts to the main theme).[19] D. W. Gotshalk identifies harmony (consisting of repetition or recurrence and gradation or partial similarity), balance (consisting of symmetry and contrast), rhythm (patterned movement), centrality (a dominant theme) and development as the elements of artistic form.[20]

These artistic principles are the basis of all the arts, which differ only with regard to their medium. Music presents these elements through the medium of sound, painting through the medium of color and texture and literature through the medium of words. I wish to illustrate what I mean by the beauty of literary form with an analysis of both poetry and story. The three poems that I have selected come from antiquity, the Renaissance and the modern period.

Psalm 1. My first example is the ostensibly simple poem
that opens the book of Psalms in the Old Testament:

1	Blessed is the man
2	who walks not in the counsel of the wicked,
3	nor stands in the way of sinners,
4	nor sits in the seat of scoffers;
5	but his delight is in the law of the LORD,
6	and on his law he meditates day and night.
7	He is like a tree
8	planted by streams of water,
9	that yields its fruit in its season,
10	and its leaf does not wither.
11	In all that he does, he prospers.
12	The wicked are not so,
13	but are like chaff which the wind drives away.
14	Therefore the wicked will not stand in the judgment,
15	nor sinners in the congregation of the righteous;
16	for the LORD knows the way of the righteous,
17	but the way of the wicked will perish.

Artistic form involves *pattern,* and Psalm 1 is carefully
structured as a sequence of alternating positive and negative statements. The poet begins on the immensely positive note conveyed by the conventional biblical form
known as the beatitude: "Blessed is the man." This is followed by three parallel clauses that define the godly person
negatively, in terms of what he does not do:

who walks not in the counsel of the wicked,
nor stands in the way of sinners,
nor sits in the seat of scoffers.

This negative description is balanced by a positive description:

but his delight is in the law of the LORD,
and on his law he meditates day and night.

The next unit contains a sequence of positive-negative-

positive statements:
> He is like a tree
> planted by streams of water,
> that yields its fruit in its season,
> and its leaf does not wither.
> In all that he does, he prospers.

The subsequent assertion about the wicked has a negative-positive pattern:
> The wicked are not so,
> but are like chaff which the wind drives away.

This is followed by a negative description:
> Therefore the wicked will not stand in the judgment,
> nor sinners in the congregation of the righteous.

The last two lines culminate the pattern of alternating statements by describing the positive results of godliness and the negative results of wickedness:
> for the LORD knows the way of the righteous,
> but the way of the wicked will perish.

What do we make of this carefully designed alternation between positive and negative statements? Whatever its thematic importance may be, the patterned movement of the poem satisfies our artistic instinct for order and shapeliness and design. I would go so far as to claim that in any poem there is a purely artistic element, quite apart from the content of the poem, and that this purely artistic ingredient is part of the beauty that every poet in some measure communicates through his form, whatever the subject matter may be.

In addition to the alternation between positive and negative statements, Psalm 1 has an envelope structure. Lines 1-4 contain two main images—the path or way and the assembly. These images are also present at the end of the poem, in lines 14-17. In the middle the poet uses two nature or harvest images—the tree that produces fruit and the chaff that the wind blows away in the process of winnowing. This A-B-A image pattern is a further aspect of the poem's artistry or symmetry.

Contrast is also part of the architecture of Psalm 1. The

poem is a prolonged contrast between two ways of life, the godly and the wicked. Or, since the poem belongs to a timeless type known as the character sketch, the poem can be viewed as a contrast between two types of people. The psalm is also based on the contrast between blessing and judgment.

Unity is an important part of the artistry of a poem. Psalm 1 has three image patterns that unify the poem. They are the image of the path or way, the image of the assembly and harvest imagery. The idea of choice also unifies the poem, since the contrast between the two ways (the godly and the wicked) focuses attention on the necessity to choose between them.

Balance is an important part of poetic form, especially in Hebrew or biblical poetry. Biblical poetry is based on the principle known as parallelism. Parallelism consists of a construction of two or more lines in which the second or third lines balance the first, either by repeating the thought in different words by completing a thought that was left incomplete in the first line or by introducing a contrast. Lines 2-4 of Psalm 1 are an example of synonymous parallelism, in which the lines repeat the same idea in different words:

> who walks not in the counsel of the wicked,
> nor stands in the way of sinners,
> nor sits in the seat of scoffers.

Lines 14-15 illustrate the same technique:

> Therefore the wicked will not stand in the judgment,
> nor sinners in the congregation of the righteous.

Antithetic parallelism, in which the second line states the truth of the first in a contrasting way, is present in the last two lines of the poem:

> for the LORD knows the way of the righteous,
> but the way of the wicked will perish.

A final aspect of the artistic form of the poem is its unified *progression*. Lines 1-6 introduce the reader to two kinds of persons. Lines 7-13 elaborate the description through the use of two similes, which describe what happens to the two persons. Lines 14-17 utter a final verdict on the ways of life by describing the future judgment of the two kinds of people.

It is evident, it seems to me, that the writer of Psalm 1 not only had something he wished to say but was concerned with saying it in a beautiful and artistic way. He asked, whether consciously or instinctively, "What kind of poem do I wish to make? How can I make my utterance beautiful and eloquent?"

John Milton, Sonnet 19. Milton's "Sonnet 19" is an occasional poem written upon his becoming blind at the age of forty-three or forty-four. It reads as follows:

1   When I consider how my light is spent,
2   Ere half my days, in this dark world and wide,
3   And that one talent which is death to hide
4   Lodged with me useless, though my soul more bent
5   To serve therewith my Maker, and present
6   My true account, lest he returning chide,
7   "Doth God exact day-labor, light denied?"
8   I fondly ask. But Patience, to prevent
9   That murmur, soon replies: "God doth not need
10   Either man's work or his own gifts; who best
11   Bear his mild yoke, they serve him best. His state
12   Is kingly: thousands at his bidding speed,
13   And post o'er land and ocean without rest;
14   They also serve who only stand and wait."

The poem is a Petrarchan or Italian sonnet, which almost always rests on a balanced, two-part structure. The octave, or first eight lines, rhymes abba abba and is used to present a problem, raise a doubt or conflict or ask a question. The sestet, or last six lines, has a rhyme scheme that varies from one poem to another (Milton's sestet in this poem rhymes cde cde) and is used to solve the problem, resolve the doubt or answer the question. Milton's sonnet is based on this principle of *balance.* In the first seven and a half lines the poet struggles with his despair over the fact that his blindness prevents him from serving God actively. The last six and a half lines resolve the problem and alleviate the despair by discovering an alternate way of service to God, the passive way of submission and contemplation.

Another element of artistic form is centrality, or *unity*. Milton's poem is built around the idea of service to God. Without the premise that a person can be justified or approved before God only by faithful service, the argument of the poem could not exist. The verb "serve" occurs three times in the poem (lines 5, 11 and 14) and becomes the focal point of the whole argument. Service, in turn, falls into two contrasting categories. Active service, denied to the poet, is the subject of the first part, while passive service, declared to be equally valid, dominates the conclusion of the poem. Every part of the poem contributes to this unifying motif of service to God.

The poem also displays a unified *progression* from beginning to end. For one thing the poem is structured as a quest. The speaker is in quest for justification before God and inner peace of mind. He is searching for a way in which he can stand approved before his God and be personally satisfied. As the speaker proceeds toward the attainment of his goal, he first pursues one possibility to its foredoomed failure and then discovers a triumphant alternative.

Furthermore, despite the hopelessly involved series of clauses in the octave, the ongoing dynamic of the speaker's meditation is based on a very simple principle: "I ask" (lines 1-7½)—"Patience replies" (lines 7½-14). When diagramed, these elements constitute the entire core of the sonnet. Within this easily grasped unity the poem progresses with a firm linear movement through the argument, from the opening formula ("When I consider") to the final, climactic aphorism ("They also serve who only stand and wait"). One could not find a better illustration of how a poem progresses from its opening statement of theme to its final illumination.

Another element of artistic form that calls for appreciation in the poem is *contrast*. There is, for example, a contrast of *mood* between the increasing despair of the octave and the peaceful submission of the sestet. There is the contrast of *theme* or topic between the active service discussed in part one and the passive service of submission and contemplation of part two. A contrast in *focus* is evident in the self-centeredness of the octave and the emphasis on God in the sestet. The best index to this is the shift in pronouns—in the octave "I" and "my" (line 1), "my" (2), "me" and "my" (4), "my" (5), "my" (6), and "I" (8), and in the sestet "his" (10), "his," "him" and "his" (11), and "his" (12). The poem, in other words, contrasts despairing introspection on the one hand and self-abnegation or self-transcendence on the other. Finally, the poem is a case study in contrasting *syntax*, or sentence structure. The syntax of the first seven and a half lines collapses under its weight and mirrors the disordered rebellion of the speaker. These lines pile up one subordinate clause after another, finally coming to rest with the main clause ("I fondly ask" in line 8). By contrast, the reply of "Patience" is direct, easily grasped and simple in syntax.

This analysis of what may be the greatest sonnet in the world is far from a complete explication of the poem. Nor does it exhaust what one would find beautiful about the poem. The poem's beauty also entails the eloquence and memorability of the words and phrases, the multiplicity of meanings in many of the images, the aptness of the images and metaphors, the skill with which Milton matches his biblical allusions to the content (allusions chiefly to the parables in Matthew about the workers in the vineyard and the talents) and the rhythm or meter of the poetry. But the elements of balance, unity, development and contrast that I have demonstrated are good illustrations of how a full enjoyment and admiration of Milton's poem depend on an awareness of its sheer artistry and technique.

E. E. *Cummings, "in Just–"*. For my third illustration of

artistry in poetry I have chosen a blatantly modern poem that at first reading may appear to have none of the formal elements that I have ascribed to the first two poems. The poem is entitled *"in Just–"* and was written by E. E. Cummings:

1   in Just-
2   spring   when the world is mud-
3   luscious the little
4   lame balloonman

5   whistles   far   and wee

6   and eddieandbill come
7   running from marbles and
8   piracies and it's
9   spring

10   when the world is puddle-wonderful

11   the queer
12   old balloonman whistles
13   far   and   wee
14   and bettyandisbel come dancing

15   from hop-scotch and jump-rope and

16   it's
17   spring
18   and
19   the

20   goat-footed

21   balloonMan   whistles
22   far
23   and
24   wee

In terms of syntax and versification, we might be inclined

to call the poem formless. It is an extreme example of free verse, that is, poetry without rhyme and with lines of variable length. It has none of the external shapeliness of Hebrew parallelism or the sonnet (with its intricate rhyme scheme). Upon analysis, however, Cummings's poem turns out to be built on the familiar elements of artistic form.

There is *pattern or design* in the three-part structure of the poem. Three successive times a happy springtime setting, accompanied by children's playing, is described and then followed by the introduction of the balloonman into the scene. The cycle falls into sections, each of which begins with the naming of the spring season—"in Just-spring," "it's spring," "it's spring"—as follows: (1) lines 1-8a; (2) lines 8b-15; (3) lines 16-24.

Part of the artistry of any poem is the selection of apt words. In this poem Cummings uses colloquial words and children's constructions to capture the language actually used by children: "Just-spring," "mud-luscious," "puddle-wonderful." Furthermore, the run-together "and" clauses and names ("eddieandbill," "bettyandisbel") reproduce the way in which children talk in their excitement. The genius of the poem, in short, is that it allows us to see the springtime world through the eyes and consciousness of a child.

Along with the pattern based on repetition and the suitability of the language, the poem makes significant use of *progression*. The key to the poem's meaning, in fact, is the progressive characterization of the balloonman. In part 1 he is "little" and "lame." In part 2 he is "queer" and "old." In part 3 he is "goat-footed" and is identified as "Man," with a capital "M." This is an increasingly sinister portrait. The "goat-footed" balloonman turns out to be a figure from classical mythology—the lustful satyr or faun, half animal and half man. In classical mythology the satyrs and fauns are associated with sensuality, and some of the stories are about their seduction of nymphs in a forest setting. The cloven feet of the satyrs and fauns became a part of Christian iconography during the Middle Ages, when the devil was pictured as having goat's feet. There is also the biblical imagery of sheep and goats in the background.

Form, we have noted, includes the idea of *unity*, or a central theme. As we stand back from this poem its controlling motif is obvious. The poem is built around a literary theme of universal significance—the Fall from innocence. The poem's topic is the same as that of Genesis 3 and *Paradise Lost* and Hawthorne's short story "Young Goodman Brown." Every part of Cummings's poem contributes toward the theme of the "seduction" of children from childhood into adulthood. The balloonman's call of the children from their play (the pied piper motif, but with negative overtones) is a symbolic act, which is why Cummings inserts the capital letter into the final occurrence of the word "balloonMan." The poem does not have a precise conclusion. Instead, the whistle of the balloonman trails off into the distance, as if to suggest the way in which the innocent play of the children passes imperceptibly into adulthood.

It is evident, then, that an important part of the poem's technique is *contrast*. There are contrasts throughout the poem between youthfulness and old age, child and adult, the natural springtime setting and the unnatural figure of the lame and goat-footed balloonman, the innocence of the children's games and the implied evil of the adult world to which the children are called, and between the contemporary urban setting and the old mythic world of satyrs and fauns and pied pipers.

Does Cummings's poem give the reader enjoyment and delight? Is it an object of beauty? How can it be, if at the level of content it uncovers something morally ugly? I have chosen the poem for analysis partly because it delineates something that has been true of literature throughout the centuries but is especially prominent as a feature of modern literature. Most modern poets will disavow that their aim is to create beauty. They are much more likely to say that the poet's task is to get beneath the beautiful surfaces of life and expose the ugliness that is there. But a look at the skill with which such poets express themselves, and a scrutiny of their sheer proficiency at their craft, shows that their poems are just as thoroughly artistic—and artistic in the same ways—as poets who define poetry (as Poe did) as the creation of beauty. I return to my earlier assertion that there is a purely artistic dimension to literature, a residue of aesthetic beauty, that is part of any poem, regardless of its subject. We are left, then, with a paradox: a poem can simultaneously present ugliness (at the level of content) and beauty (at the level of form).

If "beauty" strikes some readers as the wrong term for poetry whose subject is ugliness or misery, I am content with such synonyms as "craftsmanship" or "skill in expression." But in using these substitutes it is quite important that people who claim, for example, that gruesome tragedies such as *King Lear* or *Oedipus Rex* cannot be considered beautiful realize that at the technical level these works use exactly the same elements of artistic form that I have discussed above.

The Art of Narrative

Art—the art of fiction also—is man's acknowledgement and reflection of the divine beauty revealed in and beyond nature and life. That is what fiction is for. Its function is in its own aesthetic way, not in a deliberately practical, or moral, or esoterically religious way, to disclose God's glory for God's and man's delight. □ Henry Zylstra, Testament of Vision

A literary creation can appeal to us in all sorts of ways—by its theme, subject, situations, characters. But above all it appeals to us by the presence in it of art. □ Yurii Andreievich, in Boris Pasternak's novel Doctor Zhivago

The artistry of literature is easiest to see in poetry, the most concentrated form of writing and the most self-consciously artistic kind of expression. But stories and plays rely just as heavily for their effect on unity, progression, contrast, balance and rhythm as poetry does. While the basic building block of poetry is the image, the basic building block of narrative is larger, consisting of the episode or scene (in a play). As the following outline suggests, the list of things to look for in a story or play can be formulated in terms of the usual elements of artistic form.

Form. If we stand back at a distance from a story, it is possible to identify a unifying narrative principle that constitutes the pattern or design of the whole work. In the actual experience of reading a story or viewing a play, the sequential process is, of course, all-important. But at a later stage of response, or even during the process of the initial reading or viewing, we begin to fit the parts into a coherent, unified pattern.

Some stories, for example, are built around the life and exploits of a central hero and can be said to belong to the literary family best termed "heroic narrative." The overall design in tragedy is a gradual decline from prosperity to calamity. The moving spirit in a comic plot (I am speaking now of the shape of a story) is the gradual overcoming of obstacles to happiness. In satire we can observe how all the details in the story contribute to an attack on human vice or folly. Often the unifying principle in a story is what in a later chapter I will call an "archetypal plot motif" (a basic story pattern that recurs again and again in literature), such as the quest, the journey, crime and punishment, the rescue or the temptation motif.

Progression. Sequence and movement are obviously of central importance in narrative, which unfolds in linear fashion from beginning to end. The artistry of any story or play consists to a significant degree of the ongoing development of the story. Good storytellers place their episodes or scenes in a meaningful order, and it is a reader's task to sense how a given episode is related to the one that precedes and follows it. As Aristotle first insisted, a plot is not simply a random succession of events but a sequence of logically related events. In one form or another the progress of a story or play will be what one critic calls the pattern of "spiritual quest that leads to illumination, of moving from problem to solution or meaning."[21]

One test of a carefully designed story is the degree to which it adheres to what literary critics call a "well made plot." This scheme identifies seven phases in a story: (1) exposition—the initial background information; (2) inciting moment, or inciting force—the thing that gets the plot conflict under way; (3) rising action; (4) turning point —the point at which, certainly in retrospect, if not at the time, we can see how the plot conflict will be resolved; (5) further complication; (6) climax, or moment of epiphany (insight) for the protagonist and/or reader; (7) denouement—tying up of loose ends. Any story that fits easily into this pattern has been constructed with care and craftsmanship, and a writer does not need to be aware of this scheme (a framework that has, after all, grown out of modern literary criticism) in order for his or her works to adhere to it.

Rhythm. Most stories and plays are built on the principle of rhythm—not the recurrence of sounds, as in poetry, but the back-and-forth movement of bigger elements. Throughout a typical story tension is built up and released, built up and released again and so forth. Or there may be a back-and-forth movement between good and evil actions, tragic and comic events, sympathetic and unsympathetic sides of a character or separate threads of action. The possibilities are many, and a reader's enjoyment of stories and plays will be enhanced if he or she is aware of how the storyteller has organized the events around constantly recurring rhythms.

Variety in unity. An important part of narrative artistry is the way in which the writer elaborates the central motif by inventing the variety of details that make up the story. This principle is sometimes called "the same in the other," and it should lead a reader to observe the balance between what is new and what is repeated in the episodes of a story or the scenes in a play. In a well constructed story, every episode is, in one way or another, a variation on a theme. The great narrative pitfall that a storyteller has to avoid is monotony, and the principle that allows him to avoid it is variety of adventure or variety of event. Part of a reader's appreciation of narrative technique is based on attention to the writer's skill in selecting events that fill out the general theme or unifying motif of the story.

Contrast and balance. The essence of any plot is conflict, which is the narrative version of what we usually call contrast in poetry. In addition to plot conflict some specific narrative types of contrast are the following: (1) *foils*—characters or events that set off a leading character or plot line by being a contrast; (2) *dramatic irony*—the contrast between a reader's superior knowledge about what is happening and a literary character's ignorance; (3) *thematic or imagistic contrasts*—light and darkness in Milton's stories, for example, or youth and age in *King Lear*, or heaven and earth in the book of Revelation; (4) *reversal*—an event in which a character produces the opposite of the effect intended.

Style. If enjoying a story or play for its artistry means delighting in *how* the action is recounted, as distinct from *what* is said, then one of the terms that we must include under the category of artistic beauty is simply style. Style is composed of the small elements that are part of the way in which a writer expresses himself—the words, sentences and images. This kind of narrative and dramatic artistry is as varied as the compressed, aphoristic style of biblical narrative, the imagistic richness of Shakespeare's plays, the colloquial vigor of *Huckleberry Finn* and the sensory concreteness of Camus's *The Stranger*.

Homer's Odyssey. To illustrate the art of narrative I have selected the *Odyssey*, one of the oldest extant stories in the world (though not nearly as Old as the Old Testament Pentateuch, despite the fact that this illusion is often foisted on us by literary critics). The *Odyssey* is not only one of the best stories ever told and a glorious reminder that the basic ingredients of story have remained fairly constant through the centuries. It is also one of the best models of narrative technique in existence, so that if a person spends enough time looking at the inner workings of Homer's story, he or she will be well on the way toward understanding the technique of any story.

In writing a long epic story, Homer (regardless of whether he was a single author or a committee of oral poets) needed to impose a firm overriding *unity* on his material. The unifying principle is the quest in which the hero, Odysseus, journeys for ten years from Troy to his home (which in the *Odyssey* means both family and a kingdom) in Ithaca. As a quest story with a happy ending, the story has what is known as a comic plot, that is, a U-shaped story that descends into potential tragedy but rises to a happy ending as a series of obstacles are overcome one by one. The plot of the *Odyssey* falls into three well-defined sections: the search of Telemachus for his father (Books 1-4), the wanderings of Odysseus (Books 5-12) and the homecoming or return of Odysseus (Books 13-24). Readers sometimes wonder how the first four books, in which the protagonist does not even play an active part (he enters the story in Book 5), can be a unified part of the story. But Homer knew what he was doing. Books 1-4 establish with great impact the goal of the quest: a faithful and beautiful wife, a son reaching maturity, a rich kingdom being plundered by the villainous suitors.

Homer's story also has an abundance of *conflict*. Telemachus and Penelope are in a life-and-death struggle with the suitors, for example. At a more thematic level, there are conflicts between order and disorder, good and evil, reason and appetite, civilization and barbarism. Odysseus himself struggles against the environment (death by drowning is a constant threat on his sea voyage), the hatred of Poseidon, and the threats posed by such characters as the Cyclops, Calypso and Circe. The most subtle conflict, though, occurs within Odysseus himself and is psychological in nature. Throughout the story of his wanderings, Odysseus is torn within himself between his fixed purpose to return home and his curiosity to explore the unknown.

The element of *progression* in the story is built around the problem-solution principle that is so pervasive in literature. There are two related narrative problems that engage our attention. The main one is the absence of Odysseus from Ithaca. Subordinated to that issue, but related to it, is the question of whether Telemachus will reach maturity and become a son worthy of the family line. This is the main narrative issue of Books 1-4 (known as "the Telemachia"). The struggles of Odysseus to reach home are the main story material in the second phase of the story, the wanderings of Odysseus. Every event in this part of the story contributes toward the hero's attainment of his goal of reaching home. In the final movement of the story the development of Telemachus into adult maturity and the homecoming of Odysseus become intertwined and move toward the climactic events of destroying the wicked suitors and re-establishing order in the household and kingdom. The important thing about narrative progression, first stated by Aristotle in the *Poetics* and well illustrated in the *Odyssey*, is that there be a discernible beginning, middle and end, and that events grow out of preceding ones in a cause-effect manner. Homer's story, in which every event either moves Telemachus closer to adulthood or Odysseus nearer to his goal of arriving home, shows how such progression may occur in a story.

No story ever told illustrates the principle of *variety-in-unity* better than the story of Odysseus's twelve adventures (Books 5-12). As for the unity of the adventures, each one is (a) an obstacle that must be overcome, (b) a temptation for the hero and (c) the occasion on which Odysseus displays a virtue. Within this framework of constant elements, Homer avoids monotony with an amazing variety in the series of adventures. There is variety in the length of the episodes, with some of them narrated briefly (for example, those involving the lotus eaters and Sirens) and others at length (the Calypso and Circe episodes, for example). Some of the events are violent (such as those involving Polyphemus the Cyclops and the sea monsters

Scylla and Charybdis), while others are mild (the lotus eaters and the visit to Phaiacia). Some of the adventures involve supernatural agents such as Calypso and Circe, others involve human opponents such as the Ciconians and still others involve nature (the winds of Aeolus and the parching winds on the island of Helios, for instance). A constant factor in each adventure is the idea of temptation, but the specific sin to which the hero is tempted varies (indulgence in the food and drink of the gods in the Calypso episode, curiosity to explore the unknown in the Cyclops episode and so forth). In each episode Odysseus displays the general virtue of faithfulness to home, but the specific virtue is varied (abstinence, courage, self-control, wit).

One of the elements of narrative artistry that storytellers through the centuries have been fondest of is *dramatic irony*—a situation in which the reader knows more than a character in a story. The homecoming phase of the *Odyssey* is perhaps the most sustained performance in the art of dramatic irony in Western literature. The fact that Odysseus returns home disguised as an old beggar means that his true identity is concealed from the characters in the story. Virtually every encounter that Odysseus has with people when he returns to Ithaca is filled with dramatic irony, which is a large part of the reader's delight in reading this part of the story.

Stories also depend for their effect on *climax*. It is, of course, much harder to construct a long epic story around a single large climax than it is to build a short story or play around one. The *Odyssey* shows how the writer of long narrative can solve the major narrative problems. One thing that makes the homecoming of Odysseus so climactic is Homer's skillful use of foreshadowing. From the opening lines of the story we are never allowed to forget the eventual outcome of the action. In fact, Homer takes the first four books of the epic to establish with great clarity the goal of the hero's quest. The story is filled with references to Odysseus's need to return home and to what will happen, especially to the villainous suitors, if he ever does return. Because the climax of the story (the defeat of the suitors and the reunion of Odysseus and Penelope) has been so artfully foreshadowed, it comes with great impact when it finally occurs.

These, then, are seven of the large elements of narrative artistry in the *Odyssey*. Much more, of course, could be said on the topic if we were to look at the smaller patterns in the story. As C. S. Lewis says about narrative, "Every episode, explanation, description, dialogue—ideally every sentence—must be pleasurable and interesting for its own sake."[22] Here, too, the genius of Homer is always evident.

The lesson to be learned from all that can be said about the sheer technique of Homer's story is that the author regarded storytelling as a craft and a source of enjoyment. So did his original audience. The *Odyssey* itself contains descriptions of how oral epics such as the *Odyssey* were originally performed. They were performed to a roomful of court people in a festive banquet setting. Homer's story was, in short, after-dinner entertainment, not a sermon. In the words of Odysseus, "What a pleasure it is . . . to hear a singer [the epic poet] like this. . . . I declare it is just the perfection of gracious life: good cheer and good temper everywhere, rows of guests enjoying themselves heartily and listening to the music."[23]

The principles of narrative artistry that I have illustrated from Homer's *Odyssey* are universal. I could have illustrated them from the stories of Abraham, Joseph, Ruth or Esther in the Bible, from Chaucer, Shakespeare, Milton, Dickens, Mark Twain or Faulkner. The stories that live on and continue to delight their readers are those that offer beauty of form as well as significance of content. Someone has said that entertainment, as a quality of a story, "is like a qualifying examination. If a fiction can't provide even that, we may be excused from inquiry into its higher qualities."[24]

What are the rewards of being alert to the artistry of a story? They include pleasure, aesthetic enjoyment in the work of someone else's imagination and a sense of discovery. Someone has put it this way:

> The critic is interested, like the artist, in technique, ... in structure, the esthetic properties of the thing made, its architectonic features such as unity, balance, emphasis, rhythm, and... the shapely pattern resulting when all the materials... have been brought into more or less complete interplay and fullness of tension. When the whole work finally springs to life in his mind, the critic experiences a delight, a joy in the thing of beauty, akin to that of the artist when his vision at length fell into shape.[25]

The narrative techniques that I have been discussing represent one level at which a good story can be enjoyed—the level of sheer technique and form. At this level we enjoy a story as an achievement of a craftsman and as a performance intended to dazzle us with its skill. To move beyond a simple concern with *what* a story says to the pleasure of observing *how* it is constructed is a relatively sophisticated way of reading a story. Lest it appear that I think this is the only way in which a story can be enjoyed, I wish to conclude by listing other levels at which stories can please.

At the simplest level we read a story at the level of *plot suspense*, that is, in order to find out what happens. This kind of narrative pleasure can be gained equally well by reading a plot summary, which suggests at once the superficiality of a reading experience that never moves beyond this level. If excitement and momentary plot suspense are all there is to a story or play, and if we are bored by a second or third reading or viewing, this is an index to the story's shallowness. And if a person's pleasure in stories is consistently limited to the outline of events, so that he or she seldom or never rereads a story, this is a sign that the person needs a more generous set of critical tools that allow him or her to see more in the stories they read. But if reading a story at this level is insufficient, it remains the necessary foundation for other levels of response. C. S. Lewis writes in his classic essay entitled "On Stories," "We do not enjoy a story fully at the first reading. Not till the curiosity, the sheer narrative lust, has been given its sop and laid asleep, are we at leisure to savour the real beauties. . . . The children understand this well when they ask for the same story over and over again, and in the same words."[26]

A second kind of pleasure we can derive from a story is the delight of *entering an imagined world.* Here we are less interested in the specific events than in the atmosphere or world that the story leads us into. Whether or not a story invites this level of response seems often to depend on the writer's skill at description. In describing his interest in the fiction of James Fenimore Cooper, Lewis comments, "I wanted not the momentary suspense but that whole world to which it belonged—the snow and the snow-shoes, beavers and canoes, war-paths and wigwams, and Hiawatha names."[27] And in connection with *The Three Musketeers* Lewis observes that "the total lack of atmosphere repels me. There is no country in the book—save as a storehouse of inns and ambushes. There is no weather."[28] To delight in the imagined world of a story is, says Lewis, to allow the story to pierce a reader's "deeper imagination" as distinct from "only exciting his emotions."[29]

We can, thirdly, read a story for the *quality or state* or experience that it embodies. Lewis says about stories that "to be stories at all they must be series of events: but it must be understood that this series—the *plot* as we call it—is only really a net whereby to catch something else. The real theme may be, and perhaps usually is, something that has no sequence in it, something other than a process and much more like a state or quality."[30] A story, for example, might capture the quality of heroism, courage, terror, love, mystery, nature, comradeship or union with God.

A fourth kind of pleasure that we derive from some stories is the pleasure of *characterization.* We enjoy some stories because of the characters we encounter in them. The pleasure might consist of meeting universal character types, so that we are moved to say (as we read Chaucer's

Prologue to the Canterbury Tales, for example), "How like someone I know in real life." Alternately, we can encounter characters who are unique creations of the writer—literary characters who attract our interest, not because we find them in real life, but for their own sake. Examples from my own literary experience include Shakespeare's tragic heroes, Homer's Odysseus and Milton's Adam and Eve.

Yet another category of pleasure is stories that we enjoy reading for the *archetypal or conventional pattern* that we find in them. Such stories give delight by offering the reader a particular version, or reenactment, of a familiar pattern. Part of the interest that people have in detective stories, for example, consists of observing how the story unfolds according to the usual sequence of the antecedents, occurrence and aftermath of the crime. When we read a tragedy, comedy, epic or utopia, part of the pleasure is to observe how the story satisfies the expectations that we bring to it as an example of a given literary form. This kind of delight is one of the rewards of a wide acquaintance with literature and literary traditions.

Is Beauty Irrelevant?
One of the prime achievements in every good fiction has nothing to do with truth or philosophy . . . at all. □ *C. S. Lewis,* An Experiment in Criticism

I know that some readers will raise objections to the prominence I have given to artistic beauty as an essential ingredient in the literary experience. I trust that my illustrations of what I mean by artistry in literature have demonstrated that when I speak of literature as recreation and a source of enjoyment I do not envision something passive. In fact, I am urging a kind of reading that requires more participation on the part of the reader or viewer than most people give. But this demand for a more analytic awareness of the technique by which a work produces its effects will itself raise the objection that I have surrounded literature with a host of technical and unfamiliar terms.

Why not simply read literature for its ideas or vision of life?

Of course it is possible to read poems and stories and plays without being aware of the elements of literary form that I have discussed. But, then, it is possible to attend a basketball game and watch only the scoreboard because one claims to be uninterested in *how* the game is played or what the intricacies of the strategy are. Aside from the superficiality of such an appreciation of a game or a literary work, several other things need to be said.

The fact that a reader is unaccustomed to paying attention to literary technique or artistry does not mean that these things are not a part of the literary experience. The truth is probably that a person does, whether consciously or unconsciously, respond to the writer's craftsmanship. The elements of literary form are the means by which writers achieve their effects. Being alert to them adds a dimension of literary response that otherwise remains undeveloped. It is precisely the human urge not to be content with mere experience but to seek an understanding of how and why the experience is as it is. One of the functions of literary criticism, or literary analysis, is to make unconscious responses conscious and therefore richer.

Furthermore, developing the capacity to enjoy the technical artistry of a story or poem is one sure way to improve the quality of one's literary experience. The difference between mediocrity and greatness in literature is almost certain to come at the level of technique or form rather than at the level of ideas. The difference between Shakespeare's *Macbeth* and the last television suspense drama that you saw is the greater skill of expression and the greater imaginative craftsmanship that Shakespeare put into his play. C. S. Lewis, in his book *An Experiment in Criticism,* is quite emphatic in insisting that ignoring literary form is characteristic of "unliterary" readers. Such readers, says Lewis, "can hardly think of invention as a legitimate... activity" and are "quite unconscious of style."[31] To regard a work of literature primarily as a vehicle for philosophy, continues Lewis, "is an outrage to the thing the poet has made for us. I use the words *thing* and *made* advisedly." Literary works are "not merely *logos* (something said) but *poiema* (something made).... To value them chiefly for reflections which they may suggest to us or morals we may draw from them, is a flagrant instance 'using' instead of 'receiving'.... One of the prime achievements in every good fiction has nothing to do with truth or philosophy."[32]

Nor is Lewis the only lover of literature to make such a claim. One of the landmark books on the study of literature, Brooks and Warren's *Understanding Poetry*, makes the same point. In commenting on Longfellow's "A Psalm of Life," the editors observe that if "advice is what the poem has to offer us, then we can ask why a short prose statement of this good advice is not as good as, or even better than, the poem itself. But even the people who say they like the poem because of its 'message' will usually prefer the poem to a plain prose statement."[33] And T. S. Eliot has written that literature should be approached as literature and "not defined in terms of something else,"[34] that is, not as philosophy, sociology, psychology, theology or history, but as an art form.

To respond to the artistry of literature requires that a reader make a distinction (not a division) between a work's content and its form. But it is an established principle of literary theory that the aesthetic response can, and sometimes should, be separated from the intellectual or moral response. It is true that the content of a literary work cannot be understood apart from its narrative or poetic form. But it is quite possible to respond (though it is never one's total response) to the formal or artistic dimension of a work in isolation from the theme or message. W. K. Wimsatt, Jr. can write, with wide acceptance, that literature is "a system of values in which poetic is distinguished from moral" and Frederick Pottle can argue that a reader should practice "a separation of the aesthetic judgment... from the moral judgment.[35] And Norman

Foerster elaborates the point by writing,

> If there is any sense at all in the history of criticism from Greek antiquity to the present century, two kinds of value are inherent in literature, esthetic and ethical. Let it be granted at once that esthetic value and ethical value are interdependent and, in all strictness, blended inseparably; still, it has not been found possible to discuss them both adequately at one and the same time. Let it be granted also that . . . esthetic value must come first, since this determines whether a piece of writing is literature or a piece of non-literary writing.[36]

One of the particular advantages that this approach offers to Christian readers of literature is that it allows them to affirm the value of literature whose content or world view they may dislike or abhor. If God is the source of all beauty and artistry, then the artistic dimension of literature is the point at which Christian readers can be unreserved in their enthusiasm for the works of non-Christian writers. The willingness to differentiate between the purely artistic dimension of literature and the subject matter of literature may, in fact, have been a contribution of Christianity to aesthetics. John Milton, in a famous autobiographical passage in which he outlines the history of his own literary development, writes that the Roman elegiac poets exerted an early literary influence on him. Milton gradually came to deplore the ethical viewpoint of these pagan authors, but he notes that "their art I still applauded."[37] Milton's experience is representative of a whole tradition, and one scholar comments regarding that tradition that "it was the Christians who finally taught men to appraise poetry by a purely aesthetic standard—a standard which enabled them to reject most of the moral and religious teaching of the classical poets as false and ungodly, while accepting the formal elements in their work as instructive and aesthetically delightful."[38]

Failure to distinguish between the levels of form and content has led to two significant errors. On the one hand it has led Christian readers who want to avoid being provincial in their tastes to endorse, at the level of ideas or viewpoint, works that no reader of discernment should claim to be consonant with Christianity. And, on the other side, Christian readers who have shown good judgment in measuring non-Christian world views by a Christian standard have unfortunately devalued or rejected works that can offer much to a Christian's literary experience. The corrective to both errors is to distinguish the aesthetic from the moral/intellectual response and to be unreserved in affirming the value of non-Christian literature at the level of craftsmanship and beauty.

Another objection to my emphasis on literature as a quest for beauty can be phrased as a question: aren't truth and intellect more important than beauty and imagination? If so, isn't it trivial to speak of literature in terms of beauty and enjoyment and pleasure? I am not, of course, building my entire case for literature on its artistry alone. But insofar as literature *is* an object of beauty, it needs no further rationale to establish its value.

Is truth more important than beauty? I think the answer is a very qualified yes. Surely religious truth is more important than artistic beauty. A person will be eternally saved or lost on the basis of his response to truth, not on the basis of his artistic experience. But once we get beyond the matter of religious truth I would begin to quibble with the common assumption that truth is more important than beauty. It is not at all true that the facts that one learns in disciplines other than literature and the arts are necessarily more important than the ability to enjoy the arts. Behind the usual assumption is the premise that facts are important because they are useful, while enjoying artistry and beauty are useless. But not all knowledge is as useful as is claimed in our utilitarian age, and beyond that, I would appeal to human nature to support my claim that people have other important needs besides factual knowledge. The experience of beauty is one of them.

Matthew Arnold was right when he defended a literary education against the encroachment of science by appealing to human nature. "When we set ourselves to enumerate the powers which go to the building up of human life," wrote Arnold, we find that "they are the power of conduct, the power of intellect and knowledge, the power of beauty, and the power of social life and manners." Arnold then made the convincing point that "human nature is built up by these powers; we have the need for them all. . . . We feel the impulse for relating our knowledge to our sense for conduct and to our sense for beauty. . . . Such is human nature."[39]

Many of the most worthwhile things in life are of no practical use. What can a person *do*, in any utilitarian sense, with a sunset, or a snowy mountain peak, or mists on a summer morning or a beautifully shaped tree? The trees of Paradise, we must remember, were not only "good for food" but also "pleasant to the sight" (Gen. 2:9). The writer of Psalm 19 valued nature, not because it was useful to him, but simply because it gave him an opportunity to contemplate the beauty and handiwork of God.

Applying this to literature, we can conclude that we need not justify our reading of stories or poems and our viewing of plays on any ground other than enjoyment. As C. S. Lewis has stated, "A great deal (not all) of our literature was made to be read lightly, for entertainment. If we do not read it, in a sense, 'for fun' . . . we are not using it as it was meant to be used."[40] In *An Experiment in Criticism*, Lewis elaborates the point thus: "If entertainment means light and playful pleasure, then I think it is exactly what we ought to get from some literary work. . . . If it means those things which 'grip' the reader of popular romance— suspense, excitement and so forth—then I would say that every book should be entertaining. A good book will be more; it must not be less."[41]

Nor is it only the readers of literature who speak this way about literary craftsmanship. W. H. Auden said that when young writers would tell him that they wanted to write poetry, he would ask, "Why do you want to write poetry?" According to Auden, "If the young man answers:

'I have important things I want to say,' then he is not a poet. If he answers: 'I like hanging around words listening to what they say,' then maybe he is going to be a poet."[42] The Christian poet Chad Walsh writes, "Most of the time when I sit down to write a poem I am thinking about such matters of craftsmanship as form and meter and the antics of words."[43] Knowing that their art is not a substitute for religion, Walsh writes, Christian writers can give themselves to their work "in a spirit of deadly serious playfulness."[44] The poet Stephen Spender speaks of the "serious non-seriousness" of literature, claiming that the insistence on the non-seriousness of literature "is just as much a contemporary way of asserting poetry as a 'criticism of life' as was Shelley's attempt to legislate through poetry."[45]

To say that imaginative literature is, at one level, a form of play or recreation or entertainment is not to say that it is a matter of moral indifference. As Lewis says so well, "Our leisure, even our play, is a matter of serious concern. There is no neutral ground in the universe; every square inch, every split second, is claimed by God and counterclaimed by Satan. . . . It is a serious matter to choose wholesome recreations."[46] In short, recreation is one of the crucial areas of stewardship before God. The first step toward exercising good stewardship is to invest the idea of recreation and leisure with dignity and worth. To act as if recreation is unworthy of a Christian or to pretend that we do not engage in entertainment when in fact we spend a major part of our lives pursuing it is to allow our leisure pursuits to remain at a low level by default. As Harold Lehman puts it, "Leisure time is the arena of choice. . . . We cannot evade leisure-time choices, even a non-choice amounts to a choice by default."[47]

Some people will object to my emphasis on beauty and recreation by asking, "Isn't artistic beauty irrelevant and extraneous is an age of great social problems? Shouldn't people generally and Christians especially devote themselves to solving social problems instead of pursuing the arts?" The attitude implied by such questions is of course partly right. The arts are something that people cultivate after their basic needs for survival have been met. They are a form of entertainment, recreation and enrichment.

But more needs to be said. We are hardly ever faced with the absolute alternatives of combatting social problems or pursuing the arts. Whenever we have to choose between enjoying artistic beauty and showing compassion to someone in need, we should of course do the compassionate act and forget about artistic beauty. But over the long haul, this is not the kind of situation that people face. Nearly everyone's life gives an abundant opportunity to enjoy art as well as serve one's fellow humans. In fact, to encourage others in the wise use of leisure *is* increasingly an act of compassion.

Furthermore, I would dispute the common assumption that the arts are irrelevant to the solution of social problems. Many social problems have arisen precisely because our society has not taken the time and expended the energy to be truly artistic and to prize beauty as a value. It may sound simplistic, but it is nevertheless true that some inner-city problems will be solved only on an aesthetic basis. If our society would uphold beauty as a value not to be violated, our cities would not be concrete jungles and our streams would not be polluted.

Our practical modern world has regarded beauty as an extraneous luxury, and we are left in horror at the kind of world it has produced. If we look honestly and deeply within the human spirit as created by God, we will find a hunger for beauty as well as for truth and righteousness. And if we look beyond the human spirit to the God of the Bible and the God of creation, we will conclude that God does not regard beauty as the unnecessary pursuit of an idle moment.

Matthew Arnold, the eminent Victorian prophet of culture, said that the task of literature and culture was to teach people "how to live." What he had in mind was that the arts, as the vehicle of classical, humanistic values, would become a substitute for the Christian religion and assume the role of a moral and spiritual guide in modern society. The arts have not fulfilled—and for a Christian never can fulfill—what Arnold envisioned. But in a sense far different from what Arnold intended, the arts do address themselves to the question of how to live. Seen from a Christian and biblical perspective, the arts, including literature, show that life can be lived in a joyful awareness of the beauty that God has poured out on his creation and that artists have created in culture as a result of expressing the image of God in them. It is a great calling. The abundant life begins now and permeates the whole person, including his artistic impulses.

3 The World of the Literary Imagination

The Truth of the Imagination
The world of literature is a world where there is no reality except that of the human imagination. . . . The constructs of the imagination tell us things about human life that we don't get in any other way. □ *Northrop Frye,* The Educated Imagination

"My love is like a red, red rose." "Lilies that fester smell far worse than weeds." "And they lived happily ever after." Is there any doubt that the world of imaginative literature is, from any literal viewpoint, nonsense? Why, we wonder, has this nonsense held such a grip on the human race throughout history? We might even ask, as C. S. Lewis does, "What then is the good of—what is even the defence for—occupying our hearts with stories of what never happened. . . ? Or of fixing our inner eye earnestly on things that can never exist—on Dante's earthly paradise, Thetis rising from the sea to comfort Achilles, . . . or the Mariner's skeleton ship?"[1] Are the stories and poems that make up literature a form of truth? Are they indispensable? If so, how?

Even the materials from which the world of literature is made would appear to be fragile, insubstantial and easily destructible. Literature, after all, exists through the medium of words. The writer is a maker who builds out of words, and without words there would be no literature. One might suspect that this is a ridiculously fragile medium, but it is in fact one of the most durable and most capable of wide dissemination. There is only one original of a painting or statue, and most music depends for its existence on the presence of instruments or voices, but written literature can be reproduced easily and widely.

Literature appears even more illusory—ridiculously so, one might say—when one stops to consider that in the final analysis literature exists only in a person's mind. It has no tangible existence in external reality. Someone has written that "the realities of literature... cannot be scientifically proven or tested like the realities of science; they are not 'out there' in the world around us. They are all in your head. You cannot study literature with a telescope or a microscope: you can only study it with that combination of reason and emotion we call the imagination. Literature, then, is a record of what men think. Its realities are inside men's minds."[2]

On first view it might seem that no case can be made for the significance of imaginative literature. But the history of the human race refutes such a conclusion, for imaginative literature is one of the noblest monuments of civilization and one of the most enduring and universal human impulses. The history of literature and the arts is the history of what people have thought, felt and above all imagined through the centuries.

Why is the record of human imaginings important? Quite simply because it is the most accurate index to human values, longings and anxieties that exists. Literature tells us more about some aspects of human nature than the statistics and profiles of sociology and psychology do. If we want to know what people, including ourselves, are like, we can do no better than listen to the stories and poems of the human race.

The assertion that literature "tells the truth about the human heart" has no doubt often been used in superficial ways by people who wished to settle the question of the value of literature with an emotional or sentimental appeal instead of well reasoned arguments. And to define the truth of literature solely in terms of emotion, while it may help us to understand lyric poetry, will give us a shrunken view of stories and plays. But if we take the statement that literature tells us the truth about the human heart to mean that literature is a record of what people have felt most strongly about and been most intensely preoccupied with, then the assertion strikes me as exactly right and a good rationale for the whole literary enterprise.

To read imaginative literature is to enter a whole imagined world. It is a world having its own identity and its own integrity. This is an insight that I wish I had been introduced to much earlier in my literary experience than I was. The literary scholar who, more than anyone else, gave me a conviction of this truth was Northrop Frye, whom I first read during my first year of graduate study and whose book *The Educated Imagination*[3] is the indispensable source on the subject of the present chapter. Later I found the literary criticism of C. S. Lewis (especially his book *An Experiment in Criticism*) reinforcing my awareness that the world of literature is a world having its own identity and worth.

The purpose of the discussion that follows is to delineate five essential features of the landscape of the world of literature. My conviction as a Christian is that to explore the world of imaginative literature is to explore part of God's created reality. The Bible tells us that it is God who created people and who endowed them with a creative imagination. People and their imaginings, we can infer, are part of God's universe. Studying that world will tell us things that are just as crucial to human well-being and to God's glory as an exploration of the physical world around us is.

The One Story of Literature
All themes and characters and stories that you encounter in

literature belong to one big interlocking family. . . . In litera-
ture you don't just read one poem or novel after another, but
enter into a complete world of which every work of literature
forms part. □ *Northrop Frye,* The Educated Imagination

Several decades ago scholars of ancient hero stories began to perceive how similar such stories were to each other. It became evident that these stories were re-enactments of a common pattern in which the hero sets out from his homeland on a quest, endures a perilous journey in which he encounters forces of evil that momentarily defeat him, eventually emerges triumphant and returns home to become king and marry the princess. An early work that explored this pattern was Joseph Campbell's book *The Hero with a Thousand Faces*[4], whose very title draws attention to the way in which the multitude of hero stories tell a single story.

Once the idea of a single story pattern had been grasped as the foundation of the old hero stories, literary scholars began to see that the pattern was not confined to a single category of literature. All literature, regardless of whether it was ancient or modern or in between, fitted into one big story. One of the best documented theories of recent literary criticism is that literature is not many isolated stories and poems but instead adds up to one overall story.

The first thing I wish to say about the world of the literary imagination, therefore, is that it is unified. All of the persons, events and images of literature make up a single composite story. This story is called "the monomyth" because it is the "one story" of literature.

The monomyth is shaped like a circle and has four separate phases. As such, it corresponds to some familiar cycles of human experience. The cycle of the year, for example, consists of the sequence of summer-fall-winter-spring. A day moves through a cycle consisting of sunrise-zenith-sunset-darkness. A person's life passes from birth to adulthood to decline and finally to death. The monomyth, too, is a cycle having four phases.

We can picture the "one story" of literature like this:

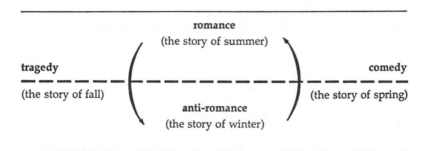

Romance (which Northrop Frye calls "the story of summer") pictures idealized human experience and is a wish-fulfillment dream of complete happiness. Its opposite, anti-romance ("the story of winter"), portrays unideal experience and is an anxiety dream of total bondage and frustration. Tragedy ("the story of fall") narrates a fall downward from bliss to catastrophe, and comedy ("the story of spring") narrates a rise from bondage to happiness and freedom. These are the four kinds of story or poem material, and together they make up the composite story of literature.

The monomyth is the most general or universal pattern to be found in literature. The circular pattern of the monomyth takes a number of specific forms, including the following:

1. The quest, in which the hero leaves the security of his home, undertakes an ordeal that tests his powers and temporarily defeats him, overcomes the obstacles, and either returns home in triumph or achieves a new state of bliss (which still constitutes a return to the initial state). Like the monomyth, the quest is circular in structure, its phases being separation, transformation through ordeal and return.

2. The death-rebirth motif, in which a hero endures death or danger and returns to life or security.

3. The initiation, in which the hero is thrust out of an existing, usually ideal, situation and undergoes a series of ordeals as he or she passes from ignorance and im-

maturity to social or spiritual adulthood.

4. The journey, in which the hero passes through threats that test him and lead to his character development.

5. Tragedy, or its more specific form of the fall from innocence.

6. Comedy, a U-shaped story that begins in prosperity, descends into tragedy, but rises to a happy ending as obstacles to success are overcome.

7. Crime and punishment, in which the order of society is destroyed and the criminal undergoes punishment as social order is re-established.

8. The temptation motif, in which an innocent person becomes the victim of an evil tempter or temptress.

9. The rescue motif (or the chase and rescue motif), in which characters undergo dire threat and then are rescued.

10. The Cinderella or rags-to-riches pattern, in which a character overcomes the obstacles of ostracism and poverty.

11. The scapegoat motif, in which a character with whom the welfare of society is identified must die for the sins of the people before prosperity can return to the people.

These eleven plot motifs are, each in its own way, reenactments of the circular monomyth that encompasses all literature.

How is the monomyth important to the study of literature? Primarily it unifies and integrates literature as a whole. It shows that the world of the literary imagination is not a collection of fragments but a coherent and unified whole. The monomyth provides a general outline where every individual story, play or poem, as well as the imagery or symbolism of a given passage, takes its place. In short, the monomyth organizes the entire content of literature. It is the shape that the human imagination gives to reality.

The monomyth is not only central to literature and literary criticism but is also central to human experience. One scholar comments that the monomyth is "the center of reality as perceived by creative man in all ages and nations and under a number of forms of expression—ritual, myth, scripture, dream, even history.... There is little doubt that the myth pattern does embody, in a simple and usable form, a principle of reality so vast as to have implications for nearly every area of life."⁵ The "one story" of literature embodies the shape of a person's life, daily routine, and psychic, emotional and spiritual experience. The Christian view of history also has this shape, since it divides human history into the sequence of life before the Fall, the Fall itself, ordinary fallen history, and the end of history, when evil will be destroyed and original perfection restored. The monomyth has a special relevance to Christian belief in a second way as well, since it tells the story of the individual Christian soul: once perfect (in Adam and Eve), fallen by virtue of its inclination to evil and redeemed and glorified through faith in Christ. The unifying story of literature, it is clear, delineates not only the landscape of literature, but also of human life.

A Simplified World
The tragedian dare not present the totality of suffering as it usually is in its uncouth mixture of agony with littleness, all the indignities and (save for pity) the uninterestingness, of grief. It would ruin his play.... He selects from the reality just what his art needs. ☐ C. S. Lewis, An Experiment in Criticism

Once upon a time there was a son who asked his father for his share of the family inheritance. After his father gave him the money, he took a journey to a distant land, where he quickly wasted all that he had on wine, women and song. Then he became so poor that he wished he could have eaten the food that he fed to his employer's hogs. Finally he came to himself and returned to his father, asking to be forgiven.

This brief story typifies an important feature of the world of imaginative literature, namely, that it is a simplified world (but not "simple") in which all of the irrelevant details have been omitted and only the essential pattern remains. We know exactly who the son is: he is the young prodigal, or wastrel, who squanders his money on riotous living and then is initiated into the world of suffering. The shape of the plot is also clear, consisting of such motifs as the journey, the initiation into evil and its consequences, transformation through ordeal and homecoming. Even if the story were elaborated into a novel, the underlying patterns would still stand out fully illuminated.

The same clarity is discernible in "The Lamb" by William Blake:

Little lamb, who made thee?
Dost thou know who made thee?
Gave thee life and bid thee feed
By the stream and o'er the mead;
Gave thee clothing of delight,
Softest clothing, wooly, bright;
Gave thee such a tender voice,
Making all the vales rejoice?
Little lamb, who made thee?
Dost thou know who made thee?

Little lamb, I'll tell thee,
Little lamb, I'll tell thee:
He is called by thy name,
For He calls Himself a lamb.
He is meek, and He is mild;
He became a little child.
I a child, and thou a lamb:
We are called by His name.
Little lamb, God bless thee!
Little lamb, God bless thee!

Blake's poem distills all that is desirable and innocent in human experience—childhood, nature, God, gentleness—and presents it in the symbolic form of a child's address to a lamb. The poem gives us a lyric version of innocence.

Literature is obviously not a journalistic report of everything that happens. It is not a recording of the mere flow of human experience. Rather, a writer distills from human experience what fits the story's pattern or theme. A love poet, for example, distills the beauty and attractiveness of his or her beloved. The writer of tragedy selects details that fit the tragic pattern of the particular story or the pessimism of his or her view of life. The writer of satire distills what is ugly or foolish in life and omits what is virtuous. Homer's *Odyssey* gives the essence of the family man, Chaucer's Troilus is the ideal lover and so forth. The world of literature is a highly organized version of the real world. It is a world in which the images, characters and story patterns are presented stripped of complexities. What C. S. Lewis says of Sidney's *Arcadia* is true of most literature: "its inhabitants are 'ideal' only in the sense that they are either more beautiful or more ugly, more stately or more ridiculous, more vicious or more virtuous, than those whom we meet every day. The world he paints is, in fact, simplified and heightened."[6]

Not only is the world of literature a simplified one, it is also a world in which we keep encountering the same characters and events over and over again. When we read literature we are continually reminded of some literary character or story pattern or passage of poetry. Television suspense stories are always busy re-enacting a story pattern known as crime and punishment, in which we observe the antecedents, occurrence and aftermath of the crime, ending with the punishment of the criminal. The stories of Cinderella, of Samson and Delilah, of Adam and Eve's expulsion from the garden or of Romeo and Juliet have been retold thousands of times.

Images, plot motifs and character types that recur again and again in literature are called *archetypes*. Northrop Frye defines an archetype as "a symbol, usually an image, which recurs often enough in literature to be recognizable as an element of one's literary experience as a whole."[7] Leslie Fiedler speaks of archetypes as "any of the immemorial patterns of response to the human situation in its permanent aspects."[8] Archetypes are the basic building blocks of literature. They are the forms by which the literary imagination organizes human experience.

The same patterns are present in actual life, but we are usually not aware of them because they are hidden under all the complexities and immediacy of actual experience. In daily living, for example, we rarely look at our own lives or the lives of others and fit them into the pattern of the quest toward a goal. But the moment we begin to read the stories of Abraham, Odysseus, Aeneas, the Joad family or Frodo, we see the quest motif as the organizing pattern of the hero's life. When a young person takes a camping trip or goes off to college or begins a new job, we are only vaguely aware of the initiation pattern, but when we read the stories of Joseph, Telemachus, Candide or Huckleberry Finn, we are fully aware that the protagonist is undergoing an initiation into the adult world. The landscapes that we encounter in real life are full of unorganized details, but the landscapes of literature have an easily discernible meaning—they are either the earthly paradise or the sinister forest or the wasteland or the idealized green world of pastoral.

To summarize, the world of the literary imagination is a simplified world made up of recurrent images, events and character types known as archetypes. To enter the world of imaginative literature is to put oneself in touch with certain powerful images (for example, God, the hero, nature, home or family, city or community) that are the essential features of our own experience in the real world. One important function of literature is to clarify and organize the features that appear more randomly and more ambiguously in actual experience. One need not agree with all of Carl Jung's psychological theories about archetypes in order to accept the validity of his comment that archetypes "make up the groundwork of the human psyche. It is only possible to live the fullest life when we are in harmony with these symbols; wisdom is a return to them."⁹

The general drift of my remarks has been to suggest that the world of the literary imagination is, from one perspective, truer than the world around us. It is truer because it is a world arranged into a meaningful pattern, in contrast to the fragmented pieces that make up our moment-by-moment living. And the world of imaginative literature is truer than what we often see in the external world because it affirms what is of enduring worth in human experience. In our harried world of daily existence, it is all too easy to let the essential get buried under the peripheral. One function of the archetypes of the literary imagination is that they keep calling us back to the fundamentals of life. Putting its readers in touch with archetypes is one of the ways in which literature validates the claim made through the centuries that literature clarifies human experience and gives a heightened awareness of reality.

The Dualistic World of Literature

There are two halves to literary experience, then. Imagination gives us both a better and a worse world than the one we usually live with, and demands that we keep looking steadily at them both. . . . Literature, then, is . . . two dreams, a wish-fulfillment dream and an anxiety dream. ☐ Northrop Frye, The Educated Imagination

The world of the literary imagination is a dualistic world clearly divided into the categories of good and bad, desirable and undesirable, comedy and tragedy. This dialectical pattern, or pattern of opposites, is, like the monomyth, an organizing principle of literature as a whole. The world of literature is full of contrasts. Northrop Frye writes, "Sometimes, as in the happy endings of comedies, or in the ideal world of romances, we seem to be looking at a pleasanter world than we ordinarily know. Sometimes, as in tragedy and satire, we seem to be looking at a world more devoted to suffering or absurdity than we ordinarily know. In literature we always seem to be looking either up or down."[10]

The best way to demonstrate the dualistic structure of literature is to list the archetypal images and character types that comprise it. See chart on pages 86-87.[11]

Category of Experience	The Archetypes of Ideal Experience	The Archetypes of Unideal Experience
The supernatural	Any beneficent deity; angels; the heavenly society.	Demons (including Satan), or malicious deities; hobgoblins, ogres; blind fate.
Human characters	The hero or heroine; the good mother or father; the innocent child; the benevolent king or ruler; the wiseman; the shepherd.	The villain; the tempter or temptress; the harlot (prostitute); the witch; the idiot; the taskmaster or tyrant; the wicked father or stepmother; the malicious parent; the outcast or wanderer; the traitor; the malicious giant; the shrewish or domineering woman; the sluggard or lazy person; any "blocking character" who stands in the way of happiness; the churl or refuser of festivities.
Human relationships	The community or city; images of symposium, communion, order, unity, friendship, love; the wedding, or marriage; the feast, meal, or supper; the family; freedom.	Tyranny or anarchy; isolation among people; images of torture, mutilation (the cross, stake, scaffold, gallows, stocks), slavery or bondage; images of war, riot, feud or family discord.
Clothing	Any stately garment symbolizing legitimate position or success; festal garments such as wedding clothes; fine clothing given as gifts of hospitality; white or light colored clothing; clothing of adornment (such as jewels); protective clothing, such as a warrior's armor.	Ill-fitting garments (often symbolic of a position that is usurped and not held legitimately); garments symbolizing mourning (the shroud, dark mourning garments, sackcloth, mourning bands); dark clothes; tattered, dirty or coarse clothing; any clothing that suggests poverty or bondage; a conspicuous excess of clothing (the overdressed person).
The human body	Images of health, strength, vitality, potency; feats of strength and dexterity; images of sleep and rest; wish-fulfillment dreams; birth.	Images of disease, deformity, barrenness, injury or mutilation; sleeplessness or nightmare, often related to guilt of conscience; death.
Food	Staples, such as bread, milk and meat; luxuries, such as wine and honey; the harvest.	Hunger, drought, starvation, cannibalism; poison or magic potions.
Animals	A community of domesticated animals, usually a flock of sheep; a lamb; a gentle bird, often a dove; a faithful domesticated animal, such as a dog; a group of singing birds; the beneficent talking animals of folktales; animals or birds noted for their strength, such as the lion or eagle.	Monsters or beasts of prey; the wolf (enemy of sheep), the tiger, the dragon, the vulture, the cold and earthbound snake, the owl (associated with darkness), the hawk; any wild animal harmful to people; the scapegoat.

Category of Experience	The Archetypes of Ideal Experience	The Archetypes of Unideal Experience
Landscape	A garden, grove, or park; the mountaintop or hill; the fertile and secure valley; pastoral settings or farms; the pathway.	The sinister or dark forest, often enchanted and in control of demonic forces; the heath or wilderness or wasteland, which is always barren and may be either a tropical place of intense heat or a place of ice and intense cold; the dark and dangerous valley; the underground cave or tomb; the graveyard; the labyrinth.
Plants	Green grass; the rose; the vineyard; the tree of life; the lily; evergreen plants (symbolic of immortality); herbs or plants of healing.	The thorn or thistle; weeds; dead or dying plants; the willow tree (symbolic of mourning).
Buildings	The city or palace or castle; the temple or church; the house or home; the tower of contemplation; the capital city, symbol of the nation; the rustic cottage.	The prison or dungeon; the wicked city of violence, sexual perversion and crime; the tower of imprisonment or wicked aspiration (the tower of Babel).
The inorganic world	Images of jewels and precious stones, often glowing and fiery; fire and brilliant light; burning that purifies and refines; rocks of refuge.	The inorganic world in its unworked form of deserts, rocks and wilderness; dry dust or ashes; fire that destroys and tortures instead of purifying; rust and decay.
Water	A river or stream; a spring or fountain of water; showers of rain; dew; flowing water of any type; tranquil pools in a formal garden.	The sea and all that it contains (sea beasts and water monsters); stagnant pools.
Forces of nature	The breeze or wind; the spring and summer seasons; calm after storm; the sun or the lesser light of the moon and stars; light, sunrise, day.	The storm or tempest; the autumn and winter seasons; sunset, darkness, night.
Sounds	Musical harmony; singing; laughter.	Discordant sounds, cacophony, weeping, wailing.
Direction and motion	Images of ascent, rising, height (especially the mountaintop and tower), motion (as opposed to stagnation).	Images of descent, lowness, stagnation or immobility, suffocation, confinement.

This chart of literary archetypes is important for several reasons. In the first place, it helps to organize our literary experience as a whole. Individual stories and poems are not self-contained fragments but are part of a coherent structure. The world of the literary imagination is, in fact, one of the most thoroughly organized constructs that exists. Second, being aware of the archetypes of literature helps us to relate works of literature to each other, since archetypes appear repeatedly throughout literature. The image of the sea in *Moby Dick*, for example, cannot be confined to Melville's novel; one's imagination reaches out to include associations from the Old Testament story of Jonah, the wanderings of Odysseus on the sea and Hemingway's old man and the sea. Third, being alert to the archetypes of literature gives a new appreciation of the relationship between literature and life, for archetypes are present in the real world as well as in literature. Archetypes thus help us to sort out and understand life itself. Finally, and most importantly, developing an awareness of archetypes enhances one's imaginative and emotional response to literature. It gives a reader a "feel" for the particular work or passage that he or she happens to be reading.

There are two ways in which the list of archetypes can be applied to a work of literature. One is to take a single archetype and place it in the context of other literary works in which it appears. A reader's emotional and imaginative experience of Milton's portrayal of paradise, for example, will be intensified many times over if the time is taken to read, at the same sitting, the descriptions of the garden in Genesis 2, Calypso's island in Homer's *Odyssey* and the garden that appears at the end of Dante's *Purgatorio*.

The second way in which the list of archetypes can be used to enhance one's response to literature is to pause after reading a given work or passage (Milton's portrayal of hell in Book I of *Paradise Lost*, let us say, or Stephen Crane's short story "The Open Boat") and read through the list of archetypes to observe how many of the images the writer has used. In this process images will begin to flow together into clusters and reinforce each other, merging finally into a total vision. I cannot overemphasize that the purpose of the list of archetypes is not pigeonholing. The list is a road map that tells a reader where to find the places that will enrich his view of the literary landscape.

Some people find that this type of emphasis on the archetypal nature of literature makes literature unoriginal. To this I would make a threefold reply. First, if works of literature actually display these archetypes, there is no sense in pretending that they do not in an effort to maintain a false theory of originality or uniqueness. In life, as well as in literature, it is impossible to be human without participating in the great archetypes, nor is this a fact to lament. Second, the presence of an archetypal pattern such as the fall from innocence does not destroy the uniqueness of each re-enactment of the pattern. J. R. R. Tolkien writes, "Spring is, of course, not really less beautiful because we have seen or heard of other like events: like events, never from world's beginning to world's end the same event. Each leaf, of oak and ash and thorn, is a unique embodiment of the pattern. . . . We do not, or need not, despair of painting because all lines must be either straight or curved."[12] This should be particularly understandable to a Christian, for whom the great realities of the faith—forgiveness, the new life, providence—are both a shared and individual experience. Third, the archetypal patterns of literature do not rob a writer of the opportunity to be original. Even if a writer is oblivious to archetypes, they will still be present in his work because they belong to life itself. And if a writer deliberately seeks out archetypal patterns, as Shakespeare did, he is free to elaborate the pattern in striking and original ways. As Northrop Frye comments, "Writers are interested in folk tales for the same reason that painters are interested in still-life arrangements: because they illustrate essential principles of storytelling. The writer who uses them then has the technical problem of making them sufficiently plausible or credible to a sophisticated audience."[13]

If we stand back from the list of archetypes, it becomes an index to the two major themes of literature as a whole. They are the things that people long for (wish fulfillment) and the things that people find wrong in the world around them (anxiety). If the world of imaginative literature is the record of what exists within the human mind, we can discern, from the perspective of the Christian faith, two theological truths underlying literature as a whole. They are the fact of sin and the Fall, and the longing for redemption and restoration. The desire to return to the garden —the quest to regain the lost paradise—is a pattern underlying most literature. It can be traced both in literature that laments the way things are and in literature that offers a better alternative to the existing world.

The Conventions of Literature

The deeds of Achilles or Roland were told because they were exceptionally and improbably heroic; . . . the saint's life, because he was exceptionally and improbably holy. . . . Attention is fixed . . . on the more than ordinary terror, splendour, wonder, pity, or absurdity of a particular case. These, not for any light they might throw hereafter on the life of man, but for their own sake, are what matters. □ C. S. Lewis, An Experiment in Criticism

Every area of human experience has its recognizable rules or conventions. When people eat dinner, they ordinarily sit on chairs around a table and use spoons and forks to get the food from plates to their mouths. There is a conventional order in which foods are eaten, with meat and potatoes preceding ice cream. If we observe street traffic from a high view, we can see at once that the flow of traffic is regulated by a definite set of rules. Cars move in opposite directions on the two halves of the street, they stop at points where roads intersect and so forth.

The world of literature also has conventions—lots of them. These conventions are part of the artistic order that the imagination imposes on reality. "Literature and life," writes Frye, "are both conventionalized."[14] Literature, in short, is full of things that happen constantly in stories and poems, but rarely or not at all in real life.

Poets, for example, expect us to believe (for the moment) that humans can go around speaking in rhyme and regular meter. Love poets are always busy praising their beloved as ideally beautiful or handsome. They picture themselves as ideally ardent lovers. Their rivals are ideally villainous. Self-respecting love poets fill their poems with vows of eternal constancy (they will love until the moon deserts the sky or until the twelfth of never), and they will of course compare their beloved to beautiful objects in nature (roses or the sun or springtime).

Storytellers have their conventions too. Jesus told stories about three passers-by who encountered an injured man on the road, about three stewards and about three people who found excuses to avoid attending a banquet. Why three? Because the story pattern of threefold repetition is one of the most universal narrative conventions. Equally prevalent is the way in which the motivation for a character's actions is clearly discernible to the reader of a story, even though in real life motives are often hidden. Storytellers are addicted to a narrative convention known as "poetic justice" (a situation in which good characters are rewarded and bad ones punished), even though we know that such justice is often lacking in real life. The novelist E. M. Forster said that "if it was not for death and marriage I do not know how the average novelist would conclude."[15] A convention of literary tragedy is that it omits, in the words of C. S. Lewis, "the clumsy and apparently meaningless bludgeoning of much real misfortune and the prosaic littleness which usually rob real sorrows of their dignity" and presents instead suffering that is "always significant and sublime."[16] Realistic fiction comes much closer to being a slice of life, but it, too, has its literary conventions, such as the ease with which one car can follow another in television dramas or the necessity that a romantic love motif be introduced into nine out of ten stories.

Drama also has its conventions. Even the placing of events in a realistic play is far more structured than the random flow of events in everyday life. The time span is greatly compressed in a play, so that we witness a complete courtship or tragedy in the space of one or two hours. The greatest dramatist of all pretended that people speak in blank verse, go around baring their inner souls in set speeches called soliloquies, become instantly virtuous when they enter the Forest of Arden, and, if they are women, become instantly unrecognizable when they put on men's clothing. It is no wonder that one scholar praises Shakespearean drama, not for its realism, but "because the inhabitants of its artificial world are constantly consistent in their remoteness from life,"[17] while another writes:

> Though all art implies an element of "imitation," without which it cannot interest or touch us, it is never quite a copy or transcript; and that which most nearly approaches faithful imitation is mediocre and dull.... Literature... requires, for strong and fine effect, a special treatment, not to say a transformation, of the raw material: condensation and contrast; emphasis or exaggeration here, slurring or understatement there; and the observance of certain traditions and conventions. Tragedy must be tragic, comedy comic, with... death at the end of the one, marriage at the end of the other.... For the essential and vital material of art is not actual experience, but... an imaginative one, from the actual often remote.[18]

The world of the literary imagination is a world replete with conventions. Harry Levin has said that "convention may be described as a necessary difference between art and life.... Without some sort of conventionalization art could hardly exist."[19] "And of the conventions of literature," states Northrop Frye, "about all we can say is that they don't much resemble the conditions of life."[20] Since some lovers of literature may find this emphasis on the unreality of literary conventions unsettling, allow me to pause and analyze the matter.

For one thing, *all* art rearranges life in this way. Music gives us combinations of sounds not present in nature. Painters do not, as photographers do, merely reproduce external appearances. The arts give an order to the raw data of external reality, and the order that they give to that data is based on the established conventions of a given art form. T. S. Eliot has said that "it is a function of all art to give us some perception of an order in life, by imposing an order upon it."[21]

Second, the conventions of literature enhance its value as entertainment. There is no other way to account for the persistence with which writers through the centuries have perpetuated these literary conventions and with which readers have enjoyed them. In their leisure time people prefer to look at the conventionalized world of the imagination instead of the random flow of actual life.

Finally, the conventions of literature are not only entertaining; they also help to illuminate reality. After all, it is not simply the arts that rearrange the external world in order to see it more precisely. What a scientist sees under the microscope is not what we see around us. The facts in a psychological profile are not what we see when we talk with a person sitting in front of us. The generalizations made in a history book are different from the immediate events that happened to a person living in a given age. It is not surprising, therefore, that the artificial or unlifelike conventions of literature can help us to see life more clearly. The exaggerated coldness of the lady in courtly love poems, or the exaggerated emotions of the male lover in the same poems, or the unrelieved misery of a naturalistic novel or the untainted piety of the speaker in devotional poetry, allows us to see the precise nature of these human experiences better.

The conventions, in other words, give us a heightened sense of reality. Sometimes they are simply an index to human longings—longings for grandeur in tragedy or justice in life, for example. Sometimes the unlifelike conventions of literature express things that are real but hidden from ordinary view. If, for example, it is true that God will ultimately judge evil, even though such justice is often absent from real life, then stories that are based on poetic justice can be truer than real life. The fact that the conventions of literature help us to see life more clearly is perhaps one reason why the Bible is so full of literary conventions. Most parts of the Bible resemble the world of imaginative literature that I have been describing in this chapter more closely than they resemble the daily newspaper or an ordinary history book.

Literature: A Window to Reality
The poet's job is not to tell you what happened, but what happens: not what did take place, but the kind of thing that always does take place. □ *Northrop Frye,* The Educated Imagination

The final thing I need to say about the world of the literary imagination is that it is a world that in some ways resembles real life. No matter how unreal some of the conventions of literature may be, the human issues that it concerns are those of actual human experience. That is why a reader's excursion into the imagined world of literature is not an escape from reality but a window *to* reality, not a flight away from what really exists but a flight *to* it.

Observe, for example, what happens in Coleridge's *Rime of the Ancient Mariner.* The protagonist is punished for his senseless killing of an albatross by having the dead albatross hung around his neck. In real life people do not wear a dead albatross around their necks, but they do go to work or to the psychiatrist haunted by the horror of unrelieved guilt. In fact, the image of the albatross around one's neck has passed into our storehouse of proverbs. When the mariner in the story blesses the water snakes that he is watching in the middle of the ocean, the albatross slides from his neck into the sea, and he is able to pray. Nothing like this literally happens to people in the everyday world, but people do lose their guilt and experience the new life. In real life people do not have the powers of strength and immortality that the mariner does, but in real life there is something called heroism. So no matter how remote the world of the *Rime of the Ancient Mariner* may be from reality, it is also so much a part of reality that every person carries that world within his or her own soul.

The Renaissance poet Edmund Spenser imagined a world so remote from everyday reality that he called it "Fairy Land." It consists of a magical and enchanted forest filled with monsters and knights and ladies in distress. But at the same time, like Coleridge's poem, it expresses the realities that lie within every person. In real life people do not journey into a dark forest and fight with a monster named Error, but they do journey to classrooms and television sets and find themselves forced to discern truth from falsehood. In real life we do not find (as we do in Spenser's story) witches who look beautiful on 364 days of the year, but we do encounter malicious and evil people who conceal their moral ugliness when they find it advantageous to do so. Only in Spenser's poem do people go to a place called the Schoolhouse of Faith, where they meet characters named Fidelia, Speranza and Charissa; but in our world people do experience the new life of faith in Christ and attain the virtues of faith, hope and charity. In the most famous episode in the *Faerie Queene*, Spenser places his hero in a garden called "the Bower of Bliss." This represents a temptation to excess, and although this is not the form that temptation takes in everyday life, C. S. Lewis is right when he comments regarding Spenser that "despite the apparent remoteness of his scenes, . . . the houses and bowers and gardens of the *Faerie Queene* . . . are always at hand."[22]

The same principle can be illustrated from broad categories of literature. In real life lovers do not speak in rhyme, nor do they actually say or do the things that love poets imagine them doing. But people do fall rapturously in love and say things they would not otherwise say. In real life people do not perform the heroic feats that they perform in epics, but in real life there are such things as heroism and courage and perseverance. Newspapers do not carry stories like that of Homer's Odysseus, who spent seven years on the shore of Calypso's island crying for his home and wife, but there are people around us who resist temptations that would destroy their faithfulness to home and spouse.

Often it is the most obviously fantastic literature that touches most powerfully and at the most points on actual experience. In his classic essay entitled "On Fairy-Stories," J. R. R. Tolkien observes that "fairy-stories deal largely, or (the better ones) mainly, with simple or fundamental things."[23] It was in fairy stories that Tolkien first sensed the wonder of such things "as stone, and wood, and iron; tree and grass; house and fire; bread and wine."[24] In a similar vein, C. S. Lewis can claim that a fantasy story with animals as characters sent him back to the real world with a renewed understanding of it because the story presented such realities as "food, exercise, friendship, the face of nature, even (in a sense) religion. . . . The whole story, paradoxically enough, strengthens our relish for real life. This excursion into the preposterous sends us back with renewed pleasure to the actual."[25]

It would be a mistake, then, to think that literature that is highly unrealistic in its literary conventions is, at the level of its real subject, remote from human experience. And realistic literature (such as modern detective stories and novels) that is close to the external appearances of life often has little significant relationship to the breadth of actual human experience. To the extent to which modern, realistic literature excludes such realities as nobility, beauty, mystery, holiness, deity or faithful love, it is less true than unrealistic literature that finds a place for them. The closeness of literature to life is ultimately judged, not at the level of literary conventions, but at the level of the realities that those conventions express.

The world of the literary imagination not only delights but also illumines. Flannery O'Connor has written, "I'm always highly irritated by people who imply that writing fiction is an escape from reality. It is a plunge into reality.... [26] T. S. Eliot has said that the function of literature consists of "imposing a credible order upon ordinary reality, ... thereby eliciting some perception of an order *in* reality."[27] And the novelist Joyce Cary comments that the world of literature

> is a world of ordered meaning, of coherent value as given by art. This is why the reader is often aware of learning more about the world from a book than he gets from actual experience, not only because in the book he is prepared to find significance in events that mean nothing in life, but because those events in the book are related to each other in a coherent valuation which sets them in ordered relation of importance, and this can reveal to him in what had seemed the mere confusion of his daily affairs new orders of meaning.[28]

The world created by the human imagination is a significant one. Harvey Cox notes that "fantasy is the richest source of human creativity. Theologically speaking, it is the image of the creator God in man. Like God, man in fantasy creates whole worlds *ex nihilo*, out of nothing."[29] The imagination, as the Romantic poets insisted, is not only a delightful agent of creativity, but also a vehicle for truth. If anyone doubts this, one has only to read the Bible, especially the Old Testament prophets and the New Testament book of Revelation. As people's revelation to people, human imaginings are an index to the values, preoccupations and anxieties of the human race. They are also a way of expressing the truth about reality. This includes supernatural reality, for although the physical and social sciences cannot put spiritual reality into a test tube or statistical survey or profile, the world of the literary imagination has always found it possible to include supernatural reality in its vision of what really exists. And whereas most disciplines explore the external world as it objectively exists, the constructs of the literary imagination, or what Northrop Frye calls man's mythologies, present that same world as it is viewed and experienced by people, who are valuing creatures and who therefore assimilate the world "in terms of what man wants and does not want."[30]

We must, of course, not overstate the case for the value of the imagination. Too many modern scholars and enthusiasts for the arts attribute inherent and magical and even religious power to myth, ritual and fantasy *in themselves*. From a Christian perspective this is nonsense; pagan myths and rituals are not infrequently cruel, animalistic, filled with terror and depraved. Like anything else in life, the imagination can be either good or bad, redemptive or depraved. We can observe this dual capacity in our own fantasies and imaginings, which are sometimes pictures of heroism, virtue and piety, and sometimes of malice, hatred and lust. But regardless of what the human imagination produces, whether good or depraved, the imagination is important as a revelation of what is inside the human person. Christians cannot give their moral or intellectual approval to every form of human imagining, but neither can they afford to ignore the world of the literary imagination. That world, after all, is nothing less than a window to human nature and the real world.

4 Is Literature Useful?

Does Literature Teach Truth?
All literatures are one; they are the voices of the natural man.
... Man will never continue in a mere state of innocence; he is
sure to sin, and his literature will be the expression of his sin.
... It is a contradiction in terms to attempt a sinless literature
of sinful man. □ *John Henry Newman*, The Idea of a University

Is literature useful? I have deliberately delayed asking this question because it is usually the one that defenders of literature feel obliged to answer first. The result has been less satisfactory than is often acknowledged. My own conviction is that the value of literature can be established quite apart from its usefulness. As a source of beauty, it has a purely artistic reason for being, and as a world of the imagination, it has its own delightfulness. The attempt to defend the importance of literature on practical grounds has usually led apologists to treat it as philosophy, psychology, theology, sociology or history. As long as literature is viewed in this way, it cannot avoid being regarded as a dispensable subdivision of other disciplines.

Having made this disclaimer, I would hasten to insist that the question about the usefulness of literature is a legitimate one. Surely none of us is ready to deny the

Horatian dictum that literature is not only pleasurable but also profitable. My concern is to distinguish good from bad ways of approaching the usefulness of literature.

The time-honored reply to the charges against literature has been the claim that literature teaches moral virtue and intellectual truth. This line of defense was of classical origin, having begun with Aristotle and Horace. It reached a definitive Christian expression in Sir Philip Sidney's *Apology for Poetry* (ca. 1580). Sidney places literature into the broad category of "knowledge," calling it "the first light-giver to ignorance" in "the noblest nations and languages that are known."[1] Of all the disciplines, Sidney then goes on to assert, literature is the most effective in moving people to moral virtue. The writer of imaginative literature "doth intend the winning of the mind from wickedness to virtue,"[2] and he is, "for instructing, ... wellnigh comparable to the philosopher, and, for moving, leaves him behind him."[3] Three centuries later Matthew Arnold gave the same argument a humanistic emphasis when he claimed that literature teaches people "how to live."[4] The argument is still a popular one among Christians, with Henry Zylstra, for example, asserting that "the novel ... can teach you of moral evil and of good as well as all the sages can."[5]

Attractive as this defense may be, it does not hold up under scrutiny. Literature as a whole does not embody and teach intellectual or moral truth. All literature has ideational *content*, but only a small part of the corpus of literature contains *truth*. In other words most literature has not presented a Christian view of reality, so that the usual equation of content with truth is totally misleading. People who have defined the value of literature in terms of truthful content have been much too facile and undiscriminating in their assertions that literature teaches or contains truth.

C. S. Lewis, in one of his most outstanding essays, has observed that "the values assumed in literature have seldom been those of Christianity."[6] The value structure of most literature is what Lewis quite correctly calls "sub-

Christian." He goes on to say, "Some of the principal values actually implicit in European literature were... (a) honour, (b) sexual love, (c) material prosperity, (d) pantheistic contemplation of nature, (e) *Sehnsucht* [longing] awakened by the past, the remote, or the (imagined) supernatural, (f) liberation of impulses."[7] One can, it is true, make a case for the *relative* accuracy of the scale of values espoused in literature as a whole. If we arrange values on a hierarchy ranging from the lowest to the highest, we can conclude, with Lewis, that literature as a whole records "man's striving for ends which, though not the true end of man (the fruition of God), have nevertheless some degree of similarity to it, and are not so grossly inadequate to the nature of man as, say, physical pleasure or money."[8] Still, this does not alter the case substantially. If literature as a whole does not present a Christian view of reality and in fact frequently contradicts Christian or biblical truth, no great claims can be made for literature as a teacher of truth.

That theory runs afoul of another fallacy as well. Literature as a whole is contradictory in the values by which it urges people to order their lives. When the classicist urges people to govern their conduct by their reason, the romanticist by their emotions, the naturalist by their drives and impulses, and when the Christian, believing all of these faculties to be fallen, urges people to order their lives by the moral law of God, the resulting body of literature contradicts itself, since all of these value structures cannot be true.

The model I am *rejecting* can be pictured like this:

literature = truth → reader → life/world view

That is, literature, which can simply be equated with truth, instructs the reader, who simply accepts or applies what literature teaches him in his life and his world view. The fallacies of this model are two: (1) literature as a whole is contradictory in its value structure and cannot therefore simply be equated with truth, nor can a person simply obey these contradictory statements, and (2) literature as a whole is nonbiblical or sub-Christian in its value system, so that a Christian reader is unable to make the simple equation of literature and truth.

The case for the usefulness of literature will have to be defined in different terms. I would define it in two complementary ways. (1) Writers are sensitive observers of reality. The truth that they give us is not necessarily a matter of intellectual truth or world view or moral slant, but consists of faithfulness to reality and human experience. Writers present human experience for the reader's contemplation. In that sense they present the truth—the truth about actual human experience. (2) Literature presents a variety of world views for the reader's analysis. Contemplating these serves the function of leading readers to evaluate, exercise and expand their own values and world view. Literature in this case is a catalyst for thought and a stimulus to the clarification of values. In the first instance (the writer as an observer of reality) a writer's Christianity or lack of it is likely to be unimportant; in the second instance (the writer as someone who offers a world view), it is the crucial issue for a Christian reader.

Literature as a Form of Knowledge

A poem . . . begins in delight and ends in wisdom. . . . It begins in delight . . . and ends in a clarification of life. □ Robert Frost, "The Figure a Poem Makes"

The concept, the label, is perpetually hiding from us . . . the real. We have to have conceptual knowledge . . . to engage in any activity at all, but that knowledge, like the walls we put up to keep out the weather, shuts out the real world and the sky. □ Joyce Cary, Art and Reality

The greatest contribution of literary theory in our century has been the insistence that literature is a special form of knowledge. The critics who have contributed most to this discovery are the formalist critics. Their theory has been admirably summarized by William J. Handy, whose book *Kant and the Southern New Critics*[9] is one of the best introductions to twentieth-century literary theory.

Modern criticism has asserted that the knowledge that writers of imaginative literature give us is different from the intellectual or factual information of science, philosophy, theology, psychology, sociology and similar disciplines. This is not to deny that literature contains ideas and propositional statements. It is to say that these ideas are not the differentia of literature. Usually, in fact, they are ideas that have been abstracted from the work at the cost of the actual story or poem. Furthermore, the ideas of literature are for the most part commonplace and even platitudinous. The theme that Shakespeare handles with such haunting power in his sonnets is that time flies, which is hardly a startling contribution to the realm of thought. Sir Philip Sidney apparently did not realize how self-defeating his defense of literature on intellectual grounds was when he wrote that literature is "the first light-giver to ignorance, and first nurse, whose milk by little and little enabled [people] to feed afterwards on tougher knowledges."[10] C. S. Lewis asserts that "many of the comments on life which people get out of Shakespeare could have been reached by very moderate talents without his assistance." [11]

The general thrust of formalist criticism is to distrust the abstract formulations of the cognitive or "idea" disciplines such as science and philosophy. Why the distrust? Because the ideas of the intellect reduce experience from what it really is. The intellect analyzes and categorizes experience as a way of controlling it. But the labels of the analytic intellect—table, love, sun, death, rose—never do justice to the reality of those things. The scientific or cognitive way of describing experience is, of course, necessary if we are to operate efficiently in the world.

But writers and lovers of literature insist that such ideas or labels are only part of the truth. Abstract ideas sacrifice both the particularity and variety of things in deference to a general category, and they omit the experiential dimension that makes up the real event or object. William Handy summarizes the position of most modern literary theorists when he writes that "the significance of literature resides in its being a unique form of knowledge, separate and distinct from scientific knowledge, from ethical knowledge, and from practical knowledge in what it seeks to formulate, but equally as important as these to man's complete knowledge of his experience."[12] Allen Tate writes, "The function of criticism should have been, in our time, as in all times, to maintain and to demonstrate the special, unique, and complete knowledge which the great forms of literature afford us. And I mean quite simply *knowledge*, not historical documentation and information."[13]

If the knowledge that literature gives is different from that of the scientific and intellectual disciplines, what is the nature of that knowledge? It is the knowledge of human experience. The writer of imaginative literature aims to present human experience through the medium of words. William Handy writes that "to 'know' scientifically is to possess information *about* an object."[14] By contrast, literature is presentational, to use the widely accepted term of Susanne Langer; literature *presents* human experience in its qualitative reality. This is what John Crowe Ransom has in mind when he entitles a book about literature *The World's Body*, and Thomas Howard when he subtitles a book on literature *The World as Image*. "The poet," writes Cleanth Brooks, "attempts to break through the pattern of 'abstract experience' and give man a picture of himself as a man."[15] The human faculty that allows both writer and reader to experience reality in this concreteness is, according to modern literary theory, the imagination.

How can the mere presentation of experience be a form of knowledge? The answer is that by looking closely at a single aspect of experience, we come to understand it better. This is not a process of teaching but of revelation, and many writers have viewed their task in these terms. Coleridge asked, "Who has not a thousand times seen snow fall on water? Who has not watched it with a new feeling from the time that he has read Burns'... 'To snow that falls upon a river/ A moment white—then gone forever!' "[16] To enable a reader to see with a new feeling or understanding or zest is the writer's way of imparting knowledge. The novelist Joseph Conrad wrote, "My task... is, by the power of the written work to make you hear, to make you feel—it is, before all, to make you *see*."[17] Flannery O'Connor said, "Any discipline can help your writing: logic, mathematics, theology, and of course and particularly drawing. Anything that helps you to see, anything that makes you look. The writer should never be ashamed of staring."[18] And whatever Aristotle meant by the theory that literature is an imitation of reality, one thing that he surely meant is that literature is in some way (though not in a literal or photographic way) a reproduction of human experience.

One aspect of human experience that literature reveals is the external world of physical objects. Here, if anywhere, Conrad's aim to make the reader hear and see is the dominant impulse of the writer. It is the aim of Mark Twain, for example, in the following description of sunrise on the Mississippi River:

> The dawn creeps in stealthily; the solid walls of black forest soften to gray, and vast stretches of the river open up and reveal themselves; the water is glass-smooth, gives off spectral little wreaths of white mist; there is not the faintest breath of wind, nor stir of leaf; the tranquillity is profound and infinitely satisfying. Then a bird pipes up.... When the light has become a little stronger, you have one of the fairest and softest pictures imaginable. You have the intense green of the massed and crowded foliage near by; you see it paling shade by shade in front of you; upon the next projecting cape, a mile off or more, the tint has lightened to the tender young green of spring; the cape beyond that one has almost lost color, and the farthest one, miles away under the horizon, sleeps upon the water a mere dim vapor, and hardly separable from the sky above it and about it. And all this stretch of river is a mirror, and you have the

shadowy reflections of the leafage and the curving shore and the receding capes pictured in it. Well, that is all beautiful; soft and rich and beautiful; and when the sun gets well up, and distributes a pink flush here and a powder of gold yonder and a purple haze where it will yield the best effect, you grant that you have seen something that is worth remembering.[19]

William Wordsworth has a similar aim in the following description of sunrise on the Thames River in London:

Earth has not anything to show more fair:
Dull would he be of soul who could pass by
A sight so touching in its majesty;
This City now doth, like a garment, wear
The beauty of the morning; silent, bare,
Ships, towers, domes, theaters, and temples lie
Open unto the fields, and to the sky;
All bright and glittering in the smokeless air.
Never did sun more beautifully steep
In his first splendor, valley, rock, or hill;
Ne'er saw I, never felt, a calm so deep!
The river glideth at his own sweet will:
Dear God! the very houses seem asleep;
And all that mighty heart is lying still![20]

Both Mark Twain's and Wordsworth's descriptions *present* one of the faces of nature. No propositional statement of theme—for example, "sunrise is beautiful and awe-inspiring"—does justice to the meaning of the works themselves. This is why Flannery O'Connor insists that "the whole story is the meaning, because it is an experience, not an abstraction"[21] and why Cleanth Brooks speaks of "the heresy of paraphrase," that is, the fallacy of thinking that a poem's meaning consists of a propositional summary of its ideas.[22]

Literature illuminates the world of human emotions as well as the world of nature. Eve's love song to Adam in *Paradise Lost*, for example, captures the contentedness of a lover in the presence of the beloved:

With thee conversing I forget all time,

All seasons and their change, all please alike.
Sweet is the breath of morn, her rising sweet,
With charm of earliest birds; pleasant the sun
When first on this delightful land he spreads
His orient beams on herb, tree, fruit, and flower,
Glistering with dew; fragrant the fertile earth
After soft showers; and sweet the coming on
Of grateful evening mild, then silent night
With this her solemn bird and this fair moon,
And these the gems of heaven, her starry train:
But neither breath of morn when she ascends
With charm of earliest birds, nor rising sun
On this delightful land, nor herb, fruit, flower,
Glistering with dew, nor fragrance after showers,
Nor grateful evening mild, nor silent night
With this her solemn bird, nor walk by moon,
Or glittering starlight without thee is sweet.[23]

Such a poem, I submit, is a form of knowledge. It expresses the truth about romantic love in a way that no analytic discussion can ever achieve.

Literature also reveals the nature of more general human problems or social issues. Homer's *Odyssey*, for instance, leads a reader to contemplate important dimensions of home and family. Psalm 23 is a meditation on God's providence, an abstraction that the poem never uses, preferring instead the concrete image of the sheep-shepherd relationship. Aldous Huxley's *Brave New World* explores in narrative form the horrors of the technological society. In all of these instances it is the actual presentation of the subject that constitutes the knowledge of literature. Even when the subject of a literary work is something as intangible as "evil" (as in Shakespeare's *King Lear*) or "guilt" (as in Shakespeare's *Macbeth*), literature allows a reader to "know" its subject as a concrete experience, not as a philosophic proposition. Often the knowledge of literature comes with greatest impact when a reader or viewer is so moved by the presentation that he or she cannot verbalize about the work of literature but only experience it.

Literature and World View

All great artists have a theme, an idea of life profoundly felt and founded in some personal and compelling experience. . . . A novelist, therefore, can give only . . . truth with an angle. . . . The writer selects his facts. He arranges their order to suit his own conception of values, his own theme. □ *Joyce Cary*, Art and Reality

Writers do not simply present experience in an objective manner. They see reality from their own perspective and mold their literary vision around their own passionately held opinions. (Writers are among the most opinionated people in the world.) The novelist Graham Greene has said that "every creative writer worth our consideration . . . is . . . a man given to an obsession,"[24] and Joyce Cary asserts that "all serious artists . . . are perfectly convinced of the truth as they see it."[25] Any major work of literature, and every body of lyric poetry (though not every individual poem), exhibits a world view. Nathan Scott has expressed it well:

> The artist wants to give a shape and a significance to what Mr. Vivas calls "the primary data of experience." He wants to contain the rich plenitude of experience within a pattern that will illumine. . . . But, of course, he cannot discover such a pattern unless he has a vantage point from which to view experience. . . . Which is to say that he can transmute . . . reality into the order of significant form only in accordance with what are his most fundamental beliefs about what is radically significant in life.[26]

And as Scott observes further, the writer's vision or belief "is precisely the element which we ought to regard as constituting the religious dimension of imaginative literature."[27]

The intellectual value or usefulness of literature lies in the fact that literature embodies the significant world views of the past and present. By doing so it furnishes the material upon which a person can increase his understanding of his own values and the world views by which other people live. For the Christian reader the world views of literary works constitute the material upon which the Christian mind, operating from the perspective of a Christian or biblical world view, can expand its understanding of the Christian world view and apply biblical principles to the situations of life.

I would define a *world view* as a set of beliefs that tells a person what to think and how to act in any situation in life. Richard Stevens and Thomas J. Musial have written one of the most helpful books on the topic.[28] According to their framework a reader must make two assumptions as he or she attempts to understand a world view as presented in a work of literature: "First, he must assume that any world view has a central concept, or value. . . . Second, the reader must assume that all the other elements in the world view will derive their significance and worth from their relation to the central concept or value."[29] This means that the essential ingredient of a world view is a concept or value that integrates and gives meaning to all aspects of experience. The highest value might be God, a person (self, a specific individual, humanity in general), an institution (state, church, home), an abstract quality (love, truth, beauty, order, reason, emotion) or nature. Nathan Scott calls the central value a work's "ultimate concern," and he speaks in terms similar to those of Stevens and Musial when he talks of "some fundamental hypothesis about the nature of existence which . . . introduces structure and coherence . . . into the formless stuff of life."[30] Cleanth Brooks similarly calls a work of literature "a portion of reality as viewed and . . . rendered coherent through a perspective of valuing."[31]

An illustration will clarify how a single principle can become elevated to the status of the supreme value that gives significance and identity to all of life. A theistic world view makes God supreme. To a person living by this world view, God is the ultimate reality and the one who integrates everything that exists. For example, people are defined as creatures of God. In a theistic world view,

God defines what the self is, namely, the image of God. Moral goodness becomes defined as doing God's will, and evil is viewed as the departure from God's will. Time and history are identified as the working out of God's purpose. The state is viewed as a divinely ordained social institution established by God. Knowledge, in a theistic world view, is the truth that God reveals, and reality itself is defined as God's creation. In short, a theistic world view is one in which God is the point of reference for all experience —the one who gives meaning and identity to every aspect of life. The specifically Christian world view places the triune God of the Bible at the center of reality and orders experience by the truth that God has revealed in the Bible and the incarnate life of Christ.

To identify a world view in literature, then, a reader needs to ask questions such as the following:

1. What do the writer and/or characters in the work value most?

2. According to the writer and/or characters, what really exists? The physical world? A supernatural world? If so, what is the nature of each? Do moral qualities such as goodness or love really exist? Do human emotions?

3. According to the writer and/or characters, how should life be lived? What constitutes the good life?

4. According to the writer and/or characters, what *brings* human fulfillment or happiness? Virtue? Pleasure? Physical objects? Money? God?

These questions will elicit an awareness of world view. But how does one decide what value is central in a work or what conception of the good life is embodied in a work? How does the reader detect the allegiance of a story or poem? My answer is that the reader mainly listens to the writer and the characters in a story or poem. It is not hard to sense that Odysseus values home above all, Aeneas the state, Renaissance love poets their lady and Wordsworth nature.

More formally, we can extract a world view from a work of literature by observing closely the characters with whom we are brought into confrontation. We should consider literary characters as persons who make an experiment in living—who undertake some course of action that exemplifies and tests the kind of life in which they believe. This way of reading considers literary characters as persons who pursue an experiment in living "to its final stages and within a situation of ultimate meaning. Meaning in fiction is thus viewed as what an action leads to, results in, or implies."[32] It must be remembered that the experiment in living that a literary character undertakes tests the adequacy of his or her world view. If the experiment is successful, the work can be said to affirm the world view. If the experiment fails, the work denies the view of reality and by implication usually suggests an alternative. The additional task of readers, having determined what is affirmed and what is denied by the work of literature, is to evaluate that world view by the standard of what they themselves believe to be the truth about reality.

The methodology for arriving at an understanding of the central value in a work of literature can be summarized by the following questions:

1. What is the identity of the characters, especially the protagonist (or the speaker in a lyric poem)? What motivates the characters? What are their preoccupations, as revealed by their thoughts, words and actions?

2. What kind of action do the characters undertake? What is the nature of the experiment in living?

3. What are the results that follow from persons living and acting as these characters did?

Having answered these questions, the reader will ask another: how does the world view exhibited by the work relate to my own world view or scale of values? For the Christian reader this is equivalent to asking how the world view or moral slant measures up to biblical doctrine and the example of Jesus, since Christianity is a revealed religion based ultimately on a sacred book. Christians believe that God has revealed the nature of true reality and that his revelation, given thousands of years ago, is still the truth about life.

Wherein, then, lies the intellectual value of literature? It resides in the ability of literature to embody the world views by which people have lived and continue to live. This is a worthwhile knowledge for several reasons. For one thing, it gives a person a historical perspective. Such a perspective is important because before we can truly understand our own civilization and culture, and even our own world view, it is necessary to know how we got where we are. We need a historical perspective because we cannot afford the naiveté of beginning anew with each generation.

A second reason for concerning oneself with the world views of literature is that they help us understand people. The great world views are not simply historical specimens of a bygone age. They are enduring responses to permanent issues that are perpetually important in human experience. A hedonistic or materialistic or humanistic world view articulated hundreds of years ago can help a person understand a neighbor or acquaintance who lives by the same world view today.

Third, knowing the important world views gives us a knowledge of the alternatives by which persons may order their lives. Anyone's world view should arise from considered and responsible deliberation, and this necessitates an awareness of alternatives. When Jesus told his potential followers to sit down and count the cost before placing him at the center of their lives, was he not saying that people should compare the Christian world view with the other values by which they might order their lives? There is a sense in which everyone, regardless of his or her world view, shares an identical task—that of coming to an understanding of the truth about reality in an intelligent awareness of the alternatives. C. S. Lewis has written that "to judge between one *ethos* and another, it is necessary to have got inside both, and if literary history does not help us to do so it is a great waste of labour."[33]

For the Christian, studying the world views as embodied in literature affords an opportunity to exercise and expand an already formulated world view. That world view is given by God in the Bible and the Incarnation of Christ. Often a person's knowledge of that revelation is enhanced by the study of Christian theology as it has been articulated by gifted people through the centuries. In no sense, however, does the Christian go to literature to *find* his world view. For a Christian, studying the important world views increases his sense of discrimination as he compares his own Christian world view with the world views of literature. This model of how literature is useful can be diagramed, in a manner similar to that of the model that I rejected earlier:

biblical truth → reader → literature/world view

That is, a Christian reader finds his world view in the Christian revelation, which he or she then applies to literature and by which the world views of literature are measured. This model implies at least two important principles. (1) We assimilate literature in terms of what we bring to it. Literature tests and brings out what we already believe. This is not a conclusion that I have reached a priori but one that I have come to as a result of listening to people talk about the literature that they have read and the plays or movies they have seen. And it is a situation that is typical of non-Christians as well as Christians. (2) According to this model, the value of literature is not that it teaches truth, as the earlier model claimed. Instead, reading literature is profitable because it presents for a reader's understanding and analysis the significant world views of history, thereby supplying the material upon which the Christian mind can apply Christian principles to human experience. In short, literature is a catalyst to thought.

If my approach is correct, we should speak of the intellectual function of literature rather than the moral function. Literature sometimes leads a reader to good moral behavior, but to expect literature as a whole to do so for the majority of readers is to expect too much from fallen writers and fallen readers. It is always intellectually profitable, however, to exercise and expand one's own world view by applying it to the viewpoints encountered in literature. And literature is useful in this way regardless of whether a reader agrees or disagrees with the viewpoint of a given work.

It is evident that I cannot agree with the attempt to minimize the distinctiveness of Christianity in an effort to find some kind of common bond between a Christian's faith and every work of literature that he or she reads. This is what people who believe that literature "teaches truth" are forced to do. But it is untrue that virtually all literature merges into a unified core of common belief. At the level of world view and ethical viewpoint, a Christian should place every work of literature on trial, with Christian principles serving as the jury. The approach that I am urging is obviously the opposite of allowing ourselves to be "taken in" by a writer or lulled into intellectual or emotional acquiescence as we read. I prefer an approach in which our sense of discrimination is at its sharpest and in which we test the spirit or allegiance of a work with the most thoroughgoing rigor. Such an approach will send a reader to the Bible many times, searching for a standard of truth by which to evaluate the ideas encountered in literature. Christian criticism, in short, is a way of testing the spirits to see whether they are of God.

Hawthorne's **The Scarlet Letter**

Literature . . . extends the range of vision, intellectual, moral, spiritual; it . . . sharpens our discernment. □ *Charles G. Osgood,* Poetry as a Means of Grace

The Scarlet Letter, by Nathaniel Hawthorne, is an especially useful work with which to illustrate how to analyze world views in literature because it embodies three distinct world views. They are the Puritan, the Romantic and the Christian. In discussing these I will be concerned not simply to explore how these world views are embodied in the story, but also to measure them against a

Christian standard.

The first group of characters whose world view emerges in the story is the Puritan community. Theirs is a legalistic world view that exalts a moral code to supremacy. The narrator describes them as "a people amongst whom religion and law were almost identical" (chap. 2).[34] Their elevation of moral law to the integrating factor in their experience explains the Puritan community's tendency to view Hester Prynne, the mother of the illegitimate child Pearl, not as a person but as the violator of a moral code. For example, the impressive scene that opens the story describes how the community brings Hester out of the prison to the scaffold of the pillory in order to hold her up as an example of moral sin. The same propensity to define Hester in terms of the moral code is underscored in chapter five when we read that through the years, "giving up her individuality, she would become the general symbol at which the preacher and moralist might point, and in which they might vivify and embody their images of woman's frailty and sinful passion. Thus the young and pure would be taught to look at her . . . as the figure, the body, the reality of sin." The same thing is established by the letter "A" that the Puritan community compels Hester to wear. The symbol recurs in the book more than once every two pages and is a running reminder of the community's practice of defining Hester as an adulteress, a violator of the moral code.

The members of the Puritan community also take their own identity from the moral code that dominates their world. The spectators of Hester's exposure on the scaffold identify themselves as the self-righteous keepers of the code. Governor Bellingham, Reverend Wilson, Reverend Dimmesdale and the city magistrates are the official guardians of the moral law. Throughout the story these characters illustrate how the mainspring of action and governing principle for the Puritan community is the moral code.

How does the Puritan community's experiment in living fare in the story? It fails, to put it mildly. The Puritans are uniformly unsympathetic in the story. Hawthorne secures a negative reaction to them by making them the object of satiric attack throughout his story. He also pays his readers the compliment of assuming that their world view and moral sensitivity are healthy, so that we have no hesitation in condemning the bigotry, self-righteousness, sadism and unforgiving nature of the Puritan's legalism.

The final task is to evaluate the Puritan community's legalistic world view by the Christian standard. Too many readers equate the Puritans in Hawthorne's story with Christianity and conclude that Hawthorne is condemning Christianity. This is surely an inaccurate interpretation. *The Scarlet Letter*, when it attacks Puritan behavior, is not attacking Christianity because Puritan behavior in the story is not Christian. The attitudes and behavior of the Puritan community are condemned by a truly Christian standard, as contained in the Bible and the life of Christ.

The Christian ideal is one that forgives and restores the sinner. Christ *forgave* the woman taken in adultery (Jn. 8: 2-11); he did not *excuse* her, nor did he neglect to call adultery a sin, as evidenced by the fact that he told the woman, "Go, and do not sin again" (v. 11). Paul reinforced the same ideal of forgiveness when he wrote, "Brethren, if a man is overtaken in any trespass, you who are spiritual should restore him in a spirit of gentleness. Look to yourself, lest you too be tempted. Bear one another's burdens, and so fulfil the law of Christ" (Gal. 6:1-2). In a Christian world view, then, the standard by which people are called to order their lives is a forgiving God who calls people to forgive their fellow humans. The Puritans in Hawthorne's story have substituted for that standard a moral law that only condemns (rather than restores) the sinner.

The second world view dramatized in the story is the Romantic world view. Romanticism, that intellectual movement that became dominant early in the nineteenth century and has been influential ever since, elevated emotion, impulse and human freedom from all civilized restraints as the highest of all values. If there is a single term that covers this complex of values, it is nature.

Hester, as all the commentators point out, is the great exponent of Romantic values in the story. As the narrator says, "For years past she had looked from this estranged point of view at human institutions, and whatever priests or legislators had established; criticizing all with hardly more reverence than the Indian would feel for the clerical band, the judicial robe, the pillory, the gallows, the fireside, or the church. The tendency of her fate and fortune had been to set her free" (chap. 18). The great conflict in Romantic literature is the individual against society, and by that standard Hester is a thoroughgoing Romantic heroine.

In the view of Hester, as also of critics who share her Romantic values, Hester and Dimmesdale are the victims of society. If only they could escape from the restrictions of civilization and Christian morality, they would be free. This is exactly the view that Hester espouses in the climactic forest meeting with Dimmesdale when she urges their escape with these words: "Whither leads yonder forest-track? . . . Deeper it goes, and deeper, into the wilderness, less plainly to be seen at every step; until, some few miles hence, the yellow leaves will show no vestige of the white man's tread. There thou art free! . . . Or there is the broad pathway of the sea! . . . What hast thou to do with all these iron men, and their opinions?" Hester's attitude toward the adultery also reveals her Romantic impulse when she says to Dimmesdale, "What we did had a consecration of its own. We felt it so!" (chap. 17). It is the Romantic attitude that feeling is the norm.

What becomes of the Romantic world view in the story? Early in the story, when Hester and the Puritan community are the only antagonists on the scene, the Puritans appear in such an ugly light that for at least half of the story we sympathize rather completely with Hester and regard Romantic values as the normative viewpoint in the work. But as the story progresses we come to readjust our view of what constitutes reality in the story. Hawthorne has employed what Joseph Summers calls "the technique of the guilty reader,"[35] in which the author leads the reader to sympathize initially with a character and viewpoint that the reader later comes to see as wrong. Such a strategy, says Summers, is a way of "involving the reader directly in the moral action" of a story, and there is no more brilliant example of the technique than *The Scarlet Letter*.

One commentator has documented "the progressive moral dereliction of Hester" late in the story.[36] The reader is meant to sympathize with Hester in her suffering and in the human redemption that it wins for her in the community, but late in the story her Romantic outlook is juxtaposed to a Christian world view and is shown to be false. Hawthorne does not allow his two protagonists to escape from a world of moral consequences into a world of amoral freedom. In the climactic confession scene at the end of the story it is *not* society that destroys Dimmesdale. We read that the Puritan community "remained silent and inactive spectators of the judgment which Providence seemed about to work." In fact, the Puritan society cannot have judged Dimmesdale because it is ignorant of his sins of adultery and hypocrisy.

There is, finally, the Christian viewpoint in the story, embodied in Reverend Dimmesdale. Dimmesdale's quest, throughout the story, is for forgiveness and renewed communion with God and with his fellow man. This quest reflects the Christian priority of values. Throughout the story Dimmesdale sees his problem all too clearly: he must be forgiven by God and must make a public confession of his sins of adultery and hypocrisy. James's statement, "Confess your sins to one another . . . that you may be healed" (5:16), is the great truth dramatized in the final salvation of Dimmesdale.

The Christian world view, which places the Christian God of forgiveness at the center of reality, emerges as the normative viewpoint at the end of the story with Dimmesdale's public confession, one of the greatest climaxes in all of literature. In that scene Dimmesdale sees himself, not simply as the violator of a social code, as the Romanticist would have it, but in a relationship to God. "God's eye beheld it!" he shouts regarding his sins of adultery and hypocrisy. Furthermore, Dimmesdale espouses a Christian view of reality when he asserts that his confession and the renewed communion with God that it brings are the highest values that he can attain. As he mounts the scaffold he turns to Hester and asks, "Is not this better than what we dreamed of in the forest?" And Hester, the true Romanticist who had conceived of happiness as escape from civilized restraints, replies, "I know not! I know not!" Why, in Dimmesdale's view, is it better to make a public confession of sin than to escape? Because in his world view forgiveness of sin is the highest state that a person can achieve. It is a wholly Christian view of things. That, incidentally, explains why Dimmesdale says, in his moment of exposure, "Thanks be to Him who hath led me hither!" and why he calls his confession an act of "triumphant ignominy."

To the Romanticist Hester, the adultery had "a consecration of its own." Dimmesdale takes the Christian view toward moral sin and says regarding the adultery, "We forgot our God . . . we violated our reverence for the other's soul." In his concluding words, which resolve the plot of the entire story, Dimmesdale repeatedly defines his quest in life in terms of his relationship to God, with forgiveness and salvation as the highest values: "God . . . hath proved his mercy, most of all, in my afflictions. By giving me this burning torture to bear upon my breast! . . . By bringing me hither, to die this death of triumphant ignominy before the people! Praised be his name! His will be done! Farewell!" Randall Stewart says regarding this conclusion, "Thus in his profoundest character-creation, and in the resolution of his greatest book, Hawthorne has employed the Christian thesis: 'Father, not my will, but thine be done.' "[37]

The story ultimately affirms the Christian world view

and contains within itself the antidote to the Puritan and Romantic world views. Amos Wilder correctly describes Hawthorne as a writer "freely at home in the Hebraic-Christian tradition,"[38] while Joseph Schwartz, after documenting Hawthorne's aloofness from the orthodox, institutional church of his day, states that "more than any other writer of his time, Hawthorne was a God-centered writer. He was innately religious, as his profound reverence for the mysteries of Christianity demonstrates."[39]

Is reading literature intellectually useful? It is useful because literature organizes with clarity the world views by which people have lived and continue to live. For the Christian reader, analysis of these world views within a Christian framework allows for the clarification of values. And when a work affirms, as Hawthorne's *The Scarlet Letter* does, a Christian world view, a Christian reader can participate once again in the great drama of faith in God that lies at the heart of his or her own experience.

5 A Christian Approach to Literary Criticism

Literary Criticism and Christianity
Literary criticism should be completed by criticism from a definite ethical and theological standpoint.... It is ... necessary for Christian readers to scrutinize their reading, especially of works of imagination, with explicit ethical and theological standards. □ *T. S. Eliot, "Religion and Literature"*

Most of what I have said in the preceding chapters falls under the heading "a Christian approach to literature." But it is equally crucial to ask what constitutes a Christian approach to the study of literature, which is called *literary criticism*. What do Christian readers and critics of literature do that is distinctive to their religious faith?

The worst way to arrive at an answer to that question is to read essays in which critics discuss the question theoretically. The best method is to make a survey of the essays and books in which Christian scholars actually interact with literary texts. Critics who write theoretically about the relationship between Christianity and literary criticism show a distressing inclination to be esoteric, abstruse and unhelpful. By contrast, Christian critics who apply their interests to works of literature tend to clarify at once what it means to conduct literary analysis within a religious framework. A survey of this criticism shows that

Christian readers/critics are preoccupied with the issues that I discuss in this book—the nature of the religious viewpoint in works of literature, the extent to which the world view or moral perspective in a work of literature agrees or disagrees with a Christian world view, the nature of the Christian vision in literature, the values and dangers of literature in a Christian's life, and the theological ideas that explain and give sanction to the creation of imaginative literature.

My own conviction is that literary criticism is an activity or skill that is the same in kind for a Christian reader/critic and any other person. The difference is simply that Christian critics, like Freudian or Marxist or humanist or any other critics, raise questions of a literary text that may not be of interest to people who do not share the same concerns.

What, then, is the nature of the critical activity that a Christian reader/critic shares with others? It is the ability to describe and explain a literary work as accurately as possible. I believe that Matthew Arnold was absolutely correct when he said that the aim of criticism "in all branches of knowledge, theology, philosophy, history, art, science" is "to see the object as in itself it really is."[1] The aim of biology, for example, is to see the plant or animal as it really is. The aim of sociology is to see society as it really is. And so forth. The aim of literary criticism, in this view, is to see the work of literature as it really is in itself. Cleanth Brooks has written, "Let us say that the task of literary criticism is to put the reader in possession of the work of art."[2] And T. S. Eliot is in the same camp when he states that the literary critic's "primary interest . . . is to help his readers to understand and enjoy."[3] Literary criticism, in other words, should be primarily descriptive (a contribution to knowledge), not evaluative (merely a statement of personal taste).

Morris Weitz differentiates among three types of criticism—description, explanation or interpretation and evaluation.[4] Descriptive criticism asks verifiable, true or false questions, such as, Does Hamlet delay? Is *Hamlet* a tragedy? Is Claudius a usurper? Evaluative criticism, which asks whether a work is artistically good or bad, never asks objectively verifiable questions. Explanation or interpretation may incline toward either the verifiable or subjective end of the spectrum. For example, to explain Hamlet's behavior on the basis of the conventions of the code of revenge is relatively verifiable, while interpreting Hamlet as an instance of irresolution is open to dispute.

It is impossible for literary criticism always to be purely descriptive. Its methodology should, however, be as verifiable as it can possibly be. This applies equally to literary criticism conducted within a religious framework. I wish to oppose as strongly as I can the idea (usually stated as a charge by the unsympathetic) that when Christian critics begin to operate within the area of their distinctive interests they abandon description or analysis for some type of esoteric and subjective evaluation or judgment.[5] The Christian reader/critic, like any good critic, should be interested primarily in describing the literary work as it really is. Such criticism is closely tied to the objective data of the literary text, and it is verifiable in the sense that anyone should be able to go through the same process of questioning and come to similar conclusions.

Some religious criticism is interpretive rather than descriptive, and when it is interpretive it represents one way, among several options, of viewing the work under analysis. To assert, for example, that Marlowe's Dr. Faustus uses his magical powers in increasingly cheap and trivial ways is descriptive and verifiable, but to go further and attribute this decline in Christian terms as "due to *habitude*, constant indulgence in sin"[6] is to enter the realm of interpretation. Even when operating at the level of interpretation, a critic, including the Christian critic, must tie his criticism as closely as possible to the objective data of the piece. When George Santayana praises Dr. Faustus as a humanistic hero and a martyr to everything that the Renaissance prized, he bases his interpretation chiefly on his own bias and response to the play. By contrast Leo Kirschbaum is able to support his Christian interpretation of the play by objective data—"by the Choruses; by Faustus' own recognition; by the Good Angel; by Mephostophilis . . . ; by the Old Man—and, of course, by the action itself."[7] At its best, interpreting literature in a Christian framework is never primarily a subjective evaluation.

The distinctive feature of Christian literary criticism is that Christian readers take the descriptive process a step further than other critics, or a step in a particular direction that may not interest others. Having described the work of literature as it really is in itself, the Christian reader/critic describes the work in relation to Christian belief and biblical doctrine. This is not an esoteric activity, though it may be uninteresting to a non-Christian. The additional description or interpretation that a Christian gives to a literary work is a comparative process in which the intellectual content or moral vision of the work is put alongside the Christian viewpoint on the same subject. In this comparative process a reader/critic might profitably ask three questions:

1. Do the ideas in the work of literature conform or fail to conform to Christian doctrine or ethics?

2. If some of the ideas are Christian, are they inclusively or exclusively Christian? That is, are they ideas that *include* both Christianity and other religious or philosophic viewpoints, or do they *exclude* Christianity from other viewpoints?

3. If some of the ideas in a work are Christian, are they a relatively complete version of the Christian view, or are they a relatively superficial or rudimentary version of Christian belief on a given topic?

I wish to make five observations about the process of criticism that I have described. First, it is obvious that whatever is distinctive about Christian literary criticism concerns the content rather than the form of a literary work. Readers and critics have nothing to say distinctively as Christians about the sonnet form or the narrative structure of a novel or the imagery of a poem. They have much to say relative to their interests about the ethical ideas and world view and themes of literature.

This means, second, that the preoccupations that are distinctive to Christian readers/critics cannot possibly be a complete act of criticism because content is not all there is to a work of literature. There are two levels at which Christian presuppositions add very little, if anything, to one's literary response. They are the level of artistic beauty and the level of mere presentation of human experience (as distinct from the interpretation that a writer gives to that experience). It is legitimate for Christian scholars or journals to concentrate on the distinctive interests of the Christian faith in the literary criticism that they publish, but such criticism should never be the whole of what Christians do as readers or classroom teachers. The largest fault with the religious movement in literary criticism is that in its most characteristic pose it concentrates on the distinctively or exclusively religious dimension of literary analysis to the neglect of what Christian readers/critics share with all readers and all critics.

Third, although I have disavowed evaluation as a primary goal of Christian literary criticism and have insisted that comparing the moral vision in a literary work with Christian truth is largely a descriptive process, some qualification is necessary. The comparison of literary works to Christian belief is an evaluation in the sense that a Christian is already committed to the truthfulness of the Christian faith. The evaluative dimension should remain latent rather than prominent, however, especially in published criticism. If the audience consists of Christians, the mere comparison of a work to Christian belief will be accepted simultaneously as an evaluation of the truth or falseness of the work's theme and world view. And if one's audience does not share the critic's Christian viewpoint, accentuating the evaluative as distinct from the descriptive nature of the critical process will unnecessarily alienate the audience.

A fourth implication of my methodology is that the distinctive concerns of a Christian reader/critic should be the final process that he applies to a work of literature. T. S. Eliot chose his words carefully when he said that "literary criticism should be *completed* by criticism from a definite ethical and theological standpoint" (italics mine).[8] *First* a Christian reader/critic should be rapturous over the artistry of a work. *First* one should note the illumination that the work gives of concrete human experience. *Then* a Christian should measure the philosophic or ethical viewpoint of the work from a Christian perspective.

Finally, the great pitfall of any critic, including the Christian critic, is to allow one's personal perspective to determine the description or interpretation of what a work of literature really says. If a reader likes a work, for example, he or she is inclined to interpret the work as adhering to his or her own world view. A Christian reader of Christopher Marlowe's *Dr. Faustus* is likely to see the play as affirming orthodox Christianity and a militant atheist to interpret the play as a glorification of heterodoxy and iconoclasm. A reader who disagrees with the hedonistic existentialism of Camus's *The Stranger* is likely to find that the story exposes the inadequacies of its protagonist, while a reader who shares Meursault's outlook is inclined to think that Camus presents a sympathetic hero whose viewpoint is correct. The ideal, of course, is *first* to allow the work to express its scale of values or world view and *then* to exercise the prerogative of agreeing or disagreeing with that viewpoint. There is no shortcut to the painstaking analysis of the work itself as the critic's first order of business.

I noted at the outset of this discussion about Christian literary criticism that the best way to determine what constitutes such criticism is to observe it in practice. A person's definition of Christian literary criticism will emerge, I suggest, upon deciding which of the following test cases fall into the realm of religious literary criticism:

1. Explicating the structure, biblical allusions and

imagery of Milton's sonnet "When I Consider How My Light Is Spent."

2. Explicating the structure, classical allusions and imagery in a poem by Ben Jonson or Alexander Pope.

3. Discussing image patterns in a Shakespearean tragedy.

4. Discussing the world view of a Shakespearean tragedy.

5. Explaining the structural principles of the sonnet form.

6. Explaining the ways in which Faulkner's religious views are like and unlike Christianity.

7. Demonstrating the similarities between Jonathan Swift's portrayal of the Yahoos and Christian sermons from the preceding century.

8. Demonstrating the indebtedness of the ideas in Wordsworth's poem "Tintern Abbey" to David Hartley's ideas about psychology.

These examples are, in fact, typical of the decisions I was continually making as an editor responsible for literary articles in a Christian scholarly journal.

My own position is that Christian readers/critics should perform all of the activities described above. In a Christian framework all truth is God's truth and all beauty God's beauty. Any discovery about the truth or beauty of literature is therefore a contribution toward the cultural mandate of subduing God's world for his glory. When we speak of a group of critics or a journal as belonging to something called "religious literary criticism," however, we are naturally concerned with the distinctive interests of such critics. I would include items 1, 4, 6 and 7 from the list in this category, for the following reasons. An essay that unfolds the biblical images in a Christian poem by Milton is concerned with matters of interest to Christians as Christians, while the same process applied to a classical poem is not. Image patterns in a Shakespearean play and the structure of a sonnet are purely aesthetic matters, while world view and religious ideas are areas in which the distinctives of Christian belief begin to play a role. Putting Swift's fiction into the context of Christian theology is of distinctive interest to a Christian reader as a Christian, while relating Wordsworth's poetry to Hartley's psychology is not.

Shakespeare's Macbeth *in Christian Perspective*

What I believe to be incumbent upon all Christians is the duty of maintaining consciously certain standards and criteria of criticism over and above those applied by the rest of the world; and that by these criteria and standards everything that we read must be tested. . . . We must tirelessly criticize it according to our own principles. □ T. S. Eliot, "Religion and Literature"

I have said that a Christian reader/critic performs the same type of descriptive or explanatory criticism that any good critic does. A Christian is not performing a different kind of criticism. To be a good critic a Christian must first of all be master of a skill or craft. Before relating the ethical ideas of Shakespeare's play *Macbeth* to Christian belief, the work must be seen as it really is in itself. This part of the critical act will account for at least three-fourths of what the Christian reader/critic does. Without taking the time or space to develop the topics, I would list the following as those that deserve careful description:

1. The literary genre (drama), along with what this means in terms of setting, plot and characterization.

2. The tragic pattern of the story, with all the implications that this has for characterization and plot.

3. An exploration of the powerful archetypes in the play, including the temptation motif, the crime and punishment pattern, the villain, the usurper and the futile attempt to cheat the oracle.

4. The image patterns that are always an important part of the artistry of Shakespeare's plays.

5. The elements of artistry that raise Shakespeare's play above a television melodrama—the characterization (with emphasis on the psychology of the criminal mind and the psychology of guilt), the dramatic irony, the symbols, the figures of speech, the poetry, the use of foils and contrasts.

6. The relation of the play to the Renaissance world picture, with its emphasis on the great chain of being.

Having done all this, the Christian reader/critic will now want to describe the work in its relationship to Christian belief. The aim is still to identify the work, not as it is in itself this time, but as its content touches upon biblical truth and Christian experience. Critics generally agree that *Macbeth* is, in significant ways, a Christian play. The task of a Christian reader/critic is to explore how this Christian identity manifests itself. In short, what does it mean to approach *Macbeth* from a Christian perspective?

Is a Christian approach to the play one that places it within the context of medieval or Renaissance theology? If so, what theologians or theological traditions should provide the context? Should a scholar compare the play's attitude toward ambition to the thought of Aquinas and conclude that "for Shakespeare, as it had been for Aquinas, ambition was an aspect of pride, a rebellion against the will of God and the order of nature"?[9] Should he make a detailed study of medieval beliefs about demons and then apply these ideas to the agents of evil in *Macbeth*, showing that "Shakespeare has informed *Macbeth* with the Christian conception of a metaphysical world of objective evil"?[10] Or should a critic ransack the writings of Martin Luther, John Calvin and Richard Hooker for theological parallels to Shakespeare, demonstrating that in such areas as the devil, fear and guilt "the patterns of a Christian understanding of sin seem to have contributed in marked ways to the development of Macbeth's characterization"?[11] Or are Anglican church ritual and the Book of Common Prayer the right sources to consult, as Herbert R. Coursen, Jr. does when he relates the data of the play at as many points as possible to the Anglican sacrament of the Eucharist?[12]

Does a Christian approach to *Macbeth* mean discovering biblical allusions in the work? Does it, for example, mean tracing the phrases "dusty death," "a walking shadow" and "a tale told by an idiot" in Macbeth's famous soliloquy to Old Testament wisdom psalms?[13] Does it involve linking the comment by Lady Macbeth's doctor that his patient "more needs... the divine than the physician" (V,ii,71) to the Old Testament statement (2 Chron. 16:12) that King Asa "even in his disease... did not seek the LORD, but sought help from physicians"?[14] Should a critic attempt to show that Lady Macbeth's assertion that "a little water clears us of this deed" (II,ii,68) is an implied allusion to "the ceremonial of washing hands in testimony of innocence (Deut. 21:6) and Pilate's washing his hands (Mt. 21:24)," or that the reference to Duncan as "The Lord's anointed Temple" refers to "two Biblical ideas: the king as the Lord's Anointed (2 Sam. 1:16) and the human body as a temple (1 Cor. 3:17 and 6:19)"?[15] Should the light imagery in Lady Macbeth's sleepwalking scene be related to nine verses from the Bible in an effort to show that "these images of light form... a specifically Christian pattern"?[16]

Does a Christian approach to the play mean identifying parallels or analogues between the play and the Bible, in effect allegorizing the play? Should a critic show that Macbeth's fall "parallels that of Lucifer" and that Lady Macbeth is an "Eve-figure"?[17] Or that Duncan "is a Christlike figure" and that "Macbeth, welcoming Duncan to a banquet in his castle, plays the part of Judas at the Last Supper"?[18] Or that the play "is the Adam and Eve story over again, with the Witches in the role of the Serpent"?[19] Or that Macbeth's fear and "slaughter of various innocents" is an "analogy to the biblical Herod," that Malcolm's conquest of Macbeth with the use of tree branches is a picture of "the biblical theme of a 'righteous branch' as deliverer," and that the play itself is therefore "a Christmas play"?[20] Or that there is an implied "analogy between the murder of Duncan and the crucifixion" of Jesus, and that "Macbeth, by analogy, has crucified his Lord afresh" by killing Duncan?[21] Should a critic seek to establish analogies between the Macbeth-Malcolm rivalry and the Old Testament story of Saul and David, or between Macbeth's visit to the witches and Saul's visit to the witch of Endor or between the evil that engulfs Scotland and the unleashing of Satan in the New Testament book of Revelation?[22]

Or should a Christian critic instead relate the ethical and philosophical ideas to Christian beliefs? Should he or she attempt to show that the play dramatizes Christian viewpoints about "man's evil and the conviction of sin,"[23] "the fact of temptation,"[24] "virtue and sin,"[25] "hardening of heart or incapacity for penitance,"[26] and "damnation"?[27] Is a Christian critic doing the right thing when he interprets many of the moments in the play as occasions when we observe "the constant striving of heaven . . . to induce Macbeth to repent" and concludes on the basis of this pattern that "the spirit of Christ may be discerned by the reader in, through, and above the Shakespearean scene"?[28]

Obviously there is no scarcity of options from which to choose. It is perhaps not surprising that some critics have reacted against the whole attempt to analyze Shakespeare's tragedies in a Christian context. These objections deserve to be heard, but after they have been analyzed they will, I believe, be objections to abuses or specific applications of religious criticism to Shakespeare's plays, not to the principles on which such criticism is based.

Some critics, for example, object, as I do, to readings that speculate about issues that a play itself does not raise. Critics in the religious criticism camp show a particular drive to speculate about the eternal destinies of characters in Shakespeare's plays, even when the works do not comment on the question. This relates to a second abuse, namely, the practice of taking a single piece of religious data from a play and extending it into a whole system of theology that is then applied to the play. The fact that a character in *Macbeth* believes in divine providence, as evidenced by his assertion that the forces opposed to Macbeth will defeat him "with Him above/ To ratify the work" (III, vi,32-33), does not, in my view, allow us to interpret every episode in the play, or even Macbeth's final defeat, as an illustration of God's providence. Or, to cite another instance, to conclude, on the basis of allusions to biblical wisdom literature in a soliloquy by Macbeth, that "Shakespeare's view of human life is neither more nor less than the Biblical view" is to make a bigger claim than the data allows.[29]

Tragedy tends to limit its focus to the temporal or earthly order, say some critics who dislike the religious approach to Shakespeare's tragedies. I agree. But this proves nothing against religious analysis of Shakespeare's plays, because the Christian religion sees ordinary experience and actual history as precisely the arena within which ethical issues and God's activity occur. I cannot agree with Roland Frye's equation of "temporal" with "secular" and "non-theological."[30] Such an approach distorts the way in which the Bible and the Christian faith have always viewed earthly history as the place where we can expect to find spiritual realities fleshed out and tested. Frye comments that "in Macbeth, Shakespeare has created one of the most magnificent presentations of the degeneration of the human soul which our culture affords, and he has done so in reference to Christian theology, but his purpose is still to keep the mirror up to nature and to show the course of human life in this world."[31] The curious and confusing word here is "but"; within a Christian framework it is inevitable, not contradictory, that moral or religious patterns will be embodied in "human life in this world." As R. P. Blackmur expresses it, "An age of faith comes about when religious convictions are part of—incarnate in—secular experience."[32]

Furthermore, critics who find Shakespeare's tragedies thoroughly earthly in their scope have unjustifiably minimized the ways in which these plays reach out explicitly beyond the purely earthly sphere. Surely the world of *Macbeth* includes the supernatural realm as well as the earthly one when the play contains thirty-seven images of hell and demons,[33] and when the murdered king is called "The Lord's anointed Temple" (II,iii,69), and when Macbeth speaks of the knell that summons Duncan "to Heaven, or to Hell" (II,i,64), and when Macbeth expresses a willingness to ignore "the life to come" if he can gain the world now (I,vii,7) and when Lady Macbeth's doctor says, "More needs she the divine than the physician. . . ./ God, God forgive us all" (V,ii,71-72). Whatever *Macbeth* is, it is certainly neither "secular" nor earthbound in its perspective.

A final objection that is voiced against the Christian interpreters of Shakespeare is that they are overly zealous to prove that the pattern of a given play is Christian. This, in my view, is one of the worst abuses of the religious critics of Shakespeare. Many critics apparently assume that it is the task of Christian criticism to show *that* the plays are Christian, whereas the real task of Christian criticism is to determine *whether* the plays are Christian. Surely criticism that weighs the ethos or world view of a play in the scale of Christian belief and finds it lacking has performed its rightful service just as thoroughly as when it finds agreement between Christian doctrine and a work.

It is my conviction that a Christian approach to *Macbeth* must begin by discovering the major themes of the play. This is quite different from starting with a list of religious ideas that is then applied to the play, regardless of whether the play calls for application of a given idea. Identifying the major ideas in a work is an empirical process that begins with ordinary literary criticism—with analysis of plot conflict and structure, characterization and imagery. To say that the analysis of the play must be inductive or empirical means that a critic does not interpret characters and events from a Christian perspective when the work itself does not raise the occasion for applying Christian theology to the characters and events. G. R. Elliott, for example, interprets a number of episodes in *Macbeth* as warnings sent by divine providence to call Macbeth to repentance. Now it is true that Christians interpret events as being directed by God, but in many of the instances cited by Elliott there is nothing in the play to prompt us to interpret the events in such a manner. In such cases the critic imposes a Christian framework onto the play at points where the play itself does not invite such application of Christian doctrine. When the play is silent about the matter of providence, it strikes me as more accurate to say that it lacks a Christian perspective, but this is a dubious procedure because a writer is not obliged to cover the whole territory in every work he writes. If the play does not commit itself on the issue of providence, there is no reason to measure it against that particular Christian doctrine.

When I say that a Christian analysis of *Macbeth* must begin by discovering the major themes of the play, the word "major" is important. Much religious criticism of Shakespeare has consisted of showing that specific phrases or lines in specific speeches of characters in the play have a theological or biblical content. All that such criticism shows is that a character in the play has uttered a Christian sentiment. This is rather small game to be stalking compared to the larger issues of ethics and philosophy and world view that the play as a whole embodies. Christian analysis becomes significant when it addresses itself to what has been variously called the play's "mode of thought and feeling," "its implicit world view," its "fundamental moral principles," its "philosophical patterns" and its "moral vision."[34]

Once a Christian reader/critic has identified the main themes or moral patterns of the play, he or she *then* compares them to Christian belief on the same topics. The question of what constitutes the repository of Christian belief will be answered differently by different critics. I have already indicated my conviction that the ultimate foundation of Christian belief is the Bible. Some critics base their definitions of Christianity on creedal statements, church ritual or the writings of theologians. These critics would do well to take three things into account. First, Christian creeds and theological traditions are ultimately based on something even more foundational, the Bible. Second, creeds and systematic theologies change, while the Bible has remained the one constant source of

Christian belief. And third, writers in the Christian tradition have been much more inclined to base their Christianity on the Bible and biblical theology than on the detailed constructions of the theologians. Shakespeare was much more likely to have been familiar with the stories and poems of the Bible than with the theological writings on which scholars spend hours in the library. Much of what is considered loosely as "religious criticism" is simply history-of-ideas criticism or source criticism, the aims of which are distinct from (though not incompatible with) those of readers who are interested in measuring works of literature by the standard of Christian doctrine.

What about the other options that fall within the school of "Christian criticism of Shakespeare"? They are, in my view, peripheral to the concerns of the Christian reader/ critic. I see no validity whatever in allegorizing the details of a work of literature to fit a Christian pattern if the work itself is not explicitly allegorical. Of course works of literature *can* be allegorized in this way, but so can a football field and a parking lot. Finding biblical parallels to characters and events in the play can help to clarify the work, but these analogues are usually archetypes found everywhere in literature. To cite the biblical parallels while ignoring others (those in classical mythology, for example) does not prove a Christian allegiance in the play, though critics usually imply that it does. Discovering biblical allusions in *Macbeth* has the same potential and limitations that the discovery of biblical parallels does. Biblical allusions certainly prove Shakespeare's acquaintance with the Bible, and their identification is necessary to an understanding of the play. But by themselves they do not say much about whether the play is Christian in its themes. We should never forget that writers who use biblical allusions tend also to use allusions to classical mythology. If biblical allusions are interpreted as evidence of a Christian allegiance, classical allusions can, with equal validity, be interpreted as evidence of a pagan outlook.

What, then, are the leading themes that *Macbeth* embodies? The overall design of the play is the archetypal pattern of crime and punishment. It is the story of a criminal who gets his comeuppance. This has led many readers and critics to discuss justice as a leading theme of the play, but I remain doubtful that this conclusion is correct. I frankly do not know how to interpret the narrative device known as poetic justice (a situation in which good characters are rewarded and bad ones punished). That the prevalence of poetic justice in the literature of the world captures a profound human longing for justice I do not doubt. But are some Shakespearean critics right in saying that the presence of poetic justice in Shakespeare's tragedies shows a Christian conception of providence and justice?

I remain unconvinced for two reasons. (1) The happy ending based on poetic justice is more a convention of storytelling than an expression of a view of the world. I could be wrong about this, but poetic justice is so universal in stories that if it is accepted as evidence of a Christian world view, we are left with the unlikely situation that virtually all of the stories ever told (including most television dramas) exhibit a single conception of moral justice, even though in other ways these works may be exactly opposite to each other. (2) Furthermore, biblical Christianity does not teach that true justice is always discernible in history. Battenhouse is surely correct in saying that poetic justice "is in fact not a Christian idea" and that in the Bible "we find . . . a long list of innocent martyrs, from Abel to John the Baptist and various of Christ's disciples."[35]

One of the indisputable themes of the play—and one that is in keeping with Christian belief—is an insistence on the reality of evil and the implications that this has for the view of man. Until the nineteenth century Western thought was dominated by two views of man. The humanistic tradition, reaching back to ancient Greek thought, had a generally optimistic view of human nature. A major premise of humanism, from the time of Socrates forward, has been that people will ordinarily not do something wrong if they know better, that understanding will usually lead to virtue. If people do evil acts, proponents of this tradition would agree, it is because they have not seen evil as it really is. In one way or another, they are victims of ignorance.[36] This view of knowledge as the doorway to virtue is summarized in Alexander Pope's aphorism that "Vice is a monster of so frightful mien,/ As to be hated needs but to be seen."[37]

The Christian tradition, by contrast, has taken the view that people are sinful by nature and inclined to do evil regardless of how much knowledge they have. The writer of Psalm 19 prays to be forgiven not only from "hidden faults" but "also from presumptuous sins" (that is, sins committed, like Adam's in *Paradise Lost*, against better knowledge). The theological basis of this view of human nature is laid out with great detail by Paul in his New Testament Epistle to the Romans, where he argues that all people, whether or not they have access to the moral standards of the Bible, knowingly violate their own moral ideals. Narrative embodiment of the belief can be found in most of the stories of the Bible, where a wholly idealized protagonist is a rarity and where characters who do what they know to be wrong are the rule. John Calvin, who exerted a major influence on the Christian milieu in which Shakespeare wrote, noted that whereas "the sum of opinion of all philosophers" had been that "reason . . . is a sufficient guide for right conduct, . . . all ecclesiastical writers have recognized both that the soundness of reason in man is gravely wounded through sin, and that the will has been very much enslaved by evil desires."[38]

Macbeth is a classic illustration of the human inability to live up to what a person's ideals and conscience tell him he should do. Throughout the early scenes of the play we repeatedly get the impression that Macbeth and Lady Macbeth are caught in the act of doing something that they know to be monstrously wicked but which they are attracted to nevertheless. This explains Macbeth's titanic struggle with his own conscience, which torments him before, during and after the murder. The thought of murdering Duncan is to Macbeth a "horrid image" that unfixes his hair and makes his heart knock at his ribs (I,iii,135-36).[39] The soliloquy in which Macbeth tallies up the reasons why he should not murder Duncan (I,vii,1-28) likewise shows how clearsighted he is about the sinfulness of the contemplated murder. As Kenneth Muir comments, "Macbeth is never in doubt of the difference between good and evil; nor is Lady Macbeth, not even in the speech in which she deliberately chooses evil as a means of achieving the 'good' of the crown."[40] Or as Virgil Whitaker puts it, "*Macbeth* is the tragedy of a man who, in full knowledge of what he was doing, destroyed his own soul."[41]

The inclination of Macbeth and Lady Macbeth to evil is stronger than their ability to do it. Lady Macbeth prays for evil forces to unsex her and fill her, "from the crown to the toe, top-full/ Of direst cruelty" (I, v, 42-43). She must take the stimulant of wine before she can go through with the murder (II,ii,1-2). And Macbeth, it is clear, would never have perpetrated the murder if Lady Macbeth had not intimidated him into doing it.

A second principle that the play enacts is that people are morally responsible for the evil they do. In other words, the play challenges the naturalistic view which maintains that people are the helpless victims of psychological and environmental and cosmic determinism. Shakespeare's play, it must be granted, depicts all sorts of forces, both within Macbeth and outside of him, that push him in the direction of committing the murder. As in the Bible, however, external forces of evil are not responsible for the evil that people do. External promptings to evil are only *the occasion for* what Dorothy Sayers calls (in connection with Dante's *Divine Comedy*) "the drama of the soul's choice."[42]

Until Macbeth ceases to obey his conscience (it is misleading to say that he kills his conscience, since it continues to plague him after he violates it), he could have chosen the good. This is implied by the scenes in which he vacillates in his intention to kill Duncan. Early in the play, in fact, Macbeth elicits our sympathy because, although he is tempted by ambition, he resists the temptation. The presence of virtuous characters in the play is also a continual reminder that in the world of the play people are not forced to be criminal in their actions. The play thus affirms the Christian, biblical view of human responsibility. Roland Frye summarizes the biblical teaching on the matter thus: "Man's difficulties do not arise out of the hostility of inanimate 'things,' but out of the operation of human choice in history. . . . This basic conception pervades the Bible: man's responsible choices in history are the heart of the matter."[43]

The play is also Christian in its insistence on the reality of guilt. Unlike so much modern psychological theory, Shakespeare's play does not treat guilt as an illusion that needlessly troubles people. On the contrary, there are few works of literature that depict with such clarity and conviction the experience of guilt stemming from moral evil. Shakespeare has given English literature its classic story of human guilt, as Hawthorne did for American literature in *The Scarlet Letter*. The five episodes that dramatize the destructive effects of guilt in *Macbeth* are the dagger scene (II,i), Macbeth's mental collapse immediately after the murder (II,ii), the scene in which Macbeth and Lady Macbeth share their mutual fears and misery (III,ii), the appearance of Banquo's ghost at the banquet (III,iv) and Lady Macbeth's sleepwalking (V,i). Each of these scenes is, from the viewpoint of Christianity, impeccable in its theological premise that evil does something to the human psyche. For the biblical parallels one need only read some of the Old Testament psalms.

Macbeth is, furthermore, an anatomy of temptation. In keeping with the Bible and Christian tradition the play asserts, by means of the archetypal temptation motif, that there are forces both within and outside the individual that tempt him or her to do what is wrong. As we read or view Shakespeare's play we are made to feel the force of the temptation. We feel it in the ladderlike series of prophecies

that the witches make, in the circumstances of Macbeth's
rising political fortunes, in the tug of ambition within Macbeth and in the browbeating of Lady Macbeth. The latter
agent of temptation, particularly, makes us feel how
terrible life will be around the Macbeth household if Macbeth resists the temptation to usurp the throne. But once
we have been made to feel the weight of the reasons for
succumbing to the temptation, the play comes down with
its stern judgment against the crime.

This anatomy of temptation runs true to the teaching of
the Bible, Christian theology and Christian literature. Biblical stories that show the dynamics of human temptation
include the stories of Eve, Samson and Delilah, Saul (who
is tempted by circumstances to disobey Samuel's command), David and Bathsheba, Jesus (tempted by Satan in
the wilderness) and Peter (tempted by circumstances to
deny Jesus). The apostle James explains the theology of
temptation when he writes that "each person is tempted
when he is lured and enticed by his own desire. Then desire when it has conceived gives birth to sin; and sin when
it is full-grown brings forth death" (Jas. 1:13-14). This
same attitude toward temptation to immorality is anato-
mized in imaginative literature by such giants of the
Christian tradition as Spenser in the *Faerie Queene* and
Milton in *Paradise Lost* and *Paradise Regained*.

Shakespeare's play has as one of its chief aims to affirm
order, conceived largely in terms of the Renaissance concept of the great chain of being. According to this scheme,
the whole scale of creation exists as a hierarchy that begins
at the top with God and descends through the angels, the
planets, man, animals, plants and minerals. This principle
of hierarchy extends to the state (where the king is expected to rule), the family (where the husband is the head)
and the individual (where reason must rule the emotions
and appetites).

In Shakespeare's play, order is affirmed, as it usually is
in tragedy, by negative example. That is, we witness the
destructive results that follow from its violation. We see

the tragedy of the passion of ambition overcoming its rightful superior, reason. We observe the inversion of order in the family when Lady Macbeth begins to dominate Macbeth, and in the state when Macbeth usurps the throne from the rightful king, his natural superior in the great chain of being. In keeping with the idea of the corresponding planes of reality, disorder in the individual, family and state produces disorder in nature and the cosmos as well.

This affirmation of order is consonant with biblical teaching. A glance at the moral commands of both the Old and New Testaments shows, for example, the pervasive biblical concern for adherence to the order that God has prescribed for human life. The enormity of rebellion against legitimate civil authority is a recurrent theme of the epic of the Exodus, and it is the main political theme in the story of the civil war instigated by Absalom against his father David (2 Sam. 14—18). The idea of hierarchy in the family begins with Genesis 3:16 and culminates in statements by the apostles Paul and Peter. This is not to say, of course, that the specific formulation that the Renaissance gave to the ideal of order and hierarchy—the great chain of being—is biblical or Christian in its origin, although it is important to realize that contemporary Christian traditions in Shakespeare's day would have supported the great chain of being concept.

A final emphasis in the play, less central and more subjectively discerned, perhaps, than the themes I have mentioned thus far, is the horror of murder. The image pattern of blood that broods over the play dramatizes the special kind of guilt that attaches to the act of murder. The play captures the mysterious and profound principle of the sanctity of human life and the guilt that inevitably follows from its violation.

Here, too, the play is Christian in its thematic design. Macbeth's famous aphorism, "It will have blood, they say: blood will have blood" (III,iv,121), is paralleled by the biblical principle, "Whoever sheds the blood of man, by man shall his blood be shed" (Gen. 9:6). The archetype of the blood that is shed in murder is nearly as pervasive in the Bible as it is in Shakespeare's play, beginning with the blood of Abel that cries from the ground (Gen. 4:10) and stretching to the spilled blood of the saints and martyrs in the book of Revelation.

These, then, are the leading ideas that I find in the play: the reality of evil and the human inclination toward it, moral responsibility, the reality of guilt and temptation, the ideal of order and the horror of murder. I have already suggested how each of these ideas agrees with Christian belief. Having identified these themes, the Christian reader/critic should ask two additional questions. One is, Are these themes inclusively or exclusively Christian? Do they set Christianity off from other ethical and religious viewpoints? Or do they include both Christianity and other systems of belief?

As we look at the list of Christian principles embodied in the play, it is clear that they are inclusively rather than exclusively Christian. This is always the case with Shakespeare's plays, which arose from a generally Christian culture but which lack the explicitly Christian emphasis of Milton's work, for example. Christianity is not the only religion that recognizes the reality of evil, the crucial importance of moral choice, the reality of guilt and temptation, the importance of order and the horror of murder. This does not make these principles any less Christian, but it should serve as a caution to critics who apply the term "Christian literature" so broadly that it loses its usefulness as a term that distinguishes explicitly Christian writers from those who are simply in accord with Christian belief in the broad areas of morality. Roland Frye correctly concludes that the Christian ideas in Shakespeare's plays are "not exclusively Christian, but universally human," and that Shakespeare's ethical ideas "might be drawn with equal propriety from non-Christian as from Christian sources."[44] If it strikes us as nonsensical to call *Macbeth* a Buddhist play because it condemns murder, it is equally frivolous to say that "Shakespeare's villains... embody values destructive to the ideal of Christian humanism."[45] If, on the other hand, the view of human nature in *Macbeth* is that people make free moral choices and are inclined to use that freedom to make evil choices, we have an idea that comes much closer to being distinctively Christian, and we can, with better reason, speak of the play as showing a Christian orientation in this area.

In addition to asking whether the Christian ideas in the play are exclusively or inclusively Christian, a Christian reader/critic should consider whether the play's version of these ideas is complete or rudimentary. This is an even more demanding exercise than simply discovering whether the ideas conform to the Christian pattern of belief.

The play, we have seen, depicts the reality of evil. Yet it can hardly be said to suggest the Christian concept of evil, namely, that it is disobedience to the moral law of God. The play approaches evil and disorder in a rather utilitarian way. Disorder is bad because it leads to social problems and civil unrest, as well as to personal misery. In the soliloquy in which Macbeth considers the reasons why he should not murder Duncan (I,vii,1-28), he is "deterred only by the thought of the immediate, earthly consequences."[46] He cites the fact that Duncan is in double trust to him, since Macbeth is both subject and host to the king. When the young Joseph was tempted in Potiphar's house, he rejected the solicitation to evil not only because it would be an act of treason against his master, but also because the act would be "sin against God" (Gen. 39:9). The biblical view that all sin, regardless of its obvious social effects, is ultimately sin against God is similarly captured in David's cry after Nathan had confronted him with his sin of adultery. In his prayer of confession to God, David asserts, "Against thee, thee only, have I sinned" (Ps. 51:4). *Macbeth* dramatizes the horror that evil brings to a society, and it may even be, as G. Wilson Knight calls it, "Shakespeare's most profound and mature vision of evil."[47] But the vision of evil stops short of being a biblically complete vision. It does not accurately perceive the sinfulness of sin.

It is much the same with the play's depiction of guilt. I have praised the play for its magnificent portrayal of the dynamics of human guilt. Yet it cannot be said to embody the whole Christian doctrine on the topic. Harold S. Wilson notes that Macbeth suffers from "a terrible anxiety that is a sense of guilt without becoming ... a sense of sin. It is not a sense of sin because he refuses to recognize such a category."[48] The play, in other words, does not picture guilt as having a spiritual or supernatural identity as well as a psychological one. The best illustration of this is the scene in which Macbeth and Lady Macbeth share their fears and insecurity and death wish (III,ii). Throughout this entire dialog neither character shows any awareness that the real enemy is guilt stemming from sin. In two scenes late in the play, the soliloquy in which Macbeth laments that his old age is not accompanied by the human values that should attend it (V,iii,22-28) and the "tomorrow, and tomorrow, and tomorrow" soliloquy (V,v,19-28), Macbeth similarly realizes that something has gone wrong without ever perceiving the deeper issue of guilt and sin. For the contrast one might profitably observe the analysis of guilt that David gives us in penitential psalms such as Psalms 32 and 51. Macbeth expresses remorse that he got caught, while David is devastated by his guilt before God.

If we took time to pursue the other ideas in the play to their logical conclusions, the results would be similar to those I have been discussing. The play seldom if ever relates the leading issues to God. This suggests that the Christian patterns in the play are incomplete, stopping short of the God-centered world view of the Bible and the Christian faith. In part this is a comment on the nature of drama, since it is impossible to put God on stage and difficult to dramatize the inner thought processes of a character (though the Shakespearean soliloquy is one way to do it). Still, a comparison between *Macbeth* and Milton's *Samson Agonistes* will show the difference between a play that is inclusively and incompletely Christian in its thought patterns and one that is exclusively and thoroughly Christian.

What does it mean to approach *Macbeth* from a Christian perspective? I hope that my analysis of the play has illustrated T. S. Eliot's plea that literary criticism "be completed by criticism from a definite ethical and theological standpoint" and that Christian readers scrutinize their reading "with explicit ethical and theological standards."[49]

The Problem of Literature and Belief

In principle, I should ... expect the Christian reader ... more enthusiastically to give his suffrage to a literature that was Christianly oriented than to one which was not. But ... the Christian reader will actually respond to the various constructions of the human story that he encounters in literature with a latitudinarianism that will ... be akin to that which any other sensitive reader brings to bear upon his dealings with literary art. ☐ Nathan A. Scott, Jr., "The Modern Experiment in Criticism: A Theological Appraisal"

When a Christian reader measures the moral or intellectual vision of a literary work by his or her own world view, how should that assessment affect the overall literary response? If a Christian reader finds the viewpoint of a work untruthful, is this a flaw in the work? Does a Christian perspective in a story or poem make it a better piece of literature?

These questions belong to what is known as "the problem of literature and belief." Briefly stated, this problem raises the question, How do a reader's personal beliefs affect his response to a work of literature? Ultimately this is a question of the place of truth in a complete literary response. The problem of literature and belief has been a leading concern of twentieth-century literary theory. One critic calls it the "chief problem of poetic criticism,"[50] and another claims that it is "the problem which is not only the most vexing but probably the most vital to the criticism of our time."[51] It is not a problem that is unique to Christians. S. L. Bethell, after noting that a Christian will judge a writer's "degree of insight into character by . . . his Christian experience," adds, "And the non-Christian critic—let us be clear about this—will also judge a writer's insight into character (or into anything else, of course) by the standard of his own insight, however derived. There is no 'impartial criticism' in this sense."[52]

One of the perennially popular approaches to the problem of literature and belief is to resolve the problem by denying that it exists. If we only read at a sufficiently general level, simply as fellow members of the human race, we will encounter no major disagreements with the authors whose works we read. Douglas Bush has championed the view that the works of literature that belong to the central Western tradition have a common core of ethical belief with which any reader can agree.[53] If we will only ignore "the particular creed and personality" of an author, we will find a message "which grows out of and embraces general human experience."[54] After surveying the work of such Christian giants as Dante, Spenser and Milton, Bush concludes that "their full and enduring appeal to us . . . depends upon the degree to which their vision of the world and human experience transcends particular articles of belief."[55] And Bush ends his essay by asserting that "we may say of the greatest pagan and Christian poets that they 'are folded in a single party.' "[56]

Such a position is grossly undiscriminating. Instead of viewing the reading of literature as something that exercises and sharpens a reader's intellectual perceptions, it asks that we level everything we read down to a monotonous common denominator. But even if we discard the particularities of a writer's world view (something that writers themselves would despise, incidentally), it is simply not true that all works of literature are saying the same thing. An epic poet who glorifies war and a modern anti-war poet are not asserting a common vision. A courtly love poet who idealizes adulterous love does not share the same ethos as a poet such as Spenser, who had as one of his chief aims to discredit the courtly love tradition. Bush's theory is perhaps least acceptable to Christian readers, because it asks them to hold their Christianity in abeyance while they read, whereas a Christian relates all of life to his faith. C. S. Lewis speaks slightingly of the "L. C. M." (lowest common multiple) approach to literature, and he rejects this "doctrine of the unchanging human heart" for the following reasons:

> If we are in search of the L. C. M. then, in every poem, we are tempted to treat as the most important those elements which... remain when we have finished the stripping-off process. But how if these are not really the most important elements in the actual balance of the poem we are reading? Our whole study of the poem will then become a battle between us and the author in which we are trying to twist his work into a shape he never gave it, to make him use the loud pedal where he really used the soft. .... The truth is that when you have stripped off what the human heart actually was in this or that culture, you are left with a miserable abstraction totally unlike the life really lived by any human being.[57]

We can best see a tree, Lewis concludes, "by following the branches of the tree, not by cutting them off."[58]

Another well-known attempt to resolve the conflict between literature and belief has been that of I. A. Richards.[59] Richards distinguishes between intellectual belief and emotional belief and argues that when we are reading literature we should exercise emotional belief in ideas or attitudes that we disbelieve intellectually. Richards sometimes calls the ideas of a literary work "pseudo-statements," which are "free from belief." In a particularly notorious application of this theory, Richards concludes that "we need no beliefs, and indeed we must have none, if we are to read *King Lear*."[60] Such a theory is as weak as Bush's. It is untrue that people regularly find it possible to discount their own beliefs as they read a poem or watch a movie. And even when they give emotional assent to something that they find untrue, we have to question whether this is a desirable activity. Ideally our emotions should be based on truth, not falsehood.

Many formalist critics have tried to resolve the problem of literature and belief by declaring the complete autonomy of the literary work. An early and famous statement of this theory was that of A. C. Bradley in his essay "Poetry for Poetry's Sake." Poetry, said Bradley, is "a world by itself, independent, complete, autonomous; and to possess it fully you must enter that world, conform to its laws, and ignore for the time the beliefs, aims, and particular conditions which belong to you in the other world of reality."[61] Many formalist critics have agreed. But if we proceed empirically and make a survey of how people actually respond to literature, we find that the work of literature is not isolated from the world of the reader's belief. Nathan Scott argues well for the view that "great literature does, in point of fact, always open outward to the world,"[62] and this "world" includes the reader's own values and experience.

If there is a theory of literature that dissolves once and for all any difficulty that might be posed by literary works whose world view we reject, it would be that of C. S. Lewis. "None of us," writes Lewis, "can accept simultaneously Housman's and Chesterton's view of life, or those of Fitzgerald's *Omar* and Kipling."[63] What we can do instead is to regard works of literature as "windows" that allow us to look at the world through someone else's eyes. "Instead of stripping the knight of his armour you can try to put his armour on yourself."[64] If we approach literature in this way, insists Lewis, we will "delight to enter into other men's beliefs (those, say, of Lucretius or Lawrence) even though we think them untrue. And into their passions, though we think them depraved, like those, sometimes, of Marlowe or Carlyle."[65] This, surely, is a liberating way of reading imaginative literature. But as with any theory about literature and belief, there are many times when it fails. Readers' responses show that they do not always "delight" to see the world through some writers' eyes. Some viewpoints strike us, at least in some moods, as too frivolous or boring or depraved to interest us.

Opposite the critics who try, in one way or another, to resolve the potential tension between a reader's beliefs and those in a work of literature we can line up those who believe that a reader's dissent from a work's viewpoint has a negative effect on his response. Samuel Johnson asserts the principle that "we are affected only as we believe."[66] W. H. Auden states baldly that "false beliefs in fact lead to bad poetry," offering as an illustration his opinion that "a false conception of human nature led Thomas Wolfe to write the grandiose rubbish he mistook for great prose."[67] Yvor Winters writes that "only the convinced Christian can feel" explicitly Christian literature "at something like its true value."[68] And John Crowe Ransom sees "no necessity for waiving the intellectual standards on behalf of poets. If Dante's belief cannot be accepted by his reader, it is worse for Dante with that reader, not a matter of indifference. . . . If Shelley's argument is foolish, it makes his poetry foolish."[69]

Which of the foregoing theories about the relationship of belief to reader response is correct? I am skeptical of them all because they attempt to state a general theory that will cover every particular situation. Furthermore, they tend to be prescriptive in nature. They say, in effect, that since literature is thus and so, a reader's response *ought to be* thus and so. But no single principle can determine a priori how the content of a given work will affect our enjoyment of it.

Instead of setting up a prescriptive theory I suggest that we simply make a survey of how our own and others' response to literature is affected by agreement or disagreement with its viewpoint. We will find four different situations:

1. It is possible to respond positively to a work whose view of reality we consider untruthful but whose artistry we find magnificent.

2. It is possible that our antipathy to a work's view of reality will destroy our enjoyment of the work.

3. We can enjoy a work whose artistic quality is poor or mediocre but whose intellectual content grips us powerfully.

4. It is possible to agree with the viewpoint of a work and yet respond unfavorably to its lack of artistry.

I experience the full range of these possible responses regularly and in no predictable pattern. How, then, can a single "position" on the problem of literature and belief be "the" correct one?

Some generalizations are possible, however. Disagreement with content is more likely to overpower my literary response if it is emphatically opposed to my values than if it is simply inconsistent with, but not explicitly opposed to, my Christian beliefs. For example, a story that elevates home to the highest value does not produce the obstacle to enjoyment that a seduction poem does. I do not believe that non-Christian literature is inferior to Christian literature as art or as literature. I reject the idea that when Christian readers weigh the world view of a work in terms of their own Christian viewpoint they are thereby making a comment on the goodness or badness of the work *as a work of art or literature*. Their agreement or disagreement is with the writer's philosophy of life, not with his art.

This is a way of saying that we must operate with an awareness of the dual nature of a work of literature. It has both an intellectual and an aesthetic or imaginative aspect. In the words of C. S. Lewis, it "is not merely *logos* (something said) but *poiema* (something made)."[70] This means that a response to a work might be intellectual, aesthetic or mixed. I do not believe that Christian literature is better as art because of its Christian content. Neither do I think that there is such a thing as a purely artistic response to literature. Ultimately my fullest appreciation goes to literature that pleases me not only by its imaginative beauty but also by its truth. This, I assume, is what T. S. Eliot meant when he said that "the 'greatness' of literature cannot be determined solely by literary standards."[71] But we cannot afford the naiveté and faulty conclusions that emerge when we confuse the dual nature of the literary response, which is both aesthetic and intellectual.

John Dryden praised the variety of Chaucer's characters by applying to them the proverb, "Here is God's plenty."[72] The same zest and openness should characterize the attitude of Christian readers to the literary works that they read. When Christian readers start from a firm intellectual and emotional commitment to the Christian faith, they are freed from both manipulation by literature and a judgmental refusal to delight in it.

6 What Is Christian Literature?

The Christian Vision in Literature
Books like Resurrection *or* The Brothers Karamazov *give me an almost overpowering sense of how uniquely marvelous a Christian way of looking at life is, and a passionate desire to share it.* □ *Malcolm Muggeridge,* Jesus Rediscovered
What is the nature of the Christian vision in literature? Is it a matter of form, subject matter or interpretation of human experience? If Christian literature is literature that, regardless of its particular subject matter, reflects the Christian view of reality, what aspects of the literary work reveal that view? Must literature be exclusively or explicitly Christian before it can be considered Christian? Or does the term extend to literature that simply does not violate Christian belief? Must a Christian work give the whole truth about its particular topic, or only partial truth? Is a lyric poem that praises a springtime scene in nature, without mentioning God or anything supernatural, a Christian poem? Is a work Christian if it simply explores the problems of human existence? Or must a work suggest a Christian solution before it can be considered Christian? Is a naturalistic novel that explores the depravity of the human condition without suggesting an alternative, a Christian vision of reality?

The question of Christian literature is important for at least three reasons.[1] I have already stated that the question of whether the world view or ethos presented in a work of literature conforms or fails to conform to the standard of Christian truth is precisely the issue that is the distinctive interest of Christian literary criticism. Second, the question of what constitutes the Christian vision in literature has been important in recent literary criticism, especially Shakespearean criticism and criticism of modern literature. And third, it is, of course, the perennial question facing Christian writers.

Before attempting to answer the question of what constitutes a Christian vision in literature, I wish to clear the air of some misconceptions. One of these is that literature is totally neutral in its viewpoint and that there is no such thing as Christian literature. W. H. Auden's statement that "there can no more be a 'Christian' art than there can be . . . a Christian diet"[2] is sometimes taken seriously, but it deserves to be dismissed. Trees, rocks and cars are amoral and intellectually neutral. But ideas, opinions and statements about life are either true or false. Since literature not only presents experience but also interprets it—since it has ideational content and embodies a world view or ethical outlook—it will always be open to classification as true or false, Christian or humanist or Marxist or what not. In the long run every writer's work shows a moral and intellectual bias. It is this bias that can be determined to be either in accord with or antithetical to Christian belief.

In talking about the Christian element in literature, we are not, of course, concerned with literary form. A literary form such as the sonnet or novel or metaphor is amoral and philosophically neutral. Nor is the question of what is Christian in literature primarily a matter of subject matter. As painters decide what they are most adept at painting, writers will ordinarily write about the things that they are most effective at portraying in words. If, in a Christian view, all of life is God's, the Christian vision in literature can encompass the whole range of human experience, as indeed the Bible does. The only qualification that I would make here is that "out of the abundance of the heart the mouth speaks" (Mt. 12:34); that is, sooner or later a writer will say something about the things that matter most to him. If this is true, it is inevitable, in my view, that the Christian vision in literature will be characterized by the presence rather than the absence of such realities as God, sin, redemption and God's revelation in both Word and Son.

In talking about what is Christian in Christian literature, I am not, of course, touching upon the whole work. It should go without saying that Christian literature is first of all *literature*. It is artistic in form and its subject is human experience. These are not incidental but indispensable to Christian literature, and the Christian writer who creates a beautiful and inventive poem or story and who sees some aspect of human experience with gifted precision has fulfilled his or her calling in a Christian way. But beyond these dimensions of a story or poem is the writer's perspective on the subject that he or she chooses to write about. It is this perspective that is the focus of any discussion about Christian literature, not because the other aspects of the work are unimportant, but because this is where the distinctively Christian element will be either present or absent.

One of the most serious fallacies is that religious literature and Christian literature are identical phenomena. Such an assumption or equation is nonsense. Christian belief is only one kind of religious viewpoint. To ask what constitutes the Christian vision in literature is to undertake an inquiry that is much more specific than simply identifying the nature of religious literature or "the sacred" in literature. This explains why criticism that discusses the phenomenon of religious literature is usually of little practical use in an analysis of the Christian element in literature, particularly when the word *religious* is defined in terms of "deep thought" or "ultimate concern."

If "religious literature" is too broad a category to do justice to the Christian element in literature, the category "devotional literature" is too narrow to do justice to it. By *devotional literature* I mean literature whose subject matter is the specifically religious aspect of human experience or the theological doctrines of the Christian faith. Chad Walsh describes it as "books in which such words as God, Christ, soul, etc., frequently occur; or books dealing with Church life, ministers, devout souls, etc."[3] What makes literature Christian is "not . . . a privileged and special subject-matter but rather . . . a perspective from which 'full light' can be had on all subject matters."[4] Or as Flannery O'Connor confirms from her perspective as a Christian fiction writer, "What we call the Catholic novel is not necessarily about a Christianized or Catholicized world, but simply . . . one in which the truth as Christians know it has been used as a light to see the world by. . . . The Catholic novel can't be categorized by subject matter, but only by what it assumes about human and divine reality."[5]

In answering the question of what constitutes a Christian vision in literature we should avoid a simple criterion by which we categorize all works of literature as either Christian or non-Christian. Instead of a "great divide" approach we need a framework that identifies the variety of *ways in which* a work of literature can show a Christian allegiance. This framework, I suggest, should be viewed as a continuum that ranges from the superficially or incidentally Christian at the one end to the thoroughly and explicitly Christian at the other. Such a framework allows us to analyze, not whether a work is Christian or non-Christian, but the levels at which a work of literature engages (if it does at all) the Christian view of reality. In the discussion that follows I have attempted to identify the ways in which Christian experience and belief can enter a work of literature.

The first level is the use of *allusions to the Bible and/or to Christian doctrine or symbolism*. At the very least, such allusions show a writer's familiarity with the Christian faith. And certainly such works of literature require the Christian religion as a necessary framework for understanding them. Allusions can also be an index to a genuine Christian vision. By itself, however, a writer's use of biblical allusions or Christian symbols is the least reliable index to whether the allegiance of a work is Christian.

For one thing, many writers are interested in the Bible and in Christian symbols in the same way that they are interested in classical mythology—for primarily literary reasons. Allusion and symbol are, after all, figures of speech, just as metaphor and simile are, for example. They do not necessarily imply anything at the level of ideas or world view. When Shakespeare says regarding lust that "none knows well/ To shun the heaven that leads men to this hell" ("Sonnet 129"), he is using the Christian images of heaven and hell as metaphors or symbols of pleasure and degradation, respectively, not in the sense employed by Christian eschatology. When Wilfred Owen entitles an antiwar poem "At a Calvary near the Ancre," he is using the Christian image to represent military carnage, not to relate to the Christian doctrine of redemption. When Thomas Campion begins his most famous love poem "There Is a Garden in Her Face," by borrowing a metaphor straight from the Song of Solomon, he is not thereby identifying his romantic love ethic as specifically biblical but is simply following the model of a poetic work that exerted a powerful influence on Renaissance poetry.

Another reason why Christian references do not necessarily imply a Christian viewpoint in a work is that many writers, especially modern writers, reinterpret Christian images or biblical material to produce something entirely different from, and sometimes hostile to, the original meaning. This was never so clear to me as when my interest in the Bible as literature led me to undertake a systematic survey of poems and stories dealing with biblical characters and events. The following three examples typify much of the literature:

1. A poem entitled "The Parable of the Old Man and the Young" by Wilfred Owen, in which the Abraham and Isaac

story of Genesis 22 is inverted by having Abraham refuse to kill the "Ram of Pride" and kill instead his son, a killing that becomes a symbol for the carnage of World War 1.

2. Companion poems by Louis Untermeyer entitled "Goliath and David," in which Goliath regrets his destructive strength and David decides to throw aside his stone and invite Goliath to "come and play."

3. Archibald MacLeish's play *J. B.*, in which the moment of epiphany is not, as in the biblical Job, an insight into the glory of God and the possibility of human fellowship with him, but an affirmation of human love as the highest value.

While it is no comment either positively or negatively on the quality of these works, we must be aware of the way in which their themes have been freed from their original source, the Bible, and been transformed into a viewpoint totally new. Christian allusions do not imply a Christian perspective in such works.

Not only do writers feel free to reinterpret Christian symbols and biblical material: they are also capable of using a Christian idiom or vocabulary to express a content or world view far removed from Christianity. William Wordsworth, for example, was a master at using a biblical idiom to express a romantic world view and pantheistic religious experience. "The world is too much with us," writes Wordsworth, and the idiom comes from New Testament statements about "the cares of the world" that destroy true values (Mt. 13:22) and about how we should "not love the world or the things in the world" (1 Jn. 2:15). But by the time he reaches the end of the sonnet, Wordsworth has declared his preference for a pagan sensitivity to nature over the world of Christian belief. A poem such as "Tintern Abbey" shows Wordsworth's characteristic use of "the vocabulary of religious devotion displaced into a naturalistic mode."[6] William Butler Yeats entitled one of his most famous poems "The Second Coming," but his poem does not imply an acceptance of Christian eschatology. Instead, Yeats uses the Christian terminology to express his own theory of history as a series of cycles or "gyres," and his poem is a speculation about what kind of age is in the process of replacing Christianity.

I do not wish to leave the impression that biblical or Christian allusions are never an index to a writer's Christian allegiance. For truly Christian writers such allusions are full of Christian meaning. Sometimes they are a signpost that a writer wishes his work to be interpreted in a distinctively Christian way. For example, it is a commonplace of Spenser criticism that Book I of the *Faerie Queene*, which celebrates the distinctively Christian ideal of holiness, is filled with biblical allusions and Christian symbols, while Book II, devoted to the classical ideal of temperance, draws its allusions primarily from classical literature and philosophy. When Milton chose Genesis 1-3 instead of military warfare as his epic subject, his choice was much more than a literary decision. And when the poetry of George Herbert shows continuous reliance on the Bible and Anglican liturgy, we naturally interpret such references as an expression of his deeply felt Christian experience.

Christian allusions, however, do not *by themselves* prove much about the degree to which a work has been shaped by Christian belief. There are deeper levels of commitment within a work itself that tell us how to interpret a writer's use of Christian allusions and symbols.

A second level at which literature can show a Christian allegiance is by *embodying values or viewpoints that are inclusively Christian*. An idea or viewpoint is "inclusively Christian" when it belongs to the large area where Christian belief overlaps with other religious or ethical viewpoints. It includes both literature that exhibits Christian ideas without any explicitly Christian references and literature that uses Christian terminology to express viewpoints that are, however, not the exclusive property of Christian belief. The ways in which literature can be inclusively Christian are many.

One big category, and one that includes a great deal of

lyric poetry, is literature that is content to hold the mirror up to life without much concern to interpret reality. Poets have produced an enormous amount of nature poetry and love poetry, for example, that attempts to reproduce as accurately as possible the sights and sounds of the landscape or the emotions of love. Unless such poetry violates Christian belief, by revealing a pantheistic attitude toward nature or celebrating illicit love, for example, it can be said to be in accord with the Christian view of reality, regardless of whether or not the writer uses explicitly Christian terms.

Or, to cite another category, much modern literature portrays the misery and despair and hedonism of people living without Christian values in the contemporary world. Most of this literature is written by non-Christians, and as a result some of it is asserting that life *is* without ultimate meaning or that people *should* disregard Christian moral values. But some of this literature is trying to capture, as accurately and objectively and compassionately as possible, the plight of contemporary society. To the extent to which it succeeds it has shown a Christian view of human depravity or sinfulness or lostness, and I doubt that we could tell, simply by looking at the literature, whether the writer of a given work is a Christian or non-Christian.

It is much the same with that huge branch of modern literature that can best be termed protest literature, which denounces the forms of injustice, oppression and immorality found in the contemporary world. An important genre within this category is dystopian (or anti-utopian) fiction. Most dystopian fiction has been written by non-Christians, yet as Chad Walsh has shown, there are many "parallels between specific biblical insights and what the anti-utopians are asserting."[7] From all that we know about Aldous Huxley, he was far from Christian belief, yet it is hard for me to imagine that his protest in *Brave New World* against the decline of Christian-humanist values in contemporary life would be much different than if its author had been a Christian. After all, in the climactic encounter between the novel's normative character and the world controller, the former asserts, "But God's the reason for everything noble and fine and heroic. If you had a God. ..."[8]

I do not wish to belabor the point that one of the ways in which literature can show a Christian allegiance without being exclusively Christian is by embodying viewpoints that are in accord with Christian doctrine. Even the Bible, an avowedly religious or sacred book, contains this kind of literature. The Song of Solomon, for example, does not place human love within a context of divine love or specifically religious values. The story of Esther contains a reference to the religious practice of fasting, but beyond that it does not relate the human action to any specifically religious or supernatural framework, refraining even from the mention of God's name. If the Bible itself contains works that I have termed "inclusively Christian," we should not be surprised to find such literature in abundance in imaginative literature.

Nor should a Christian be surprised to find non-Christian writers coming up with insights that are true to Christian belief. For one thing the Christian world view has exerted a strong and steady influence over Western civilization through the centuries, so that the thought patterns of many (some would say most) non-Christian writers have naturally been molded to some extent by the Christian world view. But there is also a theological reason why Christians should accept non-Christian writers as capable of expressing insights into reality that agree with Christian belief. That theological basis is the doctrine of common grace, which in my experience is rarely articulated outside of the Calvinistic tradition.

The doctrine of common grace claims that God endows all people, believers and unbelievers alike, with some good qualities and with his natural blessings. One biblical foundation for the doctrine is the belief that God created people in his own image and that human nature is therefore possessed of a capacity for goodness, truth, creativity and so forth. With the Fall, God's image in man was marred and became directed to a bad end, but it was not destroyed. For example, in Genesis 9:6 God says to Noah, "Whoever sheds the blood of man, by man shall his blood be shed; for God made man in his own image." The continuing presence of the image of God in man leads Calvin to comment,

> Whenever we come upon these matters in secular writers, let that admirable light of truth shining in them teach us that the mind of man, though fallen and perverted from its wholeness, is nevertheless clothed and ornamented with God's excellent gifts. If we regard the Spirit of God as the sole fountain of truth, we shall neither reject the truth itself, nor despise it wherever it shall appear.... Those men whom Scripture calls "natural men" were, indeed, sharp and penetrating in their investigation of inferior things. Let us, accordingly, learn by their example how many gifts the Lord left to human nature even after it was despoiled of its true good.[9]

The New Testament several times allows us to conclude that all people, including unbelievers, are capable of true moral insight and right conduct. Jesus, for example, said, "And if you do good to those who do good to you, what credit is that to you? For even sinners do the same" (Lk. 6: 33). In the opening chapters of Romans, Paul not only argues that everyone falls short of attaining his own moral standards, whatever they are, but also that unbelievers have the capacity, *part of the time*, to "do by nature what the law requires, ... even though they do not have the law. They show that what the law requires is written on their hearts" (Rom. 2:14-15). If unbelievers are capable of this kind of right moral behavior, we should expect to find in some of their writings true insights into human experience.

Then, too, we find that Paul in his New Testament writings several times quotes from pagan poets, just as he quotes from the Old Testament to prove a theological point. In his speech in Athens to the Areopagus, for example, Paul quotes from the Greek Stoic poets Cleanthes, Aratus and Epimenides, drawing attention to his quotations by saying, "As even some of your poets have said" (Acts 17:28). "Bad company ruins good morals," (1 Cor. 15:33) is a quotation from the play *Thais* by the Greek dramatist Menander. Titus 1:12, which reads, "One of themselves, a prophet of their own, said, 'Cretans are always liars, evil beasts, lazy gluttons,' " is a quotation from Epimenides, a native of Crete. In his commentary on this verse Calvin writes, "All truth is from God; and consequently, if wicked men have said anything that is true and just, we ought not to reject it; for it has come from God."[10] Applying this to literature generally, we should expect to find many affirmations of the Christian view of reality, even when the literature is written by non-Christians.

The final way in which literature can reveal its Christian allegiance is by *exhibiting viewpoints that are exclusively Christian*. This category consists of literature whose themes are distinctive to the Christian faith. I do not have in mind only literature whose *subject matter* is distinctively Christian, that is, literature about the person and work of Christ, or literature about Christian doctrines such as providence or atonement or heaven, or works dealing with biblical characters and events. I have in mind also literature that exhibits a Christian slant on whatever topic it happens to portray.

Some examples will show the kind of literature that I call exclusively Christian. When Gerard Manley Hopkins begins a nature poem with the statement, "Glory be to God for dappled things," and when he concludes a poem with the words, "He fathers-forth whose beauty is past change:/ Praise him," the poems imply a Christian view of nature as the creation of God. When Edmund Spenser includes in his "Epithalamion" the prayer for progeny "to increase the count" of "blessed Saints" in heaven, he is giving his song a Christian cast (which it displays in other ways as well) that removes it from a purely humanistic framework.

When Milton protests the slaughter of the Waldensians in a sonnet that is structured as a prayer addressed to the God of the Bible, his poem is given a distinctively Christian meaning that makes it different from protest literature in general.

In an earlier chapter I spoke of a world view as a way of looking at reality in terms of a central value. In literature that is distinctively Christian this value is the God of the Bible. Whenever a work of literature or a given writer's corpus of works elevates God to a position of supremacy and relates all other areas of life to God, it can be identified as possessing a Christian world view.

It is important to note that a work of literature can be Christian in this way without making use of Christian terminology. Milton's elegy "Lycidas" is, on the surface, a thoroughly classical poem, replete with allusions to classical mythology. This, however, is merely the poetic vehicle. At the level of theme and idea, the poem affirms such distinctively Christian doctrines as the life everlasting, heaven, God's personal providence and the substitutionary atonement of Christ.

To summarize, when we speak of the Christian vision in literature, we should have in mind a continuum that identifies a variety of ways in which a work of literature can embody Christian viewpoints. The levels of involvement with the Christian faith include the use of Christian allusions, the embodiment of inclusively Christian themes and the embodiment of exclusively Christian concepts. Which of these merits the title "Christian literature"? There is, in my view, nothing inaccurate in calling all three types of literature "Christian." But unless the designation is reserved for the third category, it includes so much literature that it becomes virtually useless as a label. After all it is possible to find some inclusively Christian ideas in virtually every writer's work, even when the writer's ultimate allegiance is far from Christian.

What I have said about the Christian element in literature can be put into focus by a brief application to the Old

English epic *Beowulf*. A leading issue in *Beowulf* scholarship continues to be the controversy over whether the epic
merits the title "Christian." As I have suggested we can
expect the Christian data in the story to fall into several
distinct categories.

I reject as legitimate data the details in the story that can
be allegorized in keeping with Christian doctrine. M. B.
McNamee, for example, interprets the story as an allegory
of "the Christian story of salvation," with the story of the
hero symbolizing "the very life of the Savior Himself."[11]
Someone else regards the story as "a single allegorical song
intimating the Divine Mystery of Redemption," concluding that "Beowulf, offering himself for others, is Christ
redeeming man by self-sacrifice."[12] The fact that the details in a rescue story *can* be allegorized in Christian terms
proves nothing. *Any* rescue story, including the last one
we have seen on television, is a Christian work by such
logic. The Middle Ages allegorized pagan mythology in the
same way, turning the *Aeneid*, for example, into a "Christian" work.[13] But we know that neither Virgil nor his epic
was Christian in allegiance.

One category of Christian data in *Beowulf* consists of
allusions to the Bible and Christian doctrine. An early
study of these allusions identified the total number as
sixty-eight, with most of them consisting of "incidental
allusions to the Christian God, to his attributes, and to his
part in shaping the lives and fortunes of men."[14] The same
study noted the omission of any references to Christ, the
cross, the Virgin Mary, saints, the Trinity or the atonement. Later criticism also uncovered allusions to heathen
practices and ideas that contradict the Christian faith, reinforcing my earlier caution that writers who use Christian
allusions tend also to use pagan sources. By itself, therefore, the use of Christian allusions does not prove a Christian outlook in *Beowulf*. Still, the Christian allusions represent one indisputable level at which the epic interacts
with the Christian faith.

Since *Beowulf* belongs to a literary family that I call

heroic narrative (a story built around the exploits of an exemplary hero), we can expect the question of the degree to which the story is Christian to be decided most profoundly by the image of the hero in the story. The epic *Beowulf* idealizes a certain type of character. The appropriate question is whether Christianity idealizes the same type of conduct. To what extent does the epic ethos correspond to the biblical ethos?

If we look for evidence of a Christian perspective in the characterization of the hero, we will conclude that the story exhibits values that are inclusively Christian. The most important of these are hatred of evil, a spirit of self-sacrifice, loyalty in human relations and belief in a personal God of providence. The first three of these were equally characteristic of the Germanic *comitatus* ethos that provides (with Christianity) the other ethical foundation of the story. If there is anything distinctively Christian in the picture, it is of minor importance—for example, the forces of evil are occasionally associated with Christian ideas of devils and hell, and God is occasionally given attributes (for example, he is almighty, ruler and judge) that make the theology not simply theistic but something that approximates Christianity.

In addition to inclusively Christian values the hero possesses traits that violate a Christian ethical ideal. These include pride, boastfulness and a desire for earthly fame (in a manner directly antithetical to Christlike humility); a trust in military strength (in violation of the psalmist's aphorism that "a warrior is not delivered by his great strength"); and the elevation of material goods, especially treasure, to an exalted status (in antithesis to Christ's command, "Lay not up for yourselves treasure on earth"). If, in addition, we pause to ask what things would have to be added to the list of Beowulf's character traits to make the portrait explicitly Christian, the list turns out to be rather revealing: something to show that the goal of human life is more than earthly success and fame; something to show the hero's consciousness of sin; something to indicate that the highest joy in life comes from being redeemed through the atonement of Christ; something to show that the proper motivation and power for virtuous conduct are supernaturally grounded. What the evidence shows, I believe, is that the story shows an indebtedness to the Christian faith through its allusions and conformity to ethical principles that Christianity shares with other systems, while stopping short of much that is distinctively Christian and often even running counter to a Christian ethic.

The Christian Writer

I have found, . . . from reading my own writing, that my subject in fiction is the action of grace in territory held largely by the devil. ☐ *Flannery O'Connor,* Mystery and Manners

What I have said thus far about the Christian vision in literature has been concerned with the Christian reader. There are implications for the Christian writer as well. In writing about the Christian writer I speak from my perspective as a reader and teacher of literature. Anything that I say on the topic must, of course, be weighed against what Christian writers say. But we must remember that when writers speak about how the Christian faith touches upon their writing, they are actually explaining and defending their own kind of writing. They have an ax to grind and are sometimes defensive.

One must be a writer before being a Christian writer. One must first of all master the craft, just as a Christian basketball player must learn to make free throws and a Christian pianist to play the keys on a keyboard. The Christian writer must be assured, as must any writer or poet, that meaning is conveyed *through form*. The Christian view of reality will never be transmuted into literature—and it will never have great impact on the reader—unless the Christian writer has managed to incarnate it in a literary form.

The principle that any Christian writer must be alert to is that true literature works by *indirection*. To be overly abstract or explicit in expressing one's viewpoint is to kill the literary effect. I do not know exactly why this is so, nor do I wish to argue that it should be so, but it is important to recognize that it is so. The writer of imaginative literature perceives and describes the world as image and event, not as abstraction or system, and the most common feature of weak writing (by Christians, too) is a failure to operate by indirection. Cleanth Brooks has observed about the writer that "the undifferentiated generalization, the cliché, the stereotype—these are symptoms of his failure—of the kind of falsification that pertains peculiarly to art. The poet *must* be indirect, and as a consequence he always has to say to his audience: he that hath ears to hear, let him hear."[15] What this means is that a Christian poet must master the poetic idiom—metaphor, image and figures of speech. Simply to put Christian ideas into verse will not suffice. A Christian writer of narrative must learn to invent the kinds of characters and events that will completely absorb the vision or theme. Christian dramatists must learn the knack of creating characters, dialog and dramatic situations that will incarnate what they are trying to communicate.

Another area (in addition to that of literary form) where a Christian writer is on common ground with any other writer is in the ability to observe life and then transmute actual experience into words. Literature is first of all a presentation of human experience. Before a Christian writer can interpret reality, he or she must, like any other writer, *see* the world clearly. This is the point that Flannery O'Connor returns to again and again in her comments about the Christian novelist.[16]

If there is nothing distinctive about the Christian writer in regard to literary form and the need to present concrete human experience, neither is there anything different about the range of topics on which one can write. Devotional literature—literature that deals specifically with the spiritual life, with God or with Christian doctrines such as sin or the atonement—is only one kind of Christian literature. George Herbert devoted all of his poetic talents to this kind of poetry, partly, no doubt, because it was the kind of poetry he was best at. But it would be tragic if every Christian writer chose only this part of reality to portray. That would be tantamount to turning over to non-Christian writers the other great areas of human experience, such as romantic love, nature, society, death, suffering, family and human personality. The Christian faith has something to say about all of life, and Christian writers are needed to subject all of life to the light of Christianity. A Christian writer is Christian, not by virtue of the subject matter, but by virtue of the perspective that is brought to bear on the subject. Biblical narrative points the way, for there we find that spiritual reality reaches down into the very fabric of everyday life and touches upon every area of life, not simply a person's devotional life. That is why Chad Walsh can say that a Christian novelist's "plots and characters may be precisely those one would find in a naturalistic or existentialist novel. . . . It is . . . the angle of vision, the nuances that a different pair of eyes can yield, a way of understanding, not subject matter" that differentiates a Christian writer's work.[17]

What, then, will be distinctive about the perspective that Christian writers bring to their material? Must their work be explicitly or distinctively Christian? Or should they be content if their work falls into the "inclusively Christian" category? Should the literary publication on a Christian college campus have an explicitly Christian tone? Or should people sigh with relief if it contains no violations of Christian belief?

While it strikes me as undesirable to ask that every work written by a Christian exhibit a distinctively Christian identity, I believe that a Christian's overall production will show signs that label it as specifically Christian. If the Christian faith is, in vital points, unique, a Christian writer can scarcely avoid touching upon these areas as well as the areas where his or her religion shares a common ground with other systems. If it is true that any sizable body of literature implies a world view in which some value is the vital center, a Christian writer's total literary achievement should elevate God to a position of centrality. A Christian's work should not preach such a world view, but it will, I hope, reveal it implicitly. And if writers write, at least part of the time, about the things that matter most to them, a Christian writer's work will inevitably touch upon such realities as God, providence, forgiveness, salvation and the life everlasting.

While it is presumptuous and stultifying to bind a Christian writer to a list of things that must be put into his or her work, there are some general principles that would seem to apply. For example, Aristotle claimed (and centuries of literary theory have agreed) that the writer "imitates nature," that is, observes reality. For a naturalist or secularist, this means taking a look around and writing about the external world of nature and society. But if a Christian lives simultaneously in two worlds—if he or she believes that in addition to earthly reality there is a heavenly, spiritual world—then the reality that he or she presents in literature will be different from that of the non-Christian writer. In the words of Flannery O'Connor, "the Christian novelist lives in a larger universe. He believes that the natural world contains the supernatural." The Christian writer's "country," she says elsewhere, is not simply the countryside or a nation, but also "his true country, which the writer with Christian convictions will consider to be what is eternal and absolute."[18]

A Christian writer's view of humanity will also determine some features of the work. Speaking of the Christian, Flannery O'Connor observes, "It makes a great difference to his novel whether he believes we are created in God's image" and "whether he believes that our wills are free."[19] And again, "The Christian novelist is distinguished from his pagan colleagues by recognizing sin as sin. According to his heritage he sees it not as sickness or an accident of environment, but as a responsible choice of offense against God which involves his eternal future."[20] To say that a Christian writer's view of humanity will display these characteristics is not to set up a checklist of items that must be put into the work. But it is to say that when human nature is portrayed, the portrait should be theologically accurate.

One reason why Christian writers will often refuse to stay within the broad area where Christianity is like any other ethos is that by doing so they run the risk of having their own viewpoint misunderstood. Christians who write social protest literature, for example, may find their analysis of the social situation almost the same as that of a radical or Marxist, let us say. But at the level of solution they stand for something quite at odds with these people. Will the Christian writer not wish to guard against being identified with the unbeliever's camp? I assume that a Christian nature poet does not wish to be regarded as a pantheist, nor a Christian love poet as an advocate of free love, nor a Christian realist as someone who believes that the evil of the human soul is the whole truth about human potential. If I am right in this it seems to me that a Christian writer will look for literary ways to keep the record straight.

Will the overall thrust of Christian writers be positive? Will they suggest solutions in addition to exploring problems? I believe they will. A Christian's purpose in life is to be redemptive in the world. Someone who takes the example of Christ's life seriously can tolerate neither a refusal to become immersed in the flow of actual human life in this world nor a willingness to leave fallen human life where it is. The Christian writer's mission is to add to the beauty, truth and joy of the world, not its hopelessness. Flannery O'Connor put it concisely when she said, "I see from the standpoint of Christian orthodoxy. This means that for me the meaning of life is centered in our Redemption by Christ and what I see in the world I see in its relation to that."[21]

Will a Christian writer automatically write literature that reflects a Christian view of things? Is it true that a Christian cannot help but produce literature that is Christian in identity? Or should Christian writers consciously subject their work to the Christian world view? It has become a hallowed rite for many Christian writers to trot out T. S. Eliot's statement that he wanted "a literature which should be *un*consciously, rather than deliberately and defiantly, Christian."[22] Upon close scrutiny Eliot's statement should raise our suspicions. Are the two extremes that he mentions the only options? Can a Christian writer not be conscious of the Christian perspective in a given area of human experience without being "defiant" about it? If a Christian in business is reprehensible for leaving Christian ethics out of business dealings or a Christian citizen for isolating social conduct from Christian beliefs, why should we respond any differently when a Christian writer argues that "I find that *as a poet* I have had to shake loose some of what I learned in church and catechism class"?[23] One of the truths that the Christian church is waking up to is that the Christian faith is not a separate compartment of life. I see no reason why Christian writers are an exception.

The issue will be clarified if we simply view Christian writers like other Christians who speak publicly—Christian teachers or lecturers or neighbors, for example. What do we expect of such people? We expect that much of what they say will simply be the words of "a man speaking to other men" (as Wordsworth defined the poet). We expect that they will not speak contrary to the truth of the Christian faith. And sometimes, we agree, they will express viewpoints that are uniquely Christian. In order to do all these things they will have to do their homework like anyone else. They will have to know what the Christian faith has to say about issues A, B and C. I see no way in which Christian writers differ from this.

The Christian writer's calling is a great one. Milton felt called from adolescence to be a poet, and he devoted long years of tireless preparation to fulfilling his calling. Although he planned to enter the ministry, the corruptness of the church hierarchy led him eventually to reject the church as his vocation. There is plenty of evidence that he did not regard himself as having settled for something

second best by becoming a poet instead of a preacher.
Christian writers today deserve the support of the Christian church in a way that they do not come close to receiving. It is professionally disadvantageous to be a Christian
writer, just as it is often disadvantageous to be a Christian in other professions. [24] The Christian church is suspicious of the writer, partly because the writer's task is to
express the truth in perpetually new ways. But the task of
closing the gap of suspicion between the writer and the
believing community rests at least as much with the latter.
The Christian writer is, ideally, the speaker for the Christian view of things in the world of the arts. If the Christian
church extends its hands of blessing and support over its
missionaries of the gospel, should it not do the same for
those who speak the truth through imaginative literature
to an unbelieving world? And if Christian professors or
sociologists or psychologists or those in business are given
a platform to speak within the church, should not the
Christian writer be encouraged to speak through the art of
writing within the church? What the truly Christian writer
has to say is fully as important as what many another
Christian professional has to say. The time has come to
hear the voice of the Christian writer in the worship service, in the sermon or in the small group meeting. The believing community portrayed throughout the Bible did
not, we must remember, distrust the storyteller and poet.
Neither should the Christian church today.

7 Modern Literature and the Christian Reader

Preliminary Considerations

The author of a work of imagination is trying to affect us wholly, as human beings; and we are affected by it, as human beings, whether we intend to be or not.... Reading... affects us as entire human beings; it affects our moral and religious existence. □ T. S. Eliot, "Religion and Literature"

The problems posed for the Christian by modern literature are so complex that the general tendency has been to adopt simple responses. These fall into three categories. One is wholesale endorsement of modern literature combined with the attitude that anyone who finds modern literature offensive is an ignoramus. Another is wholesale condemnation of modern literature. And then there is the desire to resolve the issue with lists of approved and disapproved works. My feeling is that the issues must be handled on a much more individualistic basis. The general principles that we establish must be applied by each person in connection with every particular work of literature.

There are really two aspects to the question, How should a Christian approach modern literature? They are these: (1) How should a Christian reader cope with literary realism? Should a Christian read literature that depicts human depravity in a realistic manner? (2) How should a Christian respond to the non-Christian world views depicted in most modern literature? Should time be spent reading such literature? My thesis in both areas can be summarized under two headings: the necessity of modern literature and the dangers of modern literature. I wish to begin with some preliminary generalizations that will become relevant at various points later in the discussion.

Literature is read primarily for enjoyment—intellectual, emotional, imaginative and spiritual enjoyment. We do not read literature as though it were a duty to which we are slaves. The relevance of this principle to modern literature is simply this: if a reader finds modern literature distasteful or irrelevant to his interests, he has no obligation to force himself to read it. Reading literature is not like paying taxes, something we have to do regardless of our interests. To be repelled by evil as depicted in literature is a Christian response, but on what logic can it be argued that a person should spend leisure time seeking out ways in which to be repelled?

One must hasten to add, however, that literature is a useful vehicle for getting inside a culture. As Henry Zylstra writes, "If you really want to get at the spirit of an age and the soul of a time you can hardly do better than to consult the literature of that age and that time. In the novels and stories and poems and plays of a period you have a good indication of what, deep down, that period was about."[1] This means that we might read modern literature, not because we enjoy it, but because we recognize it as a necessary way of keeping abreast of our own culture.

Literature has two dimensions—an intellectual aspect and an aesthetic or artistic one. It is concerned with both faithfulness to reality and with beauty. Most modern literature is more concerned to present the ugliness of life than to be a source of artistic pleasure. This being the case, a reader has to be willing to waive the purely artistic element of literature in order to get out of modern literature what it aims primarily to give.

Another important principle is that the Bible itself is

literary. It will therefore answer some of our questions about realism in literature by its own example.

Literature is one of the most powerful cultural influences affecting human behavior. It affects us even if we read it only for enjoyment or recreation. T. S. Eliot puts it thus:

> The fiction that we read affects our behaviour towards our fellow men, affects our patterns of ourselves. When we read of human beings behaving in certain ways, with the approval of the author, who gives his benediction to this behaviour by his attitude toward the result of the behaviour arranged by himself, we can be influenced towards behaving in the same way.... The author of a work of imagination is trying to affect us wholly, as human beings, whether he knows it or not; and we are affected by it, as human beings, whether we intend to be or not.... What we read does not concern merely something called our *literary taste*, but... affects directly, though only amongst many other influences, the whole of what we are.[2]

Christians should be concerned about how their literary experience affects their moral behavior and their spiritual life. This, surely, is partly what T. S. Eliot had in mind when he wrote that Christians have "the duty of maintaining consciously certain standards and criteria... over and above those applied by the rest of the world."[3]

It is not a true test of a work of literature to ask whether people are consciously offended by it. We live in a day when the social pressure against admitting that one is offended by a work of literature is so intense that most people will not admit that a work of literature is spiritually or morally detrimental. T. S. Eliot comments in this regard that "it is certain that a book is not harmless merely because no one is consciously offended by it."[4] And he adds, "It is our business as honest men not to assume that whatever we like is what we ought to like."[5]

The ultimate test of whether the impact of a work is good or bad is the reader's response, not the writer's intention. This means that although we cannot always hold the writer responsible for the bad influence a work has on a given reader, we can judge *the work* as being detrimental *for a given reader*. Flannery O'Connor realizes this when she writes that "what is one thing for the writer may be another for the reader. What leads the writer to his salvation may lead the reader into sin."[6] And T. S. Eliot acknowledges the same thing when he comments that "even the effect of the better writers... may be degrading to some readers; for we must remember that what a writer does to people is not necessarily what he intends to do."[7]

Realism in Modern Literature
As a Christian I am responsible for the furniture of my mind.
□ *Frank E. Gaebelein, address delivered at Wheaton College*

In taking up the topic of literary realism I wish to speak first about its necessity and legitimacy as a literary technique. For one thing the Bible itself depicts human depravity, portraying both sex and violence in a realistic manner. In other words the Bible affirms the literary technique of realism as being legitimate. Stories of sexual immorality, presented with varying degrees of completeness, include the stories of the homosexuality of Sodom, in which "the men of Sodom, both young and old, all the people to the last man, surrounded the house"of Lot when the two angels visited Lot in the form of men (Gen. 19); the rape of Dinah (Gen. 34); Onan's interrupted intercourse with Tamar (Gen. 38:1-10); Samson and the harlot of Gaza (Judg. 16); the "Concubine at Gibeah" incident, in which sexual perverts were placated with the concubine, whom they abused to the point of death (Judg. 19); David and Bathsheba (2 Sam. 11) and the incest of Amnon and Tamar (2 Sam. 13). Stories of violence are everywhere in the Bible, especially in the Old Testament. Ehud's assassination of Eglon in Judges 3 is a good example. All of this suggests that Christians should not avoid completely the depiction of depravity in literature, because it tells them something they need to know, namely, the sinfulness of the human condition.

A second point in the case for the necessity of realism is that one of the functions of literature is to present experience as it really is. If modern life is ugly and depraved and perverted and violent, we can expect modern literature to be the same in the subject matter that it portrays. By presenting such material for our contemplation, modern literature, at its best and most responsible, aims to increase our understanding of the human predicament in the modern world. One function that such literature can fill is to open the eyes of Christians to the needs of people whose physical and moral experience they might otherwise comfortably avoid.

A third argument for the necessity of modern realism is that the literature of an age reflects the values of the age. Since this is so, we can understand our culture by reading modern literature. One of the results of such understanding should be the enlargement of a Christian reader's compassion for people who do not share the morality or hope that the Christian faith affords. As a Christian reader begins to understand the cultural attitudes and values, it will become apparent that people are often the *victims* of despair or sensuality, and that they do not necessarily enjoy the world view by which they live.

A Christian may have to put up with some objectionable material in order to appropriate the genuine insights that a work of realism offers. One critic makes a distinction between the "object matter" of literature and its "subject matter."[8] The object matter is the outward or obvious content of a work—its setting, characters and external action. The subject matter is its theme or overall message or slant on life. My claim is that a Christian may find it necessary to overlook offensive object matter—profanity, explicit portrayal of sex, violence—in order to benefit from significant subject matter. In one of the best discussions of the problem, Harold C. Gardiner writes that the effect of objectionable passages "has to be judged against the background of the whole moral import of the work."[9] Someone else has written that "to learn how to read a dirty book is to learn how to see the book *whole*."[10] The question that a Christian must answer is, "Does the moral or intellectual significance of a work exceed in value the possible offensiveness of any of its parts?" It is a question for which every work will have to be studied on its own merits and for which the answer will differ from person to person.

A final defense for reading modern naturalistic literature is that it is not the contact with such literature that contaminates but the reader's response to it. The important thing about the reading of naturalistic literature is the reader's personal response to the depravity that is depicted. We cannot completely avoid literary contact with evil; the important question is, What do we do with the evil when we run across it? It is not naturalism per se, then, that has a bad influence in a Christian's life. A Christian rejection of depravity is what is needed, and if a Christian reader responds in this way, his or her reading of naturalistic literature should not be condemned. Harry Blamires writes, "There is nothing in our experience, however trivial, worldly, or even evil, which cannot be thought about christianly"[11] If this does not establish a case for the necessity of modern literature, it at least provides a rationale and methodology for reading such literature.

As I turn now to the dangers of realism for a Christian I want to stress that these principles must be applied individually. I am definitely not talking about public censorship in the remarks that follow, partly because Christians are too small a segment of the population even to consider such a possibility. Nor am I urging that Christians as a group use these principles to reach decisions for an entire group of people. I am writing for the Christian adult as he or she tries to reach personal decisions regarding the reading of modern literature.

As I discuss the dangers of modern literature for a Christian some of my readers will conclude that I am concentrating on a selective list of sins (pornography, profanity, etc.) and ignoring such weightier matters as materialism and false values. I have no intention of minimizing the un-christian values that literature frequently embodies and is capable of lulling a reader to accept. I have already discussed the problem of false values in chapter four and do not wish to repeat that argument here. My present concern is with the kinds of behavior and attitude that modern literature can induce.

I have said that the Bible affirms realism in principle, but this, by itself, obscures an important point: the realism of the Bible is realism within certain bounds. Modern naturalistic literature, produced by non-Christians and perhaps by Christians, differs from biblical realism in the following ways:

1. The Bible does not contain a preponderance of depravity in its account of human experience. It does not leave the reader with the impression that degradation is all there is to life, or that there is no alternative to ugliness and depravity.

2. The Bible does not dwell on the sordid details of sexual immorality, nor does it dramatize profanity, using narrative summary instead of dramatization. It does not share the clinical or descriptive approach of so much modern literature in the portrayal of sex.

3. Even more crucial is that the Bible never condones the evil that it depicts. Calvin Seerveld has written, "Art is Biblically Christian when the Devil cannot stand it. If the Devil can stand it or would hand out reproductions, then there is no Biblical Christian character to it. . . . The Devil cannot stand exposure of sin as sin, dirty, devastating misery for men; it unmasks him."[12]

While I am not ready to argue that biblical literature fixes the limits for the kinds of literature that a Christian should read, I do think that it serves as a reliable model to guide a Christian regarding what should be read. As a model it strikes a balance; it gives us realism within certain bounds.

Another test of what a Christian can safely read is the test of enjoyment. Although it has often been suspect, enjoyment or delight is actually one of the most reliable criteria governing what a Christian should read. The regenerate Christian who is trying to glorify God in his literary experience will find that he or she cannot delight in three kinds of literary material: (1) literature that delights in the immorality that it depicts, or that encourages the reader to approve and emulate error or immorality; (2) pornography, or literature that elicits immoral thoughts; (3) literature that is filled with profanity, blasphemy, sacrilege (ridicule of the sacred things of the Christian religion, including God or Christ) and obscenity. The Christian mind is by definition repelled by all this and can be trusted to use restraint with such literature if it is allowed to follow the standard of Christian enjoyment. When a Christian is attracted to such literature, it is a personal lack of Christianity at that point, not the criterion of enjoyment, that is the weakness.

A third objection to naturalistic fiction concerns its clinical or descriptive approach to sex. Several things are objectionable here. If we wish to take a "sophisticated" approach, we might object to such literature on purely literary grounds. We can argue that "the primary objection to glandular fiction... is simply that it belittles man."[13] Or we can follow Edmund Fuller in his demonstration that pornographic literature is guilty of "the error of confusing cumulative detail with interpretive insight."[14] Fuller writes,

> Many writers are deluded into thinking that a four-letter-word vocabulary, carefully detailed scenes of undressing, and clinically direct anatomical descriptions add up to a profound study of the relations between men and women. This is quite... fantastic.... The criteria for every detail about sex in fiction should be: What does this illumine? What does it reveal that was not known before or that cannot be left as tacitly understood? Does this add anything to our understanding of character that was not already clear?[5]

All of this is true enough, and relevant, but it also avoids the moral issue. There have been other forms of literature that belittle people or lack interpretive insight, yet they have posed no major problem for a Christian reader.

In addition to the literary objection to pornographic literature, we should have the courage to talk about its immorality. Pornographic literature fills the mind with lustful thoughts and is capable of leading to immoral sexual behavior, especially in its most vivid form, the erotic movie. What goes through a reader's mind when he or she reads a passage or views a scene that goes into the physical details of sexual activity? The range of responses would seem to be the following: (1) embarrassment that sex, a private experience, has been dragged out into public, making a voyeur out of a reader or viewer whether or not he or she wants to be; (2) repulsion at the lust being portrayed; (3) fantasizing about sex; (4) allowing the stimulus to lead to immoral sexual activity (and on this point I am thinking of contact with such literature in bulk). No matter which of these responses is true of a given reader on a given occasion, I cannot see that any one of them is a compelling reason for a Christian to read such literature. There are certainly occasions when a Christian might read a work in spite of such descriptions but not because of them.

There is a great difference between literature that uses reticence in portraying sex as part of a thorough analysis of human experience and literature that lingers, in clinical fashion, over the details of sexual activity. The Bible portrays sex in the former but not the latter way. Immersion in literature that portrays sex in the clinical manner usually does what such literature was designed to do, namely, inflame a reader's sexual appetite. At the very least such literature fills the mind and imagination with sexual images, making voyeurs out of its readers. Jesus, the Christian reader will always remember, extended lust and adultery to include a person's thought life when he condemned the mental act of lust in one's "heart" (Mt. 5:28).

Our culture, as we know, is obsessed with sex, much to its own detriment and even more to the detriment of the Christian who tries to live by a biblical and Christlike standard. Modern literature and cinema, along with advertising, have probably done more to create the obsession than anything else has. Some will disagree with that claim, believing that our society has turned to sexual indulgence as a response to modern transience, anonymity, impersonality and technology. I am convinced, however, that modern literature has helped to create the obsession with sex. Will Durant has written that "our ancestors played this sexual impulse down, knowing that it was strong enough without encouragement; we have blown it up with a thousand forms of incitation, advertisement, emphasis and display, and have armed it with the doctrine that inhibition is dangerous."[16] Literature that portrays sexual activity in clinical detail is one of the kinds of literature that I believe creates problems for Christian readers, and when they read such literature they will do so for reasons I have defended earlier in my remarks about the necessity of modern literature.

A fourth troublesome dimension of modern literature is its frequent use of the related phenomena of profanity, blasphemy, sacrilege and obscenity. If we keep in mind that the Ten Commandments in the Old Testament are not simply particularized prohibitions but that each commandment implies a broader moral principle, we can see that the third commandment, "You shall not take the name of the LORD your God in vain," speaks about the sanctity of God's name and being and that the seventh commandment, "You shall not commit adultery," asserts the sanctity of human sexuality and the human body. If so, profanity, blasphemy and sacrilege violate the command not to take God's name in vain (and of course the command includes much in addition to blasphemy), while the seventh commandment prohibits obscenity, since obscenity defiles the sanctity of the physical body and human sexuality. Obscenity may be one of the things proscribed by the statement in Colossians 3:8 to avoid "foul talk," and it is certainly what is in view in Ephesians 5:4, which prohibits "filthiness" and "silly talk," which the New American Standard Version translates as "filthiness and silly talk, or coarse jesting." There are, incidentally, vulgarities that may violate a standard of good taste but which fall short of what I am here calling obscenity and profanity.

There are several possible difficulties posed for the Christian reader by what I have categorized together as profanity, blasphemy, sacrilege and obscenity. These things might offend a Christian's sensibility and the Holy Spirit within. They might cause the mind to cringe, a response that contradicts the reason why a person ordinarily reads literature. On the other hand a reader might be led to acquiesce in or take lightly the blasphemy or obscenity, and this is to compromise on an issue that a Christian should take seriously. The presence of profanity or obscenity in a book does not mean that the book as a whole is depraved in its viewpoint. These things are part of the "object matter" of a work and should be kept distinct from the subject matter or theme. Someone has analyzed blasphemy in literature this way:

> The mere presence of blasphemy in a book is not sufficient to condemn a book unless the author gives indication of condoning it or presenting it in a light and offensive way. Again, one must be careful, whether or not there is a real case of formal blasphemy, which requires two conditions: a) use of language which reviles God or His actions, or arrogates to creatures prerogatives of the Creator; b) advertence to the fact that such language dishonors God. Undoubtedly many of the characters in a book who are portrayed as using such language are of a type not to know that they are materially blaspheming.[17]

I return to my earlier point that every reader must resolve personally the question of how the offensiveness of some parts of a work affect, for him or her, the experience of the work as a whole. However a Christian reader resolves the question for a given work, it remains true that profanity, blasphemy and obscenity are problem areas of modern realism.

A final objection that a Christian might have to naturalistic literature is one that can be stated in different ways. It is that reading such literature, especially in quantity, often adds little that is positive to a person's spiritual well-being. I am talking about naturalistic literature that does not edify. Or about literature that leads a person to violate Paul's command to think on those things that are pure and lovely and of good report (Phil. 4:8). We know that Paul's statement does not preclude realism, since the Bible itself calls us to contemplate human depravity. Yet the overall effect of reading the Bible is clearly what Paul describes. But what can be said in defense of naturalistic literature that produces an opposite effect on a Christian reader? By immersing oneself in such literature she or he is filling the mind with the opposite of what Christians are called to affirm.

I said in my defense of realism that literature covers the whole spectrum of life and that we should not run away from what actually exists in our world. But if, in literature and life, we cannot completely avoid the depraved end of the spectrum, we can avoid most of it, particularly in literature. There is usually no good reason for a Christian deliberately to seek out literature that depicts human depravity. It is not (at least for the mature Christian) so much a matter of being swept into immoral behavior; it is much more likely to be a question of good use of time. If in life no good comes from deliberately jumping into mud puddles, in the Christian's spiritual life not much good comes from jumping into the cesspool of much naturalistic literature. And although I believe firmly what I said earlier about the ability of modern literature to keep a Christian in touch with the culture, I must also say that this argument is much less convincing than it is sometimes made out to be. How can anyone not know what is happening in society if one watches television and reads the newspaper? How much modern literature must a Christian read in order to know what lust or hatred is like? Probably none at all. Frank Gaebelein writes, "No Christian is obligated to reside in the brothels of the mind in order to know the world in which he lives."[18] In arguing as I do on this matter I have no desire to minimize the ways in which literature presents experience with greater impact and more interpretive insight than the mass media do. The question that remains, however, is, how much contact is required to make our awareness full.

To speak of the dangers of modern literature as I have implies that I am not impressed by the currently fashionable attitude that as long as a writer is serious in the portrayal of depravity, the work is thereby justified as literature. Harry Blamires subjects this popular view to careful scrutiny in his book *The Christian Mind*. He attacks "the current superstition which sets such a high value on seriousness."[19] Blamires rejects "the idea, virtually unquestioned just now, that any discussion or literary exploitation of sexual matters, perversions, or aberrations, is good *provided that it is serious*. . . . It is regarded as healthy to describe or represent intercourse, promiscuity, vice, homosexuality, lesbianism, sadism, and the like, if you do so *seriously*. . . . The increasing obsession with sexuality and vice in literature is defended today by an irrational and emotive exploitation of words like *sincere* and *authentic* which carry spurious 'moral' overtones."[20] In fact, as Blamires suggests, to portray immorality seriously may make it more, not less, blameworthy. A scene of illicit love may be portrayed "sensitively," but its sensitivity does not mitigate its depravity and may actually increase it.

The question of whether a work of literature can be called "immoral" has generally ended in semantic quibbling that obscures the real issue. What is indisputable is that literature is a stimulus to a response. The response can be either moral or immoral. Usually the response is intellectual or emotional, but sometimes it is a matter of behavior. Pornographic literature is the most obvious example of literature that can produce a direct response. As a stimulus to response literature can be as bad an influence as a person can be. To parade the biblical statement that "to the pure all things are pure" and to lay the blame entirely on the reader is, in my view, nonsense. We are responsible for the stimuli to which we expose ourselves. Furthermore, as persons we become, in significant ways, the sum of our indulgences. Christian readers are responsible for the images and thoughts that fill their minds, and the literature that they absorb is one of the major sources of such images. William Wordsworth expressed the ideal of a mind that is "a mansion for all lovely forms,"[21] which I take to be his counterpart of Paul's picture of the mind as a habitation of thoughts that are true, honorable, just, pure, lovely, gracious, excellent and worthy of praise (Phil. 4:8). One of the greatest positive values of literature is that it refines our sensibilities, but a great deal of naturalistic literature conveys a coarseness that is the opposite of refinement.

My own conclusion is that wherever an individual Christian draws the line, he or she has to draw the line somewhere and leave some works of literature unread or unfinished. The Christian is accountable to God, not to a code or a fellow human, but what is the basis for the sometimes prevalent assumption that God's standard of holiness and purity is less strict than human standards? Spiritual reality has not changed since Jesus proclaimed that it is the pure in heart who will see God.

To summarize, I feel with equal conviction both halves of my thesis that realistic literature is both necessary and troublesome for a Christian reader. The questions that will help a Christian reach personal decisions about any given work of literature include these:

1. Does my reading of this work lead me to immoral thoughts or actions?

2. Does the moral depravity that this work portrays call my attention to something about reality that I need to know?

3. Does the overall moral or social significance of this work exceed in importance the offensiveness of some of its parts? Can I minimize the impact of these parts in order to appropriate the larger insights of the work?

4. If I do not enjoy reading this work, is there a reason why I should read it anyway?

As I read naturalistic literature I am forced to a middle-of-the-road attitude that both affirms and rejects this type of literature. I affirm its importance as a force in contemporary culture. I affirm its necessity as a means of understanding my culture. I affirm the necessity to read some literature that depicts depravity in a realistic manner, since the presence of realism in the Bible leaves me no option on this score. I affirm that literature is intended to be not only a source of artistic pleasure but also a truthful reflection of reality.

On the other side of the ledger I find myself questioning the value of a Christian's spending a great deal of time reading naturalistic literature. Much of this literature condones and even glorifies the depravity that it depicts. It becomes very questionable what positive effects emerge from a Christian's reading something that offers for approval something that only elicits rejection or disgust. If reading imaginative literature is something that we do for enjoyment, much realistic fiction will fail to meet this test for a Christian reader. To read literature that goes into great detail in describing the sordid nature of evil and sexual immorality and profanity is to violate Christ's and Paul's comments on what ought to constitute the furniture of a Christian's mind.

But whenever I find myself wondering about the legitimacy of modern realism, I am pulled back by the unanswerable considerations that I cannot run away from my contemporary world, that I must face its literature and its values, and that, moreover, the Bible itself insists on my contact with realism in literature. I am left walking a tightrope between the extremes of total rejection and total affirmation of naturalistic literature. I am left with the attitude that such literature is, for the Christian, both necessary and questionable in its worth. A sense of balance is what a Christian reader needs. People who are inclined either to immerse themselves in such literature or to avoid it completely probably need to check their inclination.

The Alien Views of Modern Literature

We must remember that the greater part of our current reading matter is written for us by people who have no real belief in a supernatural order. . . . So long as we are conscious of the gulf fixed between ourselves and the greater part of contemporary literature, we are more or less protected from being harmed by it, and are in a position to extract from it what good it has to offer us. □ *T. S. Eliot, "Religion and Literature"*

How should a Christian respond to contemporary literature when it offers for approval world views and ethical attitudes that are at odds with the Christian faith and lifestyle? Should a Christian spend time reading literature that advances such alien philosophies as hedonism, despair or false optimism? If so, *how* should it be read?

I would suggest that a Christian reader should be on guard against a categorical rejection of the validity of the dominant non-Christian traditions in contemporary literature. If uncritical acceptance is one danger to avoid, another danger is the refusal to assimilate the reality of the vision of such works. The guiding principle remains the necessity and the danger of modern literature. Virginia Mollenkott comments that "once having tried the spirits and rejected those elements which are incompatible with a fearless faith, the Christian is not only in a position to gain from the insights of modern artists but is *responsible to do so.*"[22]

We must remember that non-Christian strands in modern literature embody the attitudes really held by large numbers of people in the twentieth century. Modern literature records contemporary man's quest for meaning, even when it portrays persons who search for it in such vulgar ways as sexual perversion and violence. The Christian reader cannot sweep aside the views espoused in modern literature as being unimportant, for the fact is that they are important in the culture in which we live. Christians need to be aware of how some segments of the population have given their souls to popular music and movies. The Christian needs to judge the world views of modern literature after the pattern of Christ, who was unfailingly patient in his understanding of the unregenerate mind.

Not only should a Christian look at the values expressed in modern literature carefully because such literature is a significant force in modern society, but also because it is a way of achieving a sympathetic understanding of non-Christians. As Virginia Mollenkott has written, "If we truly want to communicate with our contemporaries we must understand them; and there is no more readily available way of understanding them than by reading what they have written for us and for each other."[23] In a similar vein Roland Frye comments that if "we are to see clearly the ultimate problems of man's life for which Christian truth must have relevance if it has value, we can scarcely do better than to study man as his lot is clarified through enduring literature."[24] One of the main lessons that modern literature can teach the Christian is that persons who deserve moral condemnation should at the same time elicit our pity and compassion.

Yet another reason why a Christian reader cannot afford to make a simplistic rejection of non-Christian modern literature is that this literature contains elements of truth. The fact that unbelieving modern writers come up with the wrong solution to a problem does not necessarily mean that they have missed the mark in their scrutiny of the problem. The hedonistic tradition, for example, is based on a truth, namely, that people do have physical drives and appetites and that these appetites, in themselves and apart from the excesses and perversions that have grown up around them, are good and normal. The error of hedonism is its premise that any act of the appetite to which a person is inclined at any time is also good and normal. If a Christian reader sweeps aside the hedonistic philosophy in one fell swoop, he or she will have failed, perhaps, to understand either hedonism or the biblical view of the physical appetites.

When the Christian turns to the tradition of nihilism and despair and pessimistic existentialism, he or she must likewise begin with an agreement of sorts, namely, that life lived apart from God and biblical values is meaningless. This is the theme of the biblical book of Ecclesiastes, so a Christian can hardly afford a superficial rejection of the literature of despair.

Along with the necessity of reading works that affirm false world views I would stress the dangers of reading such literature. Three categories of such literature strike me as particularly troublesome: hedonism, naturalism and sentimentalism.

Hedonistic literature, if we immerse ourselves in it, or if we encounter it in its most vivid forms, wears down our resistance. It encourages a person to give in to lust and regard it lightly, or perhaps even as inevitable. The literature of hedonism is seductive. Its strategy is to make people feel that the desires they are resisting are so natural and healthy that it is perverse and abnormal to resist them. Film after film, novel after novel, popular song after popular song assures us that the sexual drive should be indulged whenever a person feels like doing so. Christians are not immune to the seductive powers of hedonistic songs and novels and movies.

Nihilistic literature does not persuade us to commit sins of the body, but it does persuade us to commit sins of the mind. Nihilism and despair—the denial of hope—are sins of unbelief. They are the opposite of what the Holy Spirit promises to produce within the believer. This point has been well stated by Hilda Graef, who begins her book *Modern Gloom and Christian Hope* with the premise, "Our point of view is solely that of the Christian, for whom hope is one of the theological virtues and despair a sin."[25] Despair of the modern variety is infectious, and that is why it is one of the dangers—a temption in some instances—of some modern literature.

My claim is that the literature of despair presents a false view of reality that can lead a reader into intellectual error.

And as Frank Gaebelein has written, "Art that distorts the truth is no more pleasing to God than any other kind of untruth."[26] One way in which naturalism falsifies reality is by its *concentration* on the ugly and violent aspects of life. If sentimental, wish-fulfillment literature is a false view of reality, so is naturalism. There is a realism of grace as well as a realism of carnality. The rose bush in front of the house is as real as the garbage can behind the house. The literature of nihilism and despair presents an incomplete vision of what is real. Addison Leitch once criticized Flannery O'Connor for distorting reality by choosing atypical characters for her stories and acting as though they were representative of humanity. He wrote, "One gets the impression that in order to make our total depravity plain, she makes too many of her characters bizarre. For example, in one of her great stories a woman with a wooden leg and a Ph.D. is seduced by a Bible salesman. That is not the sort of Reality I run into with any great frequency, which makes me wonder if that's the way it really is."[27] Naturalistic literature, in fact, is so exaggerated and therefore false that it lends itself easily to parody.

Naturalistic literature also falsifies reality by giving the impression that ugliness and depravity are the whole story about human potential. The Bible depicts human beings in a threefold manner—perfect as created by God, fallen by virtue of sin, but capable of redemption through faith in Christ. Modern literature is truthful in its depiction of fallen experience, but it is untruthful in its implication that this is the whole picture. Even its depiction of depravity tends to fall short of the biblical truth, portraying evil as inevitable, for example, or not perceiving depravity as sin against God and his moral law. It is, of course, true that a work of literature, or perhaps even the entire canon of a writer, is not obligated to cover the whole territory. But when an entire literary tradition consistently shows a particular bias and consistently omits certain data about reality, it can be charged with presenting a false view of reality.

Another branch of literature that falsifies reality is what I will call sentimental literature. This is wish-fulfillment literature that escapes from reality by ignoring or glossing over the sordid side of life. Such literature is often an implicit denial of such basic tenets of the Christian faith as the sinfulness of human nature and the fallen condition of the world. This branch of literature usually reflects a success ethic in which human and often materialistic success is offered as the ultimate achievement and goal of life, even though such success overrides values that Christianity regards as more important. Sentimental literature is often based on an optimistic humanism that offers a pleasant view of life on an inadequate basis. A typical case in point is "situation comedy," which raises potentially serious problems and uncovers flaws in human nature only to laugh them away.

We must, of course, avoid being too quick to stigmatize any branch of literature as being "escapist." C. S. Lewis is right in saying that "there is a sense in which all reading whatever is an escape. It involves a temporary transference of the mind from our actual surroundings to things merely imagined or conceived. This happens when we read history or science no less than when we read fictions. All such escape is *from* the same thing; immediate, concrete actuality. The important question is what we escape *to*."[28] Still, it is indisputable that some literature falsifies reality by evading or escaping from the problems of human existence. In its more extreme forms, chronic immersion in such literature can unfit a person for contact with real life, and it can dull a Christian's understanding and compassion for people in the real world.

In singling out the modern traditions of hedonism, naturalism and sentimentalism as ones that are potentially troublesome for a Christian reader, I am of course aware that there is nothing new about the situation of false world views posing difficulties for a reader. When C. S. Lewis, writing from his experience as a teacher of literature, illustrates his observation that he "could not doubt that the sub-Christian or anti-Christian values implicit in most literature did actually infect many readers,"[29] he is not talking only about modern literature. But the alien views of modern literature, especially the hedonistic, nihilistic and sentimental traditions, have proved particularly seductive for some readers, partly because they are reinforced in so many different forms in contemporary culture.

The world views of modern literature, like those of any period, must be weighed against the Christian world view. The person who wishes to pursue the topic can find help from published criticism. I conclude this chapter with a brief list of such books. The list typifies the variety of attempts to assimilate modern literature in terms of a Christian perspective. I have not personally found all of these works helpful, but my experience as a teacher has continuously reminded me that what one person finds unhelpful is often exactly what another person needs. The reader should be aware that these books represent a wide variety of scholarly depth and a wide range in their definitions of what constitutes a "Christian" element in literature. Some define it as biblical Christianity and others as broadly synonymous with the "religious" element. These books are surveys of groups of modern writers; for Christian criticism on a specific author, one should consult the books and articles on that writer.

1. *Christianity and Literature* (formerly called *Newsletter of the Conference on Christianity and Literature*) is the quarterly journal of the Conference on Christianity and Literature. Each issue contains an annotated bibliography of books and articles that discuss literature from a Christian perspective (broadly defined). The bibliography is arranged chronologically by literary periods, one of which is the modern era.

2. Stuart Babbage, *The Mark of Cain: Studies in Literature and Theology* (Grand Rapids: William B. Eerdmans, 1966).

3. Kay M. Baxter, *Contemporary Theatre and the Christian Faith* (Nashville: Abingdon, 1964).

4. Cleanth Brooks, *The Hidden God: Studies in Heming-*

way, Faulkner, Yeats, Eliot, and Warren (New Haven: Yale University Press, 1963).

5. *Contemporary Writers in Christian Perspective* (Grand Rapids: William B. Eerdmans). A series of 48-page pamphlets on several dozen modern writers. Users of the series should be aware of the general tendency to define the term "Christian" so broadly that virtually every modern writer turns out to be a member of the faith.

6. Ruth Etchells, *Unafraid to Be: A Christian Study of Contemporary English Writing* (London: Inter-Varsity, 1969).

7. Hoxie Neale Fairchild, *Religious Trends in English Poetry, Volume VI: 1920-1965* (New York: Columbia University Press, 1968).

8. Edmund Fuller, *Man in Modern Fiction: Some Minority Opinions on Contemporary American Writing* (New York: Vintage, 1949).

9. Hilda Graef, *Modern Gloom and Christian Hope* (Chicago: Henry Regnery, 1959).

10. John Killinger, *The Failure of Theology in Modern Literature* (Nashville: Abingdon, 1963). In contrast to so much criticism, which sees Christianity virtually everywhere in modern literature, Killinger (like Graef) defines Christianity with a refreshing sense of precision and finds modern literature generally lacking in any full-fledged presentation of the Christian faith. (This is the same author, incidentally, who a decade later repudiated his earlier standards in another book on modern literature.)

11. *The Shapeless God: Essays on Modern Fiction*, ed. Harry J. Mooney, Jr., and Thomas F. Staley (Pittsburgh: University of Pittsburgh Press, 1968). Essays by various scholars on specific authors. *The last chapter is a selective bibliography on religion and the modern novel.*

12. *The Climate of Faith in Modern Literature*, ed. Nathan A. Scott, Jr. (New York: Seabury, 1964). Perhaps the best collection of essays by various experts in modern literature.

13. *Man in the Modern Theatre*, ed. Nathan A. Scott, Jr. (Richmond: John Knox Press, 1965).

14. Nathan A. Scott, Jr., *Modern Literature and the Religious Frontier* (New York: Harper and Brothers, 1958).

15. *Religion and Modern Literature: Essays in Theory and Criticism*, ed. G. B. Tennyson and Edward E. Ericson, Jr. (Grand Rapids: William B. Eerdmans, 1975).

16. Martin Turnell, *Modern Literature and Christian Faith* (Westminster, Md.: Newman Press, 1961).

17. John Van Zanten, *Caught in the Act: Modern Drama as Prelude to the Gospel* (Philadelphia: Westminster Press, 1971).

18. Amos N. Wilder, *The Spiritual Aspects of the New Poetry* (New York: Harper and Brothers, 1940).

19. Amos N. Wilder, *Modern Poetry and the Christian Tradition* (New York: Charles Scribner's Sons, 1952).

20. J. Rodman Williams, *Contemporary Existentialism and Christian Faith* (Englewood Cliffs: Prentice-Hall, 1965). Not a work of literary criticism, but the best survey and Christian critique of existentialism that I have seen.

21. A. S. P. Woodhouse, *The Poet and His Faith: Religion and Poetry in England from Spenser to Eliot and Auden* (Chicago: University of Chicago Press, 1965).

8 The Bible and the Study of Literature

The Critic's Sourcebook
Without some knowledge of the Bible one simply does not know what is going on in English literature. □ Northrop Frye, On Teaching Literature

The Bible is an indispensable book for anyone who wishes to understand literature. Northrop Frye has for some time been asserting that the Bible should be the foundation for literary education. He writes, "The Bible forms the lowest stratum in the teaching of literature. It should be taught so early and so thoroughly that it sinks straight to the bottom of the mind, where everything that comes along later can settle on it.... The Bible... should be the basis of literary training."[1] William R. Mueller has written that "it is impossible for any writer to disengage himself from the profound influence which the Bible has had throughout many centuries: he may try to shout the Bible down, but he can hardly ignore it."[2] And T. R. Henn calls the Bible the "single greatest source" of Western literature.[3]

In this chapter I have tried to outline the ways in which the Bible contributes to the study of literature. My topic is how literary critics use the Bible, not primarily how writers use it. Several of my points will have already been illustrated in previous chapters, and I will treat these summarily in this chapter. The use of the Bible as a sourcebook of archetypes, however, will merit a more detailed analysis.

My first conviction is that *the Bible should be studied as literature* in high-school and college literature courses. It deserves to be studied as literature because that is what it is in many of its parts. C. S. Lewis has written that "there is a . . . sense in which the Bible, since it is after all literature, cannot properly be read except as literature; and the different parts of it as the different sorts of literature they are."[4]

We have recently witnessed a resurgence of academic interest in studying the Bible as literature, and courses in the literature of the Bible are now common in high schools and colleges. I have already approached the Bible from a literary perspective in my book *The Literature of the Bible*.[5] I do, however, wish to underscore something that I have said on several occasions: to study the Bible as literature means to ask *literary* questions of the poems and stories of the Bible.[6] Not every approach to the Bible is literary in nature, and it is the business of literary critics to follow their own intuitions as literary scholars instead of using the model of biblical scholarship.

In addition to undertaking a systematic literary survey of the Bible as one studies English or American literature, *the Bible should be used to illustrate literary techniques and literary genres*. Between the covers of this single book one can find models of many of the leading literary forms and rhetorical devices, as recent anthologies have begun to acknowledge. The great advantage of using the Bible to illustrate literary forms is its familiarity and its accessibility (even to people who do not already know it). The lyric poetry of the Bible and the poetic oracles of the Old Testament prophets illustrate admirably the ingredients of the poetic idiom (image, symbol, metaphor, simile, allusion, personification and hyperbole). And biblical narrative, partly because of its characteristic brevity and the resultant emphasis on essential patterns, is one of the best sources from which to illustrate techniques of storytelling. The Bible is paradoxically both a "popular" book, accessible even to children, and a book filled with sophisticated literary craftsmanship.

Literary critics also use the Bible *to identify and interpret allusions in literature.* An allusion is a reference to past history or literature, and in the literature of the English language there have been more allusions to the Bible than to any other book. Whenever a writer alludes to the Bible, the impact and meaning of the passage depend on a reader's knowledge of the biblical source of the allusion. There is no way to avoid the necessity of acquaintance with the Bible when reading English and American literature.

The ways in which allusions work are many. Without attempting a complete analysis of the topic, I offer the following list as one that suggests something of the complexity of how biblical allusions operate in literature:

1. Writers use references to the Bible in such a way that a knowledge of the biblical source is necessary to understand the very meaning of the literary passage. William Wordsworth, for example, praises his young daughter's intuitive rapport with nature by asserting, "Thou liest in Abraham's bosom all the year,/ And worship'st at the temple's inner shrine." The statement is unintelligible unless we know Jesus' parable about the rich man and Lazarus, and the Old Testament descriptions of the temple in Jerusalem.

2. Sometimes a biblical allusion sharpens a reference that otherwise remains vague. When Milton, in his sonnet on his blindness, speaks of "that one talent which is death to hide," the statement is vaguely intelligible without a knowledge of Scripture; but the full depth of the speaker's despair becomes clear only if we realize that he is linking himself with the slothful and condemned steward of Christ's parable of the talents.

3. A biblical allusion sometimes adds a depth of emotional and spiritual response to a literary passage. For ex-

ample, Leo Tolstoy's story *The Death of Ivan Ilych* ends
with the death of the protagonist. As Ivan struggles with
his fear of death, he is pictured as suddenly falling through
a black hole into light; in the process he loses his fear of
death: "In place of death there was light." While this
"light" has vague connotations of freedom and relief for
any reader, the associations become much richer if one
realizes that the light is part of a pattern of Christian imagery in the story's conclusion and that it is a symbol of
God and salvation.

4. Writers often use allusions as titles for works or chapters in order to suggest an interpretive framework for the
literary presentation that follows. In such instances, the
writer's hint is lost on any reader who is ignorant of the
biblical source of the allusion. Graham Greene, for example, took the title of his novel *The Power and the Glory*
from the conclusion of the Lord's Prayer ("For thine is the
kingdom, and the power, and the glory, forever"). In
doing so he offers an interpretation of his story, in which
the moral weakness of the "whiskey priest" does not im-
pair either the efficacy of his ministry nor his own eligi-
bility for salvation, since it is the power and glory of God's
grace, and not human sufficiency, that produce spiritual
results.

5. Storytellers commonly base the names of their characters on the Bible, thereby suggesting one or more interpretations of the character. In *The Scarlet Letter* Pearl's
name is based on the pearl of great price, Jesus' symbol
for the kingdom of God in Matthew 13:45. In Hawthorne's
story the name suggests both the worth of Pearl (her mother's lone comfort through much of the story) and the price
that the illegitimate child cost her mother in terms of social
standing in the community.

6. In ages when biblical knowledge was a shared cultural possession, writers sometimes depended on their
readers' knowledge of a biblical passage as the background
against which to measure a statement or event in a literary
work. Thus Milton, in *Samson Agonistes*, depends on the

reader's ability to judge as a lie Dalilah's statement that she had betrayed Samson because the Philistine lords had promised to do Samson no harm, since the biblical source makes it clear that in their initial overture to Dalilah the lords expressed their intention to "bind him to subdue him" (Judg. 16:5).

7. Writers who write about the "other world" of heaven and hell and spiritual beings often use the Bible as their source of information about that world. James H. Sims, in his book *The Bible in Milton's Epics*,[7] shows how Milton uses biblical allusions to lend "authoritative reality" to his portrayal of supernatural scenes, characters and events.

8. Writers have sometimes used the literary forms of the Bible as models for how to .write in the same literary genre. John R. May's book *Toward a New Earth: Apocalypse in the American Novel*[8] for example, shows how biblical apocalypse is discernible in the apocalyptic vision of the American novel. Or consider Spenser's emblematic blazon in "Epithalamion," where he praises his bride's beauty by comparing her features to objects in nature:

Her goodly eyes like sapphires shining bright,
Her forehead ivory white,
Her cheeks like apples which the sun hath rudded,
Her lips like cherries. . . .[9]

Where did Spenser get the idea of writing like this? He got the technique straight from the Song of Solomon, which contains four emblematic blazons.

9. Sometimes writers parody a biblical passage by paraphrasing or adding to or changing the passage for a new effect. Arthur Hugh Clough's famous poem "The Latest Decalogue" is a rendering of the Ten Commandments in which each commandment is accompanied by a reason for obeying the command. The reasons that are given are the opposite of the biblical ones and represent Clough's satiric attack on the perverted values by which people actually live. Thus the Old Testament command, "You shall not make for yourself a graven image, . . . for I the Lord your God am a jealous God" becomes, "No graven images may

be/ Worshiped, except the currency."

10. Writers sometimes *reinterpret* or invert biblical passages, characters or events, with the effect often dependent
on the reader's ability to contrast the writer's treatment
with the biblical version. D. H. Lawrence wrote a number of short poems in which he quotes or paraphrases a
line from the Bible, only to repudiate the biblical viewpoint. His poem "The Hills," for example, takes as its first
line the opening line of Psalm 121 ("I lift up mine eyes unto
the hills"), but instead of affirming with the psalmist that
his help comes from the Lord, Lawrence in the second line
of his poem denies biblical transcendence, finding
strength only in "darkness."

The foregoing list will show, I trust, that allusions are
far from the simple thing that many people take them to be.
The best starting point for a complete study of the topic is
Roland Bartel's book *Biblical Images in Literature.* [10] It is essential to realize that exploring allusions in literature is not
an "approach" that one can take or leave, as the formalist
or archetypal or psychological approaches to literature can
be either used or not used, depending on the critic's taste.
Allusions are part of the writer's idiom and cannot be
avoided. And the only way to do justice to literature that
alludes to the Bible is to know the Bible well enough to
recognize and interpret the allusions. Since readers do not
know the Bible as well as they need to, editions with foot-
notes identifying the allusions become almost a necessity.

Another way in which the Bible is of service to the literary critic is to function as *the definitive source of Christian
belief.* Christianity is a revealed religion. Until recently
Christianity has never been whatever a theologian decided
it to be. The great creeds of Christendom have been interpretations and codifications of Scripture, not rivals or
additions. Christianity is by definition the faith that cen-
ters in the person and work of Christ. And the only extant
source of information about what Christ did and taught is
the New Testament.

The Christian world view and ethos have been embodied authoritatively in the Bible. The corollary of this fact is that critics of literature who would aspire to make accurate statements about Christianity and literature must know the Bible and know it well. They must have a grasp of biblical theology and must be acquainted with the resources that will lead them to biblical passages dealing with such topics as the nature of God and human beings, creation, sin, salvation and virtue. The person whose vocation is the study of literature must have as his or her avocation the study of the Bible.

Intellectual inquiry into any subject has always been obligated to answer the question, "How do you know?" One of the features of much religious literary criticism is that while the best critics insist on a detailed and rigorous scrutiny of the literary text, many of these same critics never bother to explain where they got their generalizations about what constitutes "Christianity." This is an abdication of critics' responsibility to support their statements, and the result has been inprecision and error.

One of the things that I discovered while doing the research for this book is that among many leading voices in the religious criticism movement it has apparently become passé for a Christian to believe in heaven and eternal life as the ultimate realities. In book after book critics use such concepts as "immanence" and "incarnation" as touchstones whereby writers who are most absorbed in portraying earthly reality in itself and most indifferent to any type of transcendental reality emerge as the most "Christian" or "religious" writers. In one of the more extreme statements of the position, Amos Wilder writes that "the old two-story world is a thing of the past" and that modern man must "free himself from hang-overs of old fashions in transcendence."[11]

Where did the critics get such a view of Christianity? Certainly not by reading their New Testaments. J. B. Phillips notes regarding the writers of the New Testament that "the center of gravity of their hope was in the eternal and not in the temporal world. . . . Of comparatively recent years the center of our faith has become . . . more and more earthbound. . . . Yet to have the soul firmly anchored in Heaven rather than grounded in this little sphere is far more like New Testament Christianity."[12] The stories and poems of the Bible consistently portray two levels of reality, the earthly and the heavenly, the physical and the spiritual. The transcendental world penetrates and reaches down into the earthly scene, but it does not thereby cease to exist as a separate reality. In the Bible it is the unseen spiritual world that gives ultimate meaning to human life in this world, not vice versa. And the goal toward which the individual life is headed is not temporal life in this world but eternal life in the supernatural world. If some branches of "Christian criticism" reject biblical ideas as the touchstone for Christian belief, it is quite important that both they and critics who accept the Bible realize that they are not operating on a common ground and that they do not represent a single school of literary criticism.

The actual ways in which criticism uses the Bible as a sourcebook for Christian belief are various. At one end of the spectrum we can find a book such as William R. Mueller's *The Prophetic Voice in Modern Fiction*, which devotes each of its six chapters to a single Christian theme as embodied in a single modern novel (the themes are vocation, the Fall, judgment, suffering, love and the remnant). Each chapter is divided into approximately equal thirds, and each one moves "from a thematic discussion of the novel in question, to a study of the biblical proclamation on the same theme, to a consideration of the relationship between novel and Bible in regard to their understanding of the theme." Mueller calls his approach "a series of dialogues between biblical and modern writers,"[13] and he is right in surveying a variety of biblical passages (including both Old and New Testaments) on each theme, since biblical books are not self-contained and do not give the complete biblical teaching on any topic. Mueller's book weights literary criticism more heavily in the direction of biblical or religious analysis than I think is usually desirable.

At the other end of the critical spectrum is a critic like C. S. Lewis, who does not intersperse lengthy religious analysis with his literary criticism but who, when he makes comments about a work's relationship to Christian belief, includes enough concise quotations to make it clear that he has done his homework. Depending on a critic's audience and purpose on a given occasion, the proportion of actual reference to biblical material will fall somewhere between the poles I have cited. Regardless of how much biblical or doctrinal reference literary critics include in their criticism, they are obligated to know what biblical theology says about a given issue before making pronouncements on the relationship between a given work or author and the Christian faith.

Slightly different from a critic's use of the Bible as a sourcebook of Christian doctrine is *the use of a biblical statement or aphorism as a helpful interpretation of a literary work.* This, I agree, is a minor use of the Bible in literary criticism. It is true, however, that often a single image, phrase or sentence expresses an interpretation or summary of an entire literary work or a leading motif in a work. I am not talking about a "message" that is extracted from the work and substituted for it, but rather about an interpretative or descriptive framework that makes the actual images of a poem or characters and events of a story fall into place and stand out with new clarity. If works or motifs are based on the principle of unity in variety, or theme and variation, it is crucial to articulate the unifying theme as concisely as possible.

Often the.pattern or "informing metaphor" of a work is contained by an image or sentence within the poem or story itself. The destructive effects of carnality that are dramatized in so many episodes of Dostoyevsky's *The Brothers Karamazov* are capsulized in Grushenka's comment, "Wine doesn't give peace." But a reader/critic is not limited to the work itself for the statement that best describes a poem or story. One must search for the most apt formulation that will illuminate the primary data of the text.

Now it so happens that the Bible is the most aphoristic book in existence. It is filled with concise, memorable statements about the universal, permanent aspects of human experience. The English poet Francis Thompson, writing about books that influenced him, comments regarding the Bible that "beyond even its poetry, I was impressed by it as a treasury of *gnomic* wisdom. I mean its richness in utterances of which one could, as it were, chew the cud. This, of course, has long been recognized, and Biblical sentences have passed into the proverbial wisdom of our country."[14] The function of a proverb is, as Gerhard von Rad has noted, "to wrest some form of order from chaos." It contributes to "the mastering of life," and it "starts from the unyielding presupposition that there is a hidden order in things and events."[15] This is very similar to the task of literary criticism, which also brings a body of diffuse primary data under the control of a unifying focus. The aphorism or proverb rescues human experience from diffuseness and vagueness, just as literary criticism rescues a story or poem from what might otherwise remain a fragmented series of images and events.

The tendency of the Bible toward aphorism makes it eminently usable as a source of statements that bring literary works or parts of works into focus. I have already illustrated this in earlier chapters. *The Scarlet Letter*, for example, narrates in full psychological richness the story of a man whose tragic decline is put into focus by the statement of James, "Confess your sins to one another . . . that you may be healed" (Jas. 5:16). Much of the dramatic action, psychological portrayal and imagery of Shakespeare's *Macbeth* falls into a unified pattern that is captured in the Old Testament statement, "For your lifeblood I will surely require a reckoning. . . . Whoever sheds the blood of man, by man shall his blood be shed" (Gen. 9:5-6). Dostoyevsky wrote a novel of epic scope about the father and sons of the Karamazov family; these characters' responses to the gospel of Christ, developed by Dostoyevsky for hundreds of pages, can be summarized in terms of the brief parable

in which Jesus compares the possible responses to grace
to four kinds of soil into which seed falls (the parable of the
soils in Mt. 13:1-9, 18-23). The maxims of the Old Testament book of Proverbs can be used as a gloss on Homer's
Odyssey, and the statements in Ecclesiastes about the fu-
tility of life under the sun function as a commentary on the
sun-drenched world of Camus's *The Stranger*. A framework is right for interpreting a work of literature whenever it unfolds a pattern that really exists in the work. The
Bible, because of the truthfulness of its observations about
life and its aphoristic style, is consistently useful as a
source of statements that help to describe and interpret
works of literature.

Another significant area in which the Bible serves the
student of literature is its ability to give *answers to questions
of literary theory*. Dorothy Sayers was right in asserting
that "if we commit ourselves to saying that the Christian
revelation discovers to us the nature of *all* truth, then it
must discover to us the nature of the truth about Art among
other things."[16] The Bible answers questions of literary
theory in primarily two ways—by its doctrines and by its
example. It functions by example because many parts of
the Bible are themselves literary in nature. For purposes of
illustration I wish to cite two examples of how the Bible
can function as a source of data for arriving at answers to
questions about literary theory.

One of the perennially fascinating questions is whether
there can be such a thing as "Christian tragedy." Much
of this discussion has been wasted effort because critics
have ignored the biblical data that quickly answers the
question. In my book *The Literature of the Bible*[17] I adduce
some of the evidence from both biblical doctrine and biblical example that shows the possibility and even the in-
evitability of a tragic concept in Christianity. Edwin M.
Good explicates the Old Testament story of Saul in lei-
surely detail as a full-fledged literary tragedy, and his final
conclusion is amply supported by his analysis: "We have
in the Saul story a masterpiece of structure, dramatic order

and suspense, and tragic irony. Someday, someone will turn the story of Saul into a great tragedy for the stage. . . . He will not have to alter a single episode. Then perhaps Saul will be recognized as a tragic figure of the same stature as Oedipus or Othello."[18] Someone else discusses a number of Jesus' parables from the perspective of literary tragedy as it has been understood by the standard literary authorities from Aristotle through Frye, demonstrating that "Jesus' tragic parables show . . . the tragic possibility which the Christian understanding of existence holds out."[19] These kinds of biblical data should have settled long ago the question of Christian tragedy.

The use of the Bible as the basis for an approach to an entire literary genre has been admirably demonstrated by Rolland N. Hein in his essay "A Biblical View of the Novel."[20] Beginning with the question, "What has the Bible to say to me as a reader of novels?" Hein deduces five biblical principles that can be applied to the study of the novel. (1) The Bible affirms the worth of the novelist's preoccupation with "the real qualities of human experience." (2) The Bible sanctions the novelist's "full and uninhibited probing of the meaning" of human experience. (3) The Bible "presents us with a model of movement that is in a sense archetypal and that is all but inevitable in any narrative of serious purpose. The pattern is that of spiritual quest that leads to illumination, of moving from problem to solution or meaning within an imagined real world." (4) The Bible demonstrates that the literary worth of a work of literature depends on the work's ability to validate its theme or meaning by the data of the story or poem. (5) The Bible offers, in the example of Christ, "the perfect model for making moral judgments" about the truth or falseness of a novelist's "speculations about the moral and spiritual aspects of experience and about the relation of man to God."

Whatever the literary problem might be, the Bible usually has something to say about it, whether directly or indirectly, whether by doctrine or example. The critic whose viewpoint is Christian should not ignore one of the richest sources of answers about the theoretic problems of literature.

The Bible and Literary Archetypes

The Bible is . . . the major informing influence on literary symbolism. . . . Once our view of the Bible comes into proper focus, a great mass of literary symbols from The Dream of the Rood *to* Little Gidding *begins to take on meaning.* ☐ *Northrop Frye,* Anatomy of Criticism

The prominence of the Bible in recent literary criticism has resulted partly from the emphasis on archetypes in modern literary theory. Archetypes, it will be remembered, are the recurrent images, plot motifs and character types that make up much of the content of literature. In the oldest literature of the world, the archetypes of literature appear in their explicit, simplified form, unobscured by realistic detail. As literature developed during the centuries the archetypes became displaced in the direction of realism. "By displacement," Northrop Frye writes, "I mean the techniques a writer uses to make his story . . . lifelike."[21] According to Frye, in the older forms of literature, such as myth, folk tale, fairy tale and the Bible, "we see the structural principles of literature isolated; in realism we see the *same* structural principles (not similar ones) fitting into a context of plausibility."[22] What we see clearly in the literature of undisplaced archetypes we see less clearly in realistic literature.

Once this principle of archetypes is grasped, it is easy to see why the Bible, along with other ancient literature, is so useful to the literary critic. The Bible is *the* great repository of archetypes in Western literature. By going back to the original source or manifestation of literary archetypes, a reader/critic can learn about the basic principles of later literature. Frye calls the Bible "a grammar of literary archetypes"—the place, in other words, where we can find in clear and concentrated and even systematic form the basic rules or principles of literature.[23]

The archetypal pattern of the fall from innocence will illustrate how the Bible can serve as a grammar of archetypes. If we wish to look at the fall from innocence in its pure form, Genesis 3 is the place to which we should turn, especially verses 6-7: "So when the woman saw that the tree was good for food, and that it was a delight to the eyes, and that the tree was to be desired to make one wise, she took of its fruit and ate; and she also gave some to her husband, and he ate. Then the eyes of both were opened, and they knew that they were naked." The basic pattern stands out fully illumined: the temptation to do what is forbidden, the illusory hope for beneficial results, the act of sinful choice, the disillusionment with the results and the operation of guilt and self-consciousness stemming from the sinful act. This same pattern of loss of innocence and initiation into evil can be discerned in many works of realistic fiction, where the archetypal motif is partly concealed under a wealth of realistic detail. Examples include Milton's *Paradise Lost*, Coleridge's *Rime of the Ancient Mariner*, Hawthorne's *Young Goodman Brown*, Mark Twain's *Huckleberry Finn*, William Golding's *Lord of the Flies* and Camus's *The Fall*. The advantage of studying the biblical prototype is that it serves as a guide that maps out the things to look for in the works where the basic pattern is concealed by the elaborate realistic details of the narrative.

The same thing can be illustrated if we consider the paradisal or "good place" motif of utopian fiction. Utopian literature is at first reading a bewildering mass of geographic details, social rules and mores, governmental regulations and agencies, and economic procedures. Some clear pathways emerge, however, if we pause to analyze the essential features of the Bible's story about life in Paradise in Genesis 2. The basic elements of the "good place," described with endless variety throughout utopian fiction, include a beautiful natural environment, the complete satisfaction of all physical needs (including food and sex), abundance, contentment, security, and human unity with nature, God and fellow humans. Using the biblical outline to illuminate the basic ingredients, it is easy to see what the utopian visionary is driving at with his detailed blueprint for the good life. In the words of Arthur Koestler, "All Utopias... are merely revised editions of the ancient text."[24]

When we turn to some actual criticism that applies this theory to works of literature, we find some very superficial and amateurish work and some very expert criticism. Some criticism is weakened by a failure to use the Bible as a grammar of archetypes. Nathan A. Scott, for example, organizes modern literature into four "myths"—"the Myth of the Isolato, the Myth of Hell, the Myth of the Voyage, and the Myth of Sanctity."[25] This is a good and helpful way of organizing some leading features of the modern literary landscape. In his discussion, however, Scott does not call these patterns archetypes, which would automatically alert a reader to the fact that these motifs are not simply modern myths but are universal, being traceable all the way back to Homer and the Bible. Nor does Scott make any attempt to use various biblical stories and characters as models that illuminate the archetypal patterns that he finds in modern literature.

For a work that covers much of the same territory as Scott's brief discussion, we can turn to Marion A. Fairman's book *Biblical Patterns in Modern Literature*. Fairman believes that many modern writers give shape to their literary universes by basing them "upon the symbolic structural patterns drawn from Biblical archetypes."[26] These archetypes include the Fall, the exile from Eden (or, after the Fall), the belly of the fish (the attempt to escape from God, an attempt that ends in isolation and suffering), the sorrowing compromise (the rejection of God and the embracing of some alternate attempt to find meaning in life) and the prodigal way (the dual awareness of lostness and the possibility of grace). Like Scott's discussion this one suffers from the superficiality that results from an attempt merely to organize literary works into categories (for which brief plot summaries suffice) instead of detailed analysis of individual works. But Fairman's approach marks an important advance over Scott's in her consistent use of the Bible as the source of the archetypes found in modern literature. Examples include Genesis 3 as an explanation of the archetype of the Fall, the story of Jonah for the futile attempt to escape from God, the rich young ruler who "turned away, sorrowing," from Christ for the sorrowing compromise and Christ's parable of the prodigal son for the prodigal way.

Along with the legitimate use of the Bible as a source of literary archetypes, there have been some arbitrary and excessive claims regarding the presence of biblical patterns in literature. Honor Matthews, for example, has written a book entitled *The Primal Curse: The Myth of Cain and Abel in the Theatre*. This sounds promising until the author presses detail after detail of Shakespeare's *Macbeth* into the Cain and Abel archetype, despite the fact that there is no sibling rivalry, no direct divine punishment of the sinner and no exile or wanderer motif in the play. Shakespeare's play, Matthews claims, has many parallels with "the Biblical prototype." For example, "in each story two contrasted types face each other: the Christ figures of Duncan and Abel are opposed to the Satanic ones of Macbeth and Cain."[27] The patterns that Matthews discerns in *Macbeth* are entirely too general to be linked specifically to the Cain and Abel story, nor does the biblical story help us to see meanings in the play that would otherwise remain obscure (and this, after all, is the test that the kind of archetypal criticism I am urging must pass if it is valid).

Then, too, there is the whole vexing area of biblical "analogues." An analogue is a parallel story or symbol found in different cultural or literary traditions. The Garden of Hesperides in classical mythology, for example, is an analogue to the Genesis story of Paradise. An analogue is not necessarily an archetype, however, and too often the claim to find a biblical pattern in works of literature is arbitrary and fruitless.

Roy Battenhouse's approach to Shakespearean tragedy

is perhaps the best illustration of how criticism based on analogues operates. Here is how the technique looks when applied to Shakespeare's *King Lear:*

> ... its hero is analogous to the prodigal son. He wastes his portion on harlots (which Goneril and Regan literally are in the play) and riotous living, until he is driven to eating husks with swine (as Lear does in feeding on empty memories in his hovel on the heath). As this prodigal begins to come to himself and look homeward, the father who comes out to meet and embrace him is, paradoxically, Cordelia. In other words, *Lear* is an analogue of the Bible's story of mankind's journey toward revelation to a point as far as that journey can go short of the emergence of an adult New Adam.[28]

This is not archetypal criticism. It is much closer to allegorical interpretation, with details in the story being translated into something else. The ultimate test of this use of the Bible is whether it helps to elucidate what is really in Shakespeare's play, and I cannot see that it does. I do not find that anything in *King Lear* points directly to the pattern of the prodigal son, nor, the other way around, that the parable of the prodigal son helps one perceive what is actually in the play.

The Bible becomes useful to a literary critic when its stories or images or characters express in clear outline an archetypal pattern that might otherwise remain obscure. To some extent this test will yield different results for different readers. Personally I find my understanding enhanced when Thomas Hardy's novel *The Mayor of Casterbridge* is related to the Old Testament story of Saul and David and when Milton's Samson is interpreted as a hero of faith as imaged forth in Hebrews 11, but not when Lady Macbeth is said to be an Eve figure.

In addition to supplying models of individual archetypes the overall structure of the Bible illuminates the structure of literature as a whole. In asking that a study of the Bible be the foundation of literary education, Northrop Frye makes it clear that "it's the total shape and structure of the Bible which is most important: the fact that it's a continuous narrative beginning with the creation and ending with the Last Judgment, and surveying the whole history of mankind... in between."[29]

In particular, two features of the structure of literature as a whole can be discerned in clear outline in the Bible. One is the dualistic nature of the world of the literary imagination. Like literature itself, the content of the Bible tends to fall into clearly defined dichotomies of good and evil, desirable and undesirable. Thus when Frye gives "an account... of the structure of imagery... of the two undisplaced worlds" of literature, "the apocalyptic and the demonic," he finds himself "drawing heavily on the Bible."[30] The second structural principle of literature that is particularly discernible in the structure of the Bible is the circular movement from bliss to catastrophe to restoration. "The Bible as a whole," writes Frye, "presents a gigantic cycle from creation to apocalypse.... The Bible presents an epic structure of unsurpassed range, consistency and completeness, ... extending over time and space, over invisible and visible orders of reality, and with a parabolic dramatic structure of which the five acts are creation, fall, exile, redemption, and restoration."[31] This circular pattern is also the structure of the monomyth— the "one story" of literature as a whole. Fairman describes the same pattern this way:

> The overall symbolic structure in Biblical writing is surely a cosmic journey, a journey beginning for man in the garden with God, a travelling of man away from God through murder, exile, degradation, a fleeing of man from the awesome presence of God—a flight halted by the appearance, death, and resurrection of Christ—then the beginnings of a return journey back to God, with the bittersweet promise of some final, future glory never to be realized in this life.[32]

No one who has even a passing acquaintance with English or American literature will doubt that writers have made continuous use of the Bible in their own literary works.

Similar familiarity with the Bible should characterize the work of literary critics, though often it seems to be lacking. As I have suggested in this chapter, the Bible should be a standard source for the very things with which a literary critic or reader is habitually concerned: literary genres, allusions, religious themes in works of literature, literary theory and archetypes. If the Bible is an indispensable revelation for Christians, it is no less indispensable to literary critics for what it reveals about literature.

9 Christianity and Literature: A Survey and Critique

A Survey

The great thing... is not to be nervous about God—not to try
and shut out the Lord Immanuel form any *sphere of truth.*
□ *Dorothy L. Sayers, "Towards a Christian Aesthetic"*

In this chapter I wish to make an analytic survey of the
works that I have found most helpful in thinking through
the issues involved in relating Christianity and literature.
I have limited my survey to essays and books that deal with
the integration of literature and Christianity at a *theoretic*
level. The list of works that actually analyze literature
within a Christian context would itself be a book, if not a
series of books. My survey for the most part omits the
works and scholars, some of them considered "standard"
and authoritative in the field, that I do not regard as sufficiently accurate to be considered helpful. At the end of
my survey I explain why I have omitted some of the works
that others may have expected to find here.

In making this survey I wish to emphasize that the
works that I discuss do not constitute all that is required
for a Christian to reach an understanding of the nature of
literature. The Christian critic or theorist needs to know
the whole tradition of Western criticism from Aristotle
through Northrop Frye. The works that I cite in this chap-

ter are attempts by Christian critics to assimilate the whole body of literary theory within a Christian framework. Christians, of course, do not agree among themselves on every issue, and the works that I briefly summarize should be viewed as the materials that will help Christian critics formulate their own Christian aesthetic.

If one makes a survey of the central or classic texts that comprise the canon of Western literary criticism to which modern critics return again and again (I have in mind texts such as Aristotle's *Poetics*, Horace's *Art of Poetry*, Wordsworth's *Preface to the Lyrical Ballads*, etc.), one will find two works that make a serious attempt to relate literature to the Christian faith. They are Sir Philip Sidney's *Apology for Poetry* (also called *The Defence of Poetry*) and T. S. Eliot's *Religion and Literature*. These two essays are anthologized, not as a bow to a particular "school" of criticism, but because they have been of central importance to literary theory in general. For this very reason they should be given a position of prominence in any survey of Christian literary criticism.

Sir Philip Sidney, *Apology for Poetry* (ca. 1580). I would claim without hesitation that even today Sidney's treatise contains in kernel form all that is required as a foundation for a Christian aesthetic. Of course we need to update Sidney's bibliography (acknowledging at the same time the amazing number of works that he mentions) and to provide the kind of commentary and interpretation that are always required to make an old text current. In addition to its acknowledged importance in the history of literary theory, there is another reason why Sidney, and not Nathan Scott or Amos Wilder, deserves to be our starting point for attempting a Christian aesthetic. It is that Sidney was both an important poet (*Astrophel and Stella* being a major literary landmark of the English Renaissance) and writer of prose fiction (*Arcadia*). This is to say that Sidney's intuitions are literary, not theological like those of scholars who teach in religion departments.

I wish to isolate five principles that Sidney develops or

illustrates in his treatise. These principles, I contend, still constitute the basis for relating literature to the Christian faith.

To begin, Sidney's theory of literature pays equal attention to literary form and content. Sidney accepts both the Greek concept of "poet" or "maker" and the Roman title "vates" or "visionary" as together constituting the truth about what literature is (both an artifact and a vision). To which of these two dimensions of literature does Christian doctrine apply? *Both*, Sidney would say, and at once we are in a different world from that of theorists like Scott and Wilder and many, many another contemporary theorist. For page after page Sidney discusses both the vision or content of literature and the sheer artistry and inventiveness that constitute the inner workings of a poem or story.

As a corollary to the first principle Sidney makes it clear that a Christian rationale for writing and reading imaginative literature includes *both* its status as a giver of pleasure or enjoyment and its status as a vision of reality. The end of literature, says Sidney as he echoes Horace, is "to teach and delight." The use that a Christian writer and reader should therefore expect literature to be put is not only a solemnly theological use, *à la* Nathan Scott, Wilder and others, but also a recreational use. When, in a famous sentence from the *Apology*, Sidney describes the delightfulness and allurement of poetry and story, we are given an insight about literature that I cannot recall glimpsing in 430 pages of *The New Orpheus*, an anthology of modern attempts to formulate a Christian aesthetic. The passage is as follows: "The poet . . . cometh with words set in delightful proportion. . . ; and with a tale, forsooth he cometh unto you, with a tale which holdeth children from play, and old men from the chimney corner."

A third premise that Sidney advances is that the thing that sets literature apart from other forms of thought is the writer's creative imagination. This means that the world of literature has its own unique identity and its own integrity. There is no discipline other than the arts, writes

Sidney, that does not take its content from the existing world of things and people. By contrast, "only the poet, disdaining to be tied to any such subjection, lifted up with vigor of his own invention, doth grow in effect another Nature... , freely ranging within the zodiac of his own wit." Sidney's "other nature" is the world of the imagination. The "right poets," according to Sidney, have "no law but wit" (that is, imagination) and "borrow nothing of what is, hath been, or shall be." Sidney's treatise is probably the best illustration on record of Dorothy Sayers's belief that the idea of artistic creation is the most important contribution of Christianity to aesthetic theory. According to Sidney, "the heavenly Maker,... having made man to his own likeness, set him beyond and over all the works of that second nature, which in nothing he showeth so much as in Poetry."

It is clear from Sidney's remarks about creativity that he believes imaginative literature to be different from philosophy or theology. The chasm between Sidney's position and that of philosophers and theologians who try to twist literature to fit their own categories cannot, I fear, be bridged. Father William Lynch speaks of "the theological imagination," but Sidney, with the intuitions of a storyteller and poet, is concerned with the literary imagination, which in his treatment is quite a different phenomenon.

A fourth distinctive of Sidney's contribution to literary theory is his use of biblical example (as well as biblical doctrine) as a repository of literary theory. Sidney cites the example of "the holy David's Psalms" and biblical prophecy to support the legitimacy of the literary enterprise for Christians. He adduces the parables of Jesus to defend the use of fiction as a way of achieving concreteness and experiential immediacy. As proof of "the strange effects of ... poetical invention" to reveal the true nature of reality in a moving way, Sidney cites the example of Nathan's parable that convicted David of his sin. As part of his general apology for literature, Sidney mentions that "the Holy Scripture... hath whole parts in it poetical." These uses that Sidney makes of biblical example are, admittedly, only a beginning, but what is important is the principle that Sidney has a grip on—the use of the Bible as a source, directly and indirectly, of aesthetic theory. It is this principle that is so rarely evident in the leading speakers of the religious literary criticism movement (as represented, for example, by *The New Orpheus*). A notable exception is Amos Wilder, but unfortunately his analysis of the Bible as literature leads him to *equate* literature and religion, concluding that "the poetic experience itself is basically akin to religious experience."[1] The whole drift of Sidney's argument is to keep the distinctions between literature and Christian experience clear.

A final strength of Sidney's *Apology* is that it maintains a balance among the four ingredients of the literary experience—the literary work, the writer, the world and the reader or audience. The point that Sidney stresses most overtly is the impact of the work on the reader (he perceives it as a morally beneficial impact), and this has led people who give the treatise only a superficial reading to conclude that this is all that Sidney sees in literature. Anyone who looks closely at the *Apology*, however, will find that Sidney has a great deal to say about each of the four ingredients of literature and about the relationships between the work itself and each of the three other phenomena.

This balance and comprehensiveness stand in contrast to so many current attempts to relate Christianity to literature. Nathan Scott has led the way in viewing literature mainly as a reflection of the modern world, and even more specifically of the spiritual climate in the modern world. This has led to an endless succession, by many different critics, of books and articles devoted exclusively to the relationship between the literary work and the religious or social milieu that it mirrors, and to modern literature as a prelude to the gospel. This, surely, is part of what it means to approach literature from a Christian perspective, but is it *all* that it means? Other religious critics have been preoccupied with their own response to literature or to the potential religious impact of literature on its audience. Such criticism has viewed literature as primarily didactic and as something to be used for a religious purpose. Naturally such criticism leaves whole areas of the literary work and literary experience untouched. And there is, finally, a branch of religious criticism that, as Giles Gunn notes, slights literature itself by continually escaping from the literary work to the life and philosophy of the writer.[2]

My assessment of Sidney's *Apology for Poetry* is clear: I regard it as a model that stands as a corrective to many of the modern trends in religious literary criticism, especially the theory that comes from scholars whose primary orientation is that of the theologian or philosopher.

T. S. Eliot, "Religion and Literature." First published in *Selected Essays* (New York: Harcourt, Brace and World, 1932), and reprinted in both *The New Orpheus* and *Religion and Modern Literature* (cited below). My frequent quotation from this essay in several preceding chapters has already suggested something of the nature of this essay. The reason why the essay is so often quoted and used as a basis for actual criticism is that in it Eliot articulates concisely some principles that lend themselves to almost indefinite application and elaboration. It is an essay written by a Christian to a Christian audience.

The primary thesis of the essay is that Christian readers must consciously assimilate and analyze the literature that they read in terms of their own Christian viewpoint and experience. One could not find an essay that argues more emphatically and uncompromisingly against the separation of a Christian's religious life and literary experience. As he pursues this plea for the integration of literature and Christianity, Eliot makes so many important observations that no summary of the essay can do it justice.

The New Orpheus: Essays Toward a Christian Poetic, ed. Nathan A. Scott, Jr. (New York: Sheed and Ward, 1964). This 431-page volume is without doubt the most helpful single source on the relationship of Christianity and literature. The twenty-two essays are written by many of the leading authorities in the field. Together they represent the variety of attempts made in the mid-twentieth century to formulate a Christian aesthetic, or philosophy of literature. Notably absent is any serious effort to interact with the Bible as a source of data about the problems of aesthetics.

The essays are arranged into five parts: (1) "The Problem of a Christian Aesthetic," (2) "The Nature of the Christian Vision," (3) "Moorings for a Theological Criticism," (4) "Belief and Form: The Problem of Correlation," (5) "The 'Silence, Exile, and Cunning' of the Modern Imagination."

Norman Reed Cary, *Christian Criticism in the Twentieth Century* (Port Washington, New York: Kennikat Press, 1975). This book is *a descriptive and analytic survey* of many of the leading theorists and practitioners of Christian literary criticism. As such it is the most helpful book and bibliography in existence for someone who wants to know what has been written on the subject.

Although I would concede that Cary surveys the scholars and topics that are generally acknowledged to be the leading ones in Christian literary criticism, this very fact raises (for me) a difficulty: the book devotes much of its space to issues that I regard as peripheral and to positions that strike me as too misguided to be important for a person who is trying to formulate his own Christian approach to literature. For this very reason, however, Cary's book is a good supplement to what I have tried to cover in this book, as the following chapter titles will suggest: "Critical and Theological Background"; "The Relationship of Religious Truth to Artistic Truth"; "The Creative Act in Theology and Art"; "Sacrament, Symbol, and Myth"; "The Tragic and the Comic"; "Theologies of Play and Christian Criticism."

C. S. Lewis, "Christianity and Culture," in *Christian Reflections* (Grand Rapids: William B. Eerdmans, 1967). It is this essay, and not an inferior essay entitled "Christianity and Literature" in the same volume, that constitutes

Lewis's great Christian apology for the importance of literature and the arts in the life of a Christian.

In the essay Lewis traces the stages of his own changing attitudes toward culture. The phases included the following: (1) a humanistic conviction of the inherent worth of culture, an attitude that Lewis continued to hold unconsciously for some time after his conversion to Christianity; (2) a growing conviction that "the friends of culture seemed to me to be exaggerating"; (3) a swing to the opposite extreme of belittling culture, until he "felt almost thankful for the bad hymns" and concluded that "the New Testament seemed, if not hostile, yet unmistakably cold to culture"; (4) a final, moderate conviction of the value of the arts, a conviction based on "a much humbler" foundation than "the kind of status which I had given it before my conversion."

It is this humbler "constructive case for culture" that is of interest to anyone trying to establish his own Christian aesthetic. Lewis develops four points. First, he found himself able to justify his own immersion in culture on a vocational basis. That is, Christianity believes that any vocation can be a way of glorifying God, and Lewis, a literature teacher, could view his calling as having God's sanction. Second, Lewis concluded that it was necessary for some Christians to be among "the culture-sellers" as a leaven or antidote to help curb the abuses of culture that exist. Third, Lewis observed that culture had given him "an enormous amount of pleasure" and that, since pleasure is one of God's good gifts, his enjoyment of literature was a Christian activity.

Finally, Lewis analyzed the values that had been espoused in culture generally. While "the values assumed in literature were seldom those of Christianity," he was nevertheless able to conclude "that culture is a storehouse of the best (sub-Christian) values." "For some," Lewis concluded, "it is a good beginning. For others it is not; culture is not everyone's road into Jerusalem, and for some it is a road out. . . . On these grounds I conclude that culture has a distinct part to play in bringing certain souls to Christ. Not all souls. . . ." And as for the converted, "If all the cultural values, on the way up to Christianity, were dim antepasts and ectypes of the truth, we can recognize them as such still. And since we must rest and play, where can we do so better than here—in the suburbs of Jerusalem?"

The essay also gets into some of the more technical or academic issues of literary criticism. As always, Lewis is at his best in cutting through the vagueness of so much theory on the relationship between Christianity and literature. In contrast to so much theory that regards literature and religion as synonymous, Lewis will have no part of the elevation of excellence in culture or literary taste "into a spiritual value." And as for the question of how the Christian perspective enters into literary criticism, Lewis writes, "Is it the function of the 'trained critic' to discover the latent beliefs and standards in a book, or to pass judgement on them when discovered, or both? . . . I for my part have no objection to our doing both when we criticize, but I think it very important to keep the two operations distinct."

Flannery O'Connor, *Mystery and Manners,* ed. Sally and Robert Fitzgerald (New York: Farrar, Straus and Giroux, 1957). This book is a collection of essays and addresses by a leading Christian writer of fiction. It is probably the single richest repository of insights into the nature of literature by a Christian writer. While not every Christian writer would agree with all of her opinions, no one can ignore her voice as a leading one in the relationship between Christianity and literature. Four themes recur again and again in the book:

1. The immersion of the writer in concrete human experience. Some samples: "The beginning of human knowledge is through the senses, and the fiction writer begins where human perception begins." "Fiction is about everything human and we are made out of dust, and if you scorn getting yourself dusty, then you shouldn't try to write fic-

tion." "The sorry religious novel comes about when the writer supposes that because of his belief, he is somehow dispensed from the obligation to penetrate concrete reality."

2. The direct influence of a Christian writer's religious belief on his writing: "It makes a great difference to his novel whether he believes that we are created in God's image, or whether he believes we create God in our own." "The Christian novelist is distinguished from his pagan colleagues by recognizing sin as sin." "If you believe in the Redemption, your ultimate vision is one of hope." "The universe of the Catholic writer is one that is founded on . . . the Fall, the Redemption, and the Judgment."

3. An eagerness to affirm her Christianity *as a writer* and a conviction that her Christian experience is both relevant and liberating to her task as a writer. She writes, "I see from the standpoint of Christian orthodoxy. This means that for me the meaning of life is centered in our Redemption by Christ and what I see in the world I see in its relation to that." "The Christian novelist lives in a larger universe. He believes that the natural world contains the supernatural." "When people have told me that because I am a Catholic, I cannot be an artist, I have had to reply, ruefully, that because I am a Catholic, I cannot afford to be less than an artist." " . . . Dogma is an instrument for penetrating reality."

4. A commitment to literature as a craft having its own integrity and, at the level of art, autonomy. Two examples: "A novelist is, first of all, a person who has been given a talent to do a particular thing." "What is good in itself glorifies God because it reflects God. The artist has his hands full and does his duty if he attends to his art."

The Climate of Faith in Modern Literature, ed. Nathan A. Scott, Jr. (New York: Seabury Press, 1964). This anthology contains ten essays by ten different critics, who analyze the Christian strand in modern literary criticism, poetry, drama and fiction. The material is divided between theory and practical criticism of actual literary texts. The principles that one gleans from the essays are useful to both the Christian critic and writer of imaginative literature.

Chad Walsh, "A Hope for Literature," pp. 207-33 in *The Climate of Faith in Modern Literature,* ed. Nathan A. Scott, Jr. (New York: Seabury Press, 1964). This is by all odds one of the solidest examinations, by a poet himself, of the cultural ingredients that produce great literature. Among many other excellent insights, Walsh compares the adequacy of the Christian world view with naturalism, scientific humanism, existentialism, Marxism and Oriental religion as foundations from which a writer might view the world. Walsh argues that Christianity offers writers "the best pair of eyes" and "the roomiest house."

Among the advantages that Christianity affords a Christian writer, Walsh discusses the following:

1. Christianity gives a writer "an ordering of his own personal life that makes intellectual and emotional sense."

2. Christianity gives a writer a perspective on his or her work: he is an "earthly assistant to God," but balancing this is an awareness that "art is not religion. A writer is not a god or godling. There is wisdom and illumination but not salvation in a sonnet."

3. Christianity offers the writer a community. "Living in it, drawing strength from it, the writer can move back and forth into the surrounding and interpenetrating world, and yet always have solid ground under his feet."

4. Christianity assures the writer of the reality and worth of human life in this world. "The poet, for instance, is reassured that his preoccupation with sensory observations is not... frivolous.... Things are real... because God made them." "The novelist and playwright receive the assurance that man's social and psychological life and his entire historical existence are meaningful."

Dorothy L. Sayers, *The Mind of the Maker* (1941; rpt. Cleveland: World Publishing Company, 1956). This is the classic work on the contribution of Christian doctrine to an understanding of artistic creativity. The doctrines that Sayers focuses on are God's capacity as Creator and the creation of people in the image of God. The book explores the ramifications of the thesis that "the characteristic common to God and man is . . . the desire and the ability to make things." Sayers even sees an analogy between the Trinity and the act of artistic creation, as follows: (1) the creative idea = the Father; (2) the creative energy or activity = the Word, or Son; (3) the creative power = the Holy Spirit. Or, looking at a literary work from the viewpoint of the reader, we end up with the trinity of "the Book as Thought" ("the Idea of the book existing in the writer's mind"), "the Book as Written," and "the Book as Read— the Power of its effect upon and in the responsive mind." As the book progresses, Sayers (in my view) carries her argument to some far-fetched and tenuous extremes, but after all is said, she has given the most thorough analysis to date of what artistic creativity means in a Christian framework.

Dorothy L. Sayers, "Towards a Christian Aesthetic." First published in *Unpopular Opinions* (1947), reprinted in *Christian Letters to a Post-Christian World*, ed. Roderick Jellema (Grand Rapids: William B. Eerdmans, 1969). Also reprinted in *The New Orpheus*. Beginning from the premise that "we have no Christian aesthetic—no Christian philosophy of the Arts," Sayers proceeds to discuss the Christian doctrines that she believes constitute the basis for such an aesthetic. One of these is the Christian doctrine of revelation: "If we commit ourselves to saying that the Christian revelation discovers to us the nature of *all* truth, then it must discover to us the nature about Art among other things. It is absurd to go placidly along explaining Art in terms of a pagan aesthetic." By revelation, I should add, Sayers means the historic creeds of Christendom; in *The Mind of the Maker* she shows a reverence for the authority of the creeds but virtually ignores the Bible itself. The other great Christian doctrine to which Sayers appeals is creation, concluding that "this idea of Art as *creation* is . . . the one important contribution that Christianity has made to aesthetics." This leads Sayers, correctly in my view, to reject the Aristotelian theory of literature as imitation in favor of the theory that "what the artist is doing is *to image forth* something."

Religion and Modern Literature: Essays in Theory and Criticism, ed. G. B. Tennyson and Edward E. Ericson, Jr. (Grand Rapids: William B. Eerdmans, 1975). The first of three sections in this anthology is devoted to theoretic analysis of "Relationships between Religion and Literature." This section includes T. S. Eliot's essay "Religion and Literature," and significant essays by Flannery O'Connor, Roy Battenhouse, Frederick Pottle and Joseph Summers.

Roland M. Frye, *Perspective on Man: Literature and the Christian Tradition* (Philadelphia: Westminster Press, 1961). This book is built on the thesis that "literature may be related to the Christian faith in three ways: first, as literary method in the use of symbol, metaphor, and story is applicable to the understanding of Biblical truth; second, as literature treats, in basic and universal terms, both the affirmations and the problems of human existence with which theology must come to grips; and last, as specific writers express their visions of life in terms of a Christian frame of reference." The real value of the book, and the part to which I find myself returning, is the second part (pp. 57-103), which explores how literature "furnishes insight into human life and increases the value of that life by the nurture of beauty, of understanding, and of compassion" and how literature probes "the ultimate dilemmas of the human soul."

Frank E. Gaebelein, "Toward a Biblical View of Aesthetics," *Christianity Today*, 30 August 1968, pp. 4-6. This essay can appropriately stand as representative of the author's essays and addresses on literature and the arts through the years. Beginning from the premise that "at the root of evangelical Christianity is its biblical heritage," Gaebelein develops such premises as the need for Christians to involve themselves in the arts, the dual way in which the Bible can function as the basis for a Christian aesthetic (through its references to art and through its doctrines), the importance of the Christian doctrines of creation, the image of God in man, the Fall and the incarnation in a Christian philosophy of the arts.

Henry Zylstra, *Testament of Vision* (Grand Rapids: William B. Eerdmans, 1958). The first half of this book contains a dozen essays on literature and Christianity. Zylstra is at his best on the function of literature (especially fiction) in the life of a Christian. This apologetic approach leads him, in turn, to make numerous cogent remarks about the nature of literature.

Virginia R. Mollenkott, *Adamant and Stone Chips: A Christian Humanist Approach to Knowledge* (Waco: Word Books, 1967). This book articulates the broad principles that should govern Christian involvement in culture and the arts. The first half of the book is concerned with Christian humanism as a framework for cultural affirmation, and the second half narrows the focus to literature specifically, with the last chapter devoted to modern literature in Christian perspective.

Harold C. Gardiner, *Norms for the Novel,* rev. ed. (Garden City: Hanover House, 1960). Written from a Catholic perspective, this book contains a lot of old-fashioned attitudes toward the nature and function of literature. One of the things that impresses me favorably about the book is the strategy developed in the early chapters for coming to terms with modern literature. The author asserts the following norms or standards as the ones that should govern a Christian reader's assessment of modern fiction:

1. The norm of charity, which means that when a Christian judges a writer to be wrong in his viewpoint, it must be remembered that it is the book and not the author that is being judged.

2. The norm that objectionable passages in realistic fiction must not be judged in isolation but in terms of the overall moral import of the book.

3. The insistence that if a novel is to be considered truthful from a Christian viewpoint, it must recognize sin for

what it is, "an offense against God, a loss of His friendship."

4. The norm that in order to be considered truthful, a work must not portray sin in such a manner as to become a temptation to sin for a normally well-balanced reader.

5. The norm that good literature combines truth and beauty; if it distorts the truth, the reader's pleasure is destroyed or lessened, and this is a failure in the work *as art*.

Gardiner also differentiates between realism as a legitimate literary technique and naturalism as a philosophy of life that, by Christian standards, is deficient because it fails to tell the whole truth.

Christianity and Literature, a journal published quarterly by the Conference on Christianity and Literature, is one good way to keep abreast of new developments in the religious approach to literature. Each issue contains book reviews and an annotated bibliography of articles that have dealt with topics of interest to Christian critics.

A Critique

Ever since Matthew Arnold, intelligent men have confused literature with religion; by this time all of us should know better. □ *Joseph H. Summers, "Christian Literary Scholars"*

As I turn now to a critique of works that I have omitted from my survey it will become evident that I have grave reservations about many of the main trends and figures in the area of Christian literary criticism. I have four main reservations.

In the first place *theological analysis of literature has been mistakenly substituted for Christian literary criticism.* This is a way of saying that literary scholars have abdicated their rightful position to theologians and philosophers. The result is that literature has been approached in terms partly alien to literary criticism as practiced by literary scholars. I have read book after book by Nathan A. Scott and Amos Wilder, but I do not recall ever seeing either of them conduct what I would call a full literary explication of a poem or story. Scholars of this type are preoccupied with literary theory *as theory* (they never seem to tire of treating literary theory as a self-contained discipline), and with literary texts as religious documents. I wish to make it clear that I do not question the value of their theory and theological analysis. What is objectionable is the way in which the religious content of literature is always the entire concern with these scholars, until literature emerges as a truncated caricature of what it really is.

It is encouraging to see literature studied in theological seminaries and divinity schools. But that study should not be confused with what goes on in college literature courses. Why, then, have critics whose intuitions are literary allowed scholars whose main interests are theological or philosophical to steal so much of the scene in Christian literary criticism? The time has come for literary critics to insist on the difference between Christian literary criticism and theological criticism of literature. To engage in the former is to give just as much attention to literary form as an artistic achievement as to the religious interpretation that literature gives to the experience that it presents. And it is to make a Christian approach to literature one that responds to the literature as something creative and re-creative, not simply a solemnly religious occasion that reminds one of a church service. What C. S. Lewis said about the humanists of the sixteenth century applies equally to many scholars whose field is religion or philosophy: "What they lost was the power... to respond to the central, obvious appeal of a great work. ... The humanists could not really bring themselves to believe that the poet cared about the shepherds, lovers, warriors, voyages, and battles. They must be only a disguise for something more 'adult.' "[3]

A second objection that I have to much religious criticism is that *much of the existing theory is based on an inadequate foundation.* What I mean, quite simply, is that scholars have based their aesthetic theories and criticism on everything *except* the Bible. The scholars who ignore the Bible are usually quite conscious of the gap that separates them from evangelical or biblical Christianity. Whenever a new anthology of essays of religious literary criticism appears, one can predict before the fact that there will be no adequate representation of scholarship that operates from biblical presuppositions. There are three times as many direct references to the Bible in a single essay by C. S. Lewis ("Christianity and Culture") as in 419 pages of text in *The New Orpheus*. In his book *Horizons of Criticism*, Vernon Ruland flaunts his scorn for critics who operate within a biblical framework.

The last people who seem to have realized what is happening are critics whose orientation is that of biblical Christianity. These scholars should have insisted on their own convictions about the Bible as the ultimate source of Christian doctrine and therefore of a Christian approach to literature and literary criticism, instead of being impressed with critics who ignore the Bible. Who cares about an approach to literature based on the theology of Aquinas or Barth or Tillich or Bonhoeffer, except a small coterie of people who happen to agree with the theology of one or another of these theologians? If Christian literary criticism is going to be anything more than a provincial hobbyhorse, it has to be based on the only common denominator that all forms of Christianity have in various ways shared, the Bible itself. Where, after all, do doctrines such as creation and incarnation come from? To adhere to the Bible as the common ground of all forms of Christianity is not, as is sometimes claimed, to narrow the field. On the contrary whenever a critic begins to add a specific creed or theological tradition to his foundation, he has narrowed, not broadened, his Christian base, for it is exactly these additional ingredients that divide a given religious viewpoint from other ones within the Christian framework.

If it is too much to ask from some segments of the religious criticism movement that Christian criticism be based on the Bible, it is at least something that evangelical Christians should take seriously. Thinking to make their scholarship respectable by holding their biblical orientation in abeyance, evangelical scholars have neither recieved a hearing in the world of scholarship nor been true to their own convictions. Evangelicals have articulated their perspective within the friendly confines of *Christianity Today* and the Christian college classroom, but the person looking for a biblical perspective on literary criticism will not find much help in the standard sources of literary criticism. The entire Christian criticism movement has been impoverished as a result.

Third, *Christian criticism has been cheapened by the theory that literature itself is a religious experience.* I have in mind the approach that finds parallels between religion and literature and sees in these resemblances the sanction and even the methodology for a Christian involvement in literature. In fact, finding these resemblances *is* religious literary criticism in the eyes of many of such critics, and this approach may well be the dominant strand in religious literary criticism.

The favorite line of thought for critics who equate religion and literature runs something like this. Both poetry and Christianity are preoccupied with concrete earthly reality; therefore literature is itself a Christian experience. Both poetry and Christianity are concerned with the specific and the individual; ergo the reading and writing of poetry is a religious act. Both literature and religion are concerned with values and the meaning of existence; therefore literature can be defined as a religious activity. Both literature and religion point beyond the physical world to mystery and transcendence; therefore the literary experience is itself a religious experience as well. Both literature and religion use signs and symbols; consequently the literary enterprise is at the same time a religious enterprise. Both literature and religion deal with "the primal springs of life"; both are celebrations of life; both are concerned with "Being" (the pompous capital letter seems to help); as a result, to explore literature cannot help but be a religious act.

I suspect that I will never understand how this kind of scramble to find parallels between literature and religion has been taken so seriously by some segments of the literary world, and I certainly will never understand how some scholars have found it possible to restate these self-evident parallels in high-sounding philosophic terms for page after page after page, and even book after book. Every writer, and perhaps every critic, too, becomes "religious" or "Christian" in this how-to-be-religious-without-really-trying syndrome. Literary descriptions of the physical or human world become evidence of a writer's religious, "sacramental" (the favorite and most overworked word) view of the world. Any use of symbol or metaphor or story can become a new manifestation of the mythic imagination, which for many critics is automatically the "religious" imagination. Any writer who explores the complexity of human experience has given us a religious insight, so the argument goes, into the "mystery" of existence, and since religion, as we all know, is full of mystery, literature is perforce religious when it captures the mystery of life.

The absurdity of this so-called "theological" or "religious" criticism of literature is easy to discern. The Christian religion embraces the actual stuff of human life; a garbage collector also grapples with the actual stuff of life, but this does not make garbage collection a religious experience. Literature, we are told, is religious in nature because it celebrates reality; the behavior of professional athletes in the locker room after winning a championship also celebrates reality, but who would think of calling it a religious experience? Both literature and religion use symbols; but a parking lot also has symbols and signs without thereby being transformed into a religion.

To say that something is wrong with the line of thought that I am opposing is to understate the case. Virtually everything is wrong with it: the inability to treat literature as anything other than religion (just as sociologists and psychologists find it hard to treat literature as anything besides sociology or psychology), the narrow definition of literature that invariably finds no room for artistic form and aesthetic beauty as literary values, the definition of "Christianity" and "religion" in such broad terms that they become virtually useless, and above all the mistaken assumption that a general rationale for literature on religious grounds also constitutes the *methodology* for studying literature. (It is one thing to say that the Christian faith, because it is concerned with human life in this world, validates the study of literature, but quite another to treat the actual *analysis* of literature as nothing more than demonstrating the self-evident fact that literature portrays human life in this world.)

What this kind of scholarship shows most clearly is that the sons of Matthew Arnold, who said that literature must *become* a religion in the modern world, are legion. But as J. Hillis Miller states, "Arnold... was wrong, and T. S. Eliot was right. Literature is not a means of salvation."[4] In too much religious criticism, as Sallie TeSelle asserts, "neither the integrity of art nor the specificity of the Christian faith is taken seriously."[5]

My final quibble with the religious criticism movement is that *Christian literary criticism has been trivialized by the indiscriminate use of the terms "Christian" and "religious."* A typical instance of this abuse is Charles Glicksberg's assertion that "any piece of literature which is seriously concerned with the ultimate meaning of man's life on earth is 'religious,'... regardless of its doctrinal orientation."[6] Flannery O'Connor protests, "Unfortunately, the word Christian is no longer reliable. It has come to mean anyone with a golden heart."[7] At the height of the mania to find Christ symbols in literature, Alan Paton and Liston Pope made a survey and came to the conclusion that "apparently any fictional character qualifies who is innocent, selfless, and strange, even if he is banal or amoral or utterly humanist."[8] Joseph H. Summers observes that the extreme that constitutes the danger for Christian critics today is that in an attempt to prove our tolerance (and our equality with our secular colleagues), we may attempt to approve *all* "creative writers," to find hidden Christian meanings in the most unlikely places, and to appropriate forcibly for religious purposes all the currently fashionable literature. (One sometimes glimpses an image of the professional atheist being inexorably hauled, kicking and screaming, to the baptismal font).[9]

This tendency has been carried to its logical extreme (though "illogical extreme" is a more accurate designation) by many critics, of whom John Killinger may be taken as representative. It is one thing to say that the modern literature of despair and hedonism has *implications for* the Christian faith, or that it clarifies, as Roland Frye states, "the ultimate problems of man's life for which Christian truth must have relevance."[10] But in his book *The Fragile Presence: Transcendence in Modern Literature*[11] Killinger is not content with such an approach. Instead, he is bent on finding *God* everywhere in modern literature—in the literature of anguish (even that which repudiates the Christian religion), the literature of absurdity and the literature of sensuality (à la D. H. Lawrence).

I return to two statements that I made in previous chapters. In the first place when modern writers use traditional Christian symbols or allusions, more often than not they are reinterpreting them, with the result that the mere presence of religious terminology in modern literature does not, by itself, show a religious viewpoint in the work as a whole. And second, it is the task of Christian literary criticism to determine *whether* the vision of a given work is Christian, not to show in every instance *that* it is Christian.

Toward a Biblical Theory of Literature

If we commit ourselves to saying that the Christian revelation discovers to us the nature of all truth, then it must discover to us the nature of the truth about Art among other things."
☐ *Dorothy L. Sayers, "Towards a Christian Aesthetic"*

It is appropriate to end this book by outlining the biblical doctrines that constitute the framework for a Christian approach to literature. Such an outline will summarize the principles that have been the undergirding of the chapters of this book. Since my application of these doctrines to aesthetic and literary questions represents only one approach among several, I trust that the outline that follows will be a useful agenda for anyone who wishes to formulate his or her own Christian aesthetic. I have included some questions that I think deserve attention or that remain perennially unanswered.

1. *The doctrine of Scripture or special revelation.* The Bible contributes to literary theory by both its example and doctrine. By its own example it establishes the importance of literature, affirms the significance of literary form (not simply content) and answers questions of literary theory and practice (for example, questions about tragedy and realism). On the side of doctrine the Bible functions in literary criticism by serving as the standard by which a critic measures the truth or falseness of a writer's ethos or world view. The question that will remain continuously present in Christian criticism is two-fold: exactly what does the Bible say about a given issue, and how overtly must a work of literature adhere to the biblical view in order to be considered Christian?

2. *Natural or general revelation and common grace.* If God reveals truth not only in the Bible but in creation (including culture and human reason), it follows that not all truth about aesthetic issues will be contained in the Bible. This means that a Christian critic should expect many of the principles of the discipline to come from that discipline itself. Furthermore, if God's common grace permeates the work of believer and unbeliever alike, a Christian reader is freed to relish truth and artistry wherever they appear in literature. We should be prepared to find truth and grace incognito (hidden or indirectly expressed) in writers who are not themselves Christian.

There are, of course, some accompanying questions. As

we wrestle with problems of literary theory, where does special revelation (the Bible) cease to be the authority and where does general revelation (literary criticism as a human discipline) begin to function as an autonomous authority? Exactly *how* incognito should we expect to find Christian truth in works of literature? And how enthusiastic should a Christian really be about the frequently superficial level at which the work of non-Christian writers correlates with biblical revelation?

3. *The doctrine of creation.* At least five major literary principles follow from the biblical doctrine of creation. (a) The fact that God made earthly reality and set the human race over it means that the writer's and critic's preoccupation with human experience and culture is God-ordained. (b) Since God made a world that is beautiful as well as functional, we know that the writer's and critic's concern with beauty, form and artistic joy is legitimate. (c) God's separateness from creation means that culture cannot be equated with God; the literary endeavor is God-approved but is not something that is inevitably Christian or even religious. (d) The doctrine of creation *ex nihilo* has enabled Christians to regard artists as capable of creating, through their imagination, works for which there is no existing model, and it allows Christians to revel in originality—in God's doing a new thing. (e) The fact that humans are created in God's image provides a sanction for human creativity and a theological explanation of why people create.

Along with all of these "givens," the doctrine of creation poses some questions that remain inconclusively answered. Is *all* human creativity good? If not, what further criteria will allow us to differentiate good from bad manifestations of the creative impulse? What are the limits beyond which creativity ceases to be God-glorifying? If people are to subdue creation and culture to God's glory, what are the precise forms that such control will take for the Christian writer or critic? Exactly where does a Christian writer or critic draw the line between making religious use of literature and making literature a surrogate religion or even a substitute for God? When do literary enthusiasm and immersion in literature become idolatry?

4. *The related biblical doctrines of beauty and pleasure.* The Bible affirms that God is the ultimate source of beauty, that it is one of his perfections, that God values it and that for people to value beauty as a gift from God is worthy. And the Bible's endorsement of pleasure opens the way for viewing the enjoyment of literature as a sound rationale for the literary enterprise.

The questions related to beauty and pleasure will continue to exercise thoughtful Christians. How can we distinguish between the good and perverted uses of beauty? How can we distinguish between enriching and trivial types of pleasure? When does pleasure become depraved and therefore debasing to a Christian reader? When does one's pursuit of beauty or pleasure become selfish indulgence? Why have the defense of literature on the pleasure principle and the criticism that delights in literary form been so strongly resisted through the centuries? Why has Christian criticism been so oblivious to form and beauty, preferring a solemnly religious and philosophic approach?

5. *The Fall, or original sin.* The Christian view of the world as fallen has far-reaching effects on a Christian writer's view of human nature and the world. And for the Christian critic/reader, the same doctrine leads to a need for discernment and for testing the spirits as he or she assimilates works of literature. The big, perennially unanswered question is, How negatively has the Fall affected human creativity, the attitudes embodied in works of literature and the ways in which readers assimilate literature? How often, and in what ways, does literature perpetuate the depravity of the fallen world?

6. *The inspiration of writers by the Holy Spirit.* The Bible contains an abundance of data about the inspiration of writers by the Holy Spirit. What is the nature of that inspiration for Christian writers? And what is its nature for non-Christian writers? Does the Holy Spirit equip writers

to produce the beauty of literary form? Does the Holy Spirit move writers in the content of their writings? If we cannot attribute untruthful content to inspiration by the Holy Spirit, can we be any more certain that the Holy Spirit has inspired the vision of Christian works of literature? Does the Holy Spirit inspire mediocre as well as great works of literature?

7. *Stewardship*. The Bible implies that there is a duty attached to every talent or capacity that we possess. The capacity for art, beauty, creativity and literary experience is a capacity that people should cultivate. Related to this is the Christian concept of calling, which encourages a person to whom God has given a talent (such as writing poems or stories or literary criticism) to exercise that talent. In addition to stewardship of ability, there is stewardship of time, which prescribes that a Christian use his or her time wisely and well. The question related to the idea of stewardship is exactly how *much* energy or time a person should devote to the pursuit of literature.

8. *Transcendence, or belief in the other world*. Christianity is the religion of the two worlds, both equally real. In addition to physical, earthly reality, there exists a world of spiritual reality (including God and heaven). The Christian writer and reader live simultaneously in both worlds. The earthly sphere can therefore never, by itself, constitute "reality" for the Christian writer or critic, and sheer immersion in physical sensation can never by itself be a touchstone for determining whether a literary work is Christian in its orientation. It is curious that hosts of Christian critics emphasize that the Incarnation of Christ provides a model for the writer's absorption in earthly reality, but that none of them tells us that the ascension of Jesus into heaven provides a model for transcending the earthly sphere. The perplexing question is why so much "religious criticism" of recent decades has been unable to come to grips with the ideas of heaven, eternal life, spiritual reality and a transcendent God as necessary ingredients in a Christian world view.

9. *The Incarnation*. This is perhaps the one Christian doctrine that has received its due in Christian literary theory. The Incarnation affirms forever that human, earthly reality is worthy of study and love. It affirms the writer's immersion in human experience, and it lends sanction to the critic's absorption in the products of the human imagination. The example of Christ's patience in understanding the unregenerate mind and his willingness to embrace the human predicament give a reason and methodology for a Christian reader's approach to the literature of non-Christian writers.

Perhaps there has been a one-sided emphasis on the Incarnation in Christian literary theory. One often gets the impression that to affirm every facet of earthly life, including its sin, is to follow the pattern of Christ. Yet Christ rejected as well as affirmed earthly life. He said some very deprecating things about physical reality and earthly endeavor. The question that needs exploration, therefore, is the precise nature and limits of Christ's involvement in the world, and the ways in which this affects various literary issues.

10. *Redemption and sanctification*. The doctrine of redemption shows the Christian writer that it is not sufficient to leave human experience where it is. Contrary to the statements of literary theorists who are obsessed with the Incarnation, Christ came to redeem and transform human life, not simply to affirm what he saw. As with Christian writers, so too with Christian critics: there calling is to wrest beauty and meaning from a fallen world and to help others to do so.

The Christian doctrine of sanctification or holiness defines the kinds of activity, behavior and morality that are proper and improper for a Christian reader. The Christian stands with Plato, and against modern secularists, in attaching moral earnestness to the literary enterprise. The desire to see holiness prevail also helps to define the materials and methods of the Christian writer.

11. *The Christian sacraments*. The Christian sacraments

assert that earthly reality can point to spiritual reality. The things of earth can become a vehicle for the things of heaven. By extension, literature can be viewed as an activity that leads to spiritual insight and worship. And since the sacraments use signs and symbols, the Christian writer and reader will respect the "sign-making" tendency of literature and the arts.

As with the incarnation, Christian sacramentalism has been run into the ground by some literary theorists. Does a Christian reader really say to himself or herself, "I have a reason and a methodology for reading this novel because of the sacrament of communion?" Does a Christian poet writing a sonnet derive inspiration or technique from the bread and wine served in church? In short, how can we differentiate the genuine and the superficial applications of Christian sacramentalism to literary theory?

12. *The Christian telos (purpose or end) of glorifying God.* The classic statement about the purpose of human life being to glorify God is 1 Corinthians 10:31: "So, whether you eat or drink, or whatever you do, do all to the glory of God." (That glorifying God should not become, as it sometimes does, an excuse for license is suggested by the next verse: "Give no offense... to the church of God.") Every dimension of literary activity—creativity, sheer excellence in writing, the act of reading—can become a way of glorifying God.

If the ultimate aim of life is to glorify God, it is a betrayal of that ideal and a form of idolatry to substitute anything in the place of God. The Christian faith should thus spare a Christian writer or reader from making an idol out of literature.

The questions that we can pose include the following: Exactly when is the writing or reading of literature glorifying to God and when is it not? When does one know when the claim to be glorifying God is genuine and real? When does the pursuit of literature become an idol?

Translating biblical principles into a Christian approach

to literature is (happily) a never ending task. And it is ultimately a personal task. A Christian writer or reader cannot delegate the integration of literature and Christianity to someone else. Relating literature to the Christian faith is an ongoing story to which every Christian writer and reader can add his or her own chapter. It is my cherished hope that every Christian who loves literature will participate in that story.

NOTES

Chapter 1: The Necessity of Literature

[1]Letter to Higbald, as quoted in Eleanor S. Duckett, *Alcuin, Friend of Charlemagne* (New York: Macmillan, 1951), p. 209.

[2]Tertullian, *On the Prescription against Heretics*, ch. 7.

[3]Jerome, *Letters*, XXII, 29.

[4]Dorothy Sayers is correct in saying that Plato's aesthetic "has influenced... the attitude of the Church more than the Church perhaps knows." *Christian Letters to a Post-Christian World*, ed. Roderick Jellema (Grand Rapids: William B. Eerdmans, 1969), p. 71.

[5]Plato, *The Republic*, X, in *Criticism: The Major Texts*, ed. Walter Jackson Bate (New York: Harcourt, Brace and World, 1952), p. 45.

[6]Ibid., p. 48.

[7]Ibid., pp. 46, 49.

[8]Tertullian, *Spectacles*, ch. 10.

[9]Ibid., ch. 29.

[10]Ibid.

[11]Augustine, *Confessions*, III, s. 2.

[12]Augustine, *The City of God*, II, ch. 14.

[13]Augustine, *Confessions*, I, s. 27.

[14]Ibid., I, s. 22.

[15]Philip Sidney, *Apology for Poetry*, in *Criticism: The Major Texts*, ed. Bate, p. 97.

[16]William Tyndale, *Answer to Sir Thomas More*, as quoted in W. E. Campbell, *Erasmus, Tyndale, and More* (London: Eyre and Spottiswoode, 1949), p. 207.

[17]William Perkins, "Of Writing," as quoted in Lawrence A. Sasek, *The Literary Temper of the English Puritans* (Baton Rouge: Louisiana State Univ. Press, 1961), p. 59.

[18]Cotton Mather, *Manuductio ad Ministerium,* in Perry Miller and Thomas H. Johnson, ed., *The Puritans,* rev. ed. (New York: Harper and Row, 1963), p. 686.

[19]Richard Baxter, *Treatise of Self-Denial,* in Sasek, p. 60.

[20]Richard Baxter, *Christian Directory,* in Sasek, p. 98.

[21]Ibid., p. 114.

[22]Sasek, op. cit.; Russell Fraser, *The War against Poetry* (Princeton: Princeton Univ. Press, 1970).

[23]Harvey Cox, *The Feast of Fools* (Cambridge, Mass.: Harvard Univ. Press, 1969), pp. 11-12.

[24]Marshall McLuhan, *Counterblast* (New York: Harcourt, Brace and World, 1969), p. 131.

[25]Karl Shapiro, "The Poetry Wreck," *Library Journal,* 95 (1970), 632-34.

[26]Cited by Arthur Schlesinger, Jr., "Implications of Leisure for Government," in *Technology, Human Values, and Leisure,* ed. Max Kaplan and Phillip Bosserman (Nashville: Abingdon Press, 1971), p. 77.

[27]Robert Lee, *Religion and Leisure in America* (Nashville: Abingdon Press, 1964); Harold D. Lehman, *In Praise of Leisure* (Scottdale, Pa.: Herald Press, 1974).

[28]Paul Elmen, *The Restoration of Meaning to Contemporary Life* (Garden City: Doubleday, 1958).

[29]Lee, *Religion and Leisure in America,* pp. 25-26.

[30]Schlesinger, pp. 77-78.

[31]My comments on the classical allusions in Paul's speech are indebted to E. M. Blaiklock, *The Acts of the Apostles: An Historical Commentary* (Grand Rapids: William B. Eerdmans, 1959), pp. 144-45.

[32]*The Poems of Emily Dickinson,* ed. Thomas H. Johnson (Cambridge, Mass.: The Belknap Press of Harvard Univ. Press, 1963; copyright 1951), final stanza of poem #341.

[33]*The Poems of Emily Dickinson,* ed. Johnson, poem #1078.

[34]Cleanth Brooks, *The Hidden God* (New Haven: Yale Univ. Press, 1963), p. 132.

[35]Nathan A. Scott, *Modern Literature and the Religious Frontier* (New York: Harper and Brothers, 1958), p. 52; Ralph Waldo Emerson, *The Poet,* in *Eight American Writers,* ed. Norman Foerster et al. (New York: W. W. Norton, 1963), p. 288.

[36]C. S. Lewis, *A Preface to Paradise Lost* (Oxford: Oxford Univ. Press, 1942), p. 3.

[37]C. S. Lewis, *An Experiment in Criticism* (Cambridge: Cambridge Univ. Press, 1961), pp. 137-39.

[38]Emerson, *The Poet,* p. 281.

[39]G. K. Chesterton, *The Everlasting Man* (1925; rpt. Garden City: Image Books, 1955), pp. 32-34.

[40]Lewis Mumford, *The Myth of the Machine: Technics and Human Development* (New York: Harcourt, Brace and World, 1966), pp. 5, 153.

[41]Cox, p. 11.

[42]Herbert Read, "The Function of the Arts in Contemporary Society," in *Art and Alienation: The Role of the Artist in Society* (New York: Horizon Press, 1967), pp. 15-28. The essay has been several times

reprinted under the title "The Necessity of Art."

[43]Herbert Read, *The Redemption of the Robot* (New York: Trident Press, 1966), p. 218.

[44]Northrop Frye, *The Stubborn Structure: Essays on Criticism and Society.* (Ithaca: Cornell Univ. Press, 1970), p. 18.

[45]Ibid., p. 17.

[46]Ibid., p. 53.

Chapter 2: Literature and the Quest for Beauty

[1]It is no surprise that William K. Wimsatt's defense of the practice of literary scholars "to say little about 'beauty' " occurs in an essay devoted to "defending the domain of poetry and poetics from the encircling (if friendly) arm of the general aesthetician." *The Verbal Icon* (Lexington: Univ. of Kentucky Press, 1954), pp. 221, 228.

[2]George Santayana, *The Sense of Beauty* (1896; rpt. New York: Random House, 1955), pp. 51-52.

[3]Theodore M. Greene, *The Arts and the Art of Criticism* (Princeton: Princeton Univ. Press, 1940), p. 7.

[4]Jacques Maritain, *Creative Intuition in Art and Poetry* (Cleveland: World Publishing Company, 1953), p. 122.

[5]Ernst Cassirer, *An Essay on Man* (Garden City: Doubleday, 1944), p. 204.

[6]C. S. Lewis, *Christian Reflections* (Grand Rapids: William B. Eerdmans, 1967), p. 34.

[7]Abraham Kuyper, *Calvinism* (Grand Rapids: William B. Eerdmans, 1953), p. 156.

[8]Ibid., p. 156.

[9]Chad Walsh, "A Hope for Literature," in *The Climate of Faith in Modern Literature*, ed. Nathan A. Scott, Jr. (New York: Seabury Press, 1964), p. 227.

[10]Denis de Rougemont, "Religion and the Mission of the Artist," in *The New Orpheus: Essays toward a Christian Poetic*, ed. Nathan A. Scott, Jr. (New York: Sheed and Ward, 1964), p. 64.

[11]Calvin Seerveld, *A Christian Critique of Art* (St. Catharines, Ontario: Association for Reformed Scientific Studies, 1963), pp. 31-35.

[12]H. L. Mencken, as quoted by D. G. Kehl, *Literary Style of the Old Bible and the New* (Indianapolis: Bobbs-Merrill, 1970), p. 7.

[13]Lewis, *Christian Reflections*, p. 21.

[14]John Calvin, *Institutes of the Christian Religion*, ed. John T. McNeill (Philadelphia: Westminster Press, 1960), I, 720.

[15]Norman Geisler, "The Christian as Pleasure-Seeker," *Christianity Today*, 25 Sept. 1975, p. 11.

[16]Fyodor Dostoyevsky, *The Brothers Karamazov* (New York: Modern Library, 1950), p. 127; Aldous Huxley, *Brave New World Revisited* (New York: Harper and Row, 1958), p. 52. Huxley goes on to observe that Hitler's rallies "were masterpieces of ritual and theatrical art" and to quote an observer's statement that "for grandiose beauty I have never seen any ballet to compare with the Nuremberg rally."

[17]Lewis, *Christian Reflections*, p. 10.

[18]Ralph Waldo Emerson, "The Rhodora," line 12.

[19]DeWitt H. Parker, *The Analysis of Art* (New Haven: Yale Univ. Press, 1926), pp. 31-62.

[20]D. W. Gotshalk, *Art and the Social Order*, 2nd ed. (New York: Dover Publications, 1962), pp. 108-14.

[21]Rolland Hein, "A Biblical View of the Novel," *Christianity Today*, 5 Jan. 1973, p. 18.

[22]C. S. Lewis, *An Experiment in Criticism* (Cambridge: Cambridge Univ. Press, 1965), p. 84.

[23]Homer, *The Odyssey*, trans. W. H. D. Rouse (New York: Mentor, 1937), p. 100.

[24]Lewis, *An Experiment in Criticism*, p. 92.

[25]Norman Foerster, "The Esthetic Judgment and the Ethical Judgment," in *The Intent of the Critic*, ed. Donald A. Stauffer (Princeton: Princeton Univ. Press, 1941), pp. 69-70.

[26]*Essays Presented to Charles Williams*, ed. C. S. Lewis (Grand Rapids: William B. Eerdmans, 1966), p. 103.

[27]Ibid., p. 91.

[28]Ibid., p. 93.

[29]Ibid., p. 102.

[30]Ibid., p. 103.

[31]Lewis, *An Experiment in Criticism*, p. 29.

[32]Ibid., pp. 82-83.

[33]Cleanth Brooks and Robert Penn Warren, *Understanding Poetry*, 3rd ed. (New York: Holt, Rinehart and Winston, 1960), p. 10.

[34]T. S. Eliot, *The Use of Poetry and the Use of Criticism* (Cambridge, Mass.: Harvard Univ. Press, 1933), p. 147.

[35]W. K. Wimsatt, Jr., "Poetry and Morals: A Relation Reargued," in *The New Orpheus*, p. 252; Frederick Pottle, "The Moral Evaluation of Literature," in *Religion and Modern Literature: Essays in Theory and Criticism*, ed. G. B. Tennyson and Edward E. Ericson, Jr. (Grand Rapids: William B. Eerdmans, 1975), p. 99.

[36]Foerster, p. 69.

[37]John Milton, *Apology for Smectymnuus*, in *John Milton: Complete Poems and Major Prose*, ed. Merritt Y. Hughes (New York: Odyssey Press, 1957), p. 693.

[38]Werner Jaeger, *Paideia: the Ideals of Greek Culture*, trans. Gilbert Highet (New York: Oxford Univ. Press, 1939), I, 34.

[39]Matthew Arnold, "Literature and Science," in *Prose of the Victorian Period*, ed. William C. Buckley (Boston: Houghton Mifflin, 1958), pp. 493-94.

[40]Lewis, *Christian Reflections*, p. 34.

[41]Lewis, *An Experiment in Criticism*, pp. 91-92.

[42]"Squares and Oblongs," in W. H. Auden, *Poets at Work* (New York: Harcourt, Brace and Company, 1948), p. 171.

[43]Chad Walsh, "The Wary Witness of the Poets," *Christianity Today*, 25 Oct. 1974, p. 20.

[44]Walsh, "A Hope for Literature," p. 227.

[45]Stephen Spender, "Can't We Do Without the Poets?" in *Highlights of Modern Literature*, ed. Francis Brown (New York: Mentor,

1949), pp. 152-53.

[46]Lewis, *Christian Reflections,* pp. 33-34.

[47]Harold Lehman, *In Praise of Leisure* (Scottdale, Pa.: Herald Press, 1974), p. 147.

Chapter 3: The World of the Literary Imagination

[1]C. S. Lewis, *An Experiment in Criticism* (Cambridge: Cambridge Univ. Press, 1965), p. 137.

[2]Alvin A. Lee and Hope Arnott Lee, *The Garden and the Wilderness* (New York: Harcourt Brace Jovanovich, 1973), p. 45.

[3]Northrop Frye, *The Educated Imagination* (Bloomington: Indiana Univ. Press, 1964).

[4]Joseph Campbell, *The Hero with a Thousand Faces* (New York: Bollingen Foundation, 1949).

[5]Charles Moorman, *A Knyght There Was: The Evolution of the Knight in Literature* (Lexington: Univ. of Kentucky Press, 1967), p. 33.

[6]C. S. Lewis, *English Literature in the Sixteenth Century Excluding Drama* (Oxford: Oxford Univ. Press, 1954), p. 341.

[7]Northrop Frye, *Anatomy of Criticism* (Princeton: Princeton Univ. Press, 1957), p. 365.

[8]"Archetype and Signature," reprinted in *Myths and Motifs in Literature,* ed. David J. Burrows et al. (New York: The Free Press, 1973), p. 28.

[9]*Psychological Reflections,* ed. Jolande Jacobi (Princeton: Princeton Univ. Press, 1953), p. 47.

[10]Frye, *The Educated Imagination,* p. 97.

[11]This list is an expanded version of my list in *The Literature of the Bible* (Grand Rapids: Zondervan Publishing House, 1974), pp. 24-25, and is indebted to Northrop Frye's essay "The Archetypes of Literature," in *Fables of Identity* (New York: Harcourt, Brace and World, 1963), pp. 7-20, as well as to Frye's *Anatomy of Criticism,* pp. 141-50.

[12]J. R. R. Tolkien, "On Fairy-Stories," in *Essays Presented to Charles Williams,* ed. C. S. Lewis (Grand Rapids: William B. Eerdmans, 1966), p. 73.

[13]Frye, *Fables of Identity,* p. 27.

[14]Frye, *The Educated Imagination,* p. 89.

[15]E. M. Forster, *Aspects of the Novel* (New York: Harcourt, Brace and Company, 1927), p. 143.

[16]Lewis, *An Experiment in Criticism,* pp. 79-81.

[17]Leo Kirschbaum, "Marlowe's Faustus: A Reconsideration," in *Christopher Marlowe's Dr. Faustus: Text and Major Criticism,* ed. Irving Ribner (New York: Odyssey Press, 1966), pp. 90-91.

[18]Elmer Edgar Stoll, *From Shakespeare to Joyce* (Garden City: Doubleday, Doran and Company, 1944), p. 50. See also Stoll's book *Art and Artifice in Shakespeare* (New York: Barnes and Noble, 1933).

[19]Harry Levin, "Literature as an Institution," in *Literary Criticism: An Introductory Reader,* ed. Lionel Trilling (New York: Holt, Rinehart and Winston, 1970), p. 414.

[20]Frye, *The Educated Imagination,* pp. 89-90.

[21]T. S. Eliot, *On Poetry and Poets* (New York: Farrar, Strauss and Cu-

dahy, 1957), p. 93.

[22]Lewis, *English Literature in the Sixteenth Century*, p. 391.

[23]Tolkien, *Essays Presented to Charles Williams*, p. 75.

[24]Ibid., p. 75.

[25]C. S. Lewis, "On Stories," in *Essays Presented to Charles Williams*, p. 100.

[26]Flannery O'Connor, *Mystery and Manners* (New York: Farrar, Straus and Giroux, 1957), pp. 77-78.

[27]Eliot, *On Poetry and Poets*, p. 94.

[28]Joyce Cary, *Art and Reality: Ways of the Creative Process* (1958; rpt. Garden City: Doubleday, 1961), p. 155.

[29]Harvey Cox, *The Feast of Fools* (Cambridge, Mass.: Harvard Univ. Press, 1969), p. 59.

[30]Northrop Frye, *The Stubborn Structure* (Ithaca: Cornell Univ. Press, 1970), p. 17.

Chapter 4: Is Literature Useful?

[1]Sir Philip Sidney, *Apology for Poetry*, in *Criticism: The Major Texts*, ed. Walter Jackson Bate (New York: Harcourt, Brace and World, 1952), p. 83.

[2]Ibid., p. 92.

[3]Ibid., p. 95.

[4]Matthew Arnold, "Wordsworth," in *Criticism: The Major Texts*, ed. Bate, p. 477.

[5]Henry Zylstra, *Testament of Vision* (Grand Rapids: William B. Eerdmans, 1961), p. 59.

[6]C. S. Lewis, "Christianity and Culture," in *Christian Reflections* (Grand Rapids: William B. Eerdmans, 1967), pp. 12-36.

[7]Ibid., pp. 21-22.

[8]Ibid., p. 26.

[9]William J. Handy, *Kant and the Southern New Critics* (Austin: Univ. of Texas Press, 1963).

[10]Sidney, p. 83.

[11]C. S. Lewis, *An Experiment in Criticism* (Cambridge: Cambridge Univ. Press, 1965), pp. 84-85.

[12]Handy, p. 29.

[13]Allen Tate, *Collected Essays* (Denver: Alan Swallow, 1959), p. 8.

[14]Handy, p. 71.

[15]Cleanth Brooks, *Modern Poetry and the Tradition* (Chapel Hill: Univ. of North Carolina Press, 1939), pp. 101-02.

[16]Samuel T. Coleridge, *Biographia Literaria*, ch. IV, in *The Norton Anthology of English Literature*, ed. M. H. Abrams et al., 3rd ed. (New York: W. W. Norton, 1974), II, p. 350.

[17]Joseph Conrad, "Preface" to *The Nigger of the Narcissus* (New York: Collier Books, 1962), p. 19.

[18]Flannery O'Connor, *Mystery and Manners*, ed. Sally and Robert Fitzgerald (New York: Farrar, Straus and Giroux, 1957), p. 84.

[19]Mark Twain, *Life on the Mississippi*, ch. 30 (New York: New American Library, 1961), p. 190.

[20]William Wordsworth, "Composed upon Westminster Bridge,

September 3, 1802."

[21]O'Connor, *Mystery and Manners*, p. 73.

[22]Cleanth Brooks, *The Well Wrought Urn* (New York: Harcourt, Brace and World, 1947), pp. 192-214.

[23]John Milton, *Paradise Lost*, Book 4, lines 639-56; quoted from *The Complete Poetical Works of John Milton*, ed. Douglas Bush (Boston: Houghton Mifflin Company, 1965), p. 290.

[24]Graham Greene, *The Lost Childhood* (New York: Viking Press, 1952), p. 79.

[25]*Art and Reality: Ways of the Creative Process*, ed. Joyce Cary (1958; rpt. Garden City: Doubleday, 1961), p. 127.

[26]Nathan A. Scott, Jr., "The Modern Experiment in Criticism: A Theological Appraisal," in *The New Orpheus: Essays toward a Christian Poetic*, ed. Scott (New York: Sheed and Ward, 1964), p. 155. Scott's essay is a particularly balanced attempt to do justice to both the artistic autonomy and philosophic "vision" or "belief" of a literary work.

[27]Ibid., p. 160.

[28]Richard Stevens and Thomas J. Musial, *Reading, Discussing, and Writing about the Great Books* (Boston: Houghton Mifflin, 1970). Also excellent is James Sire's *The Universe Next Door: A Basic World View Catalog* (Downers Grove: InterVarsity Press, 1976), which defines what a world view is and then analyzes seven major world views.

[29]Stevens and Musial, p. 116.

[30]*The New Orpheus*, ed. Scott, pp. 156, 163.

[31]Cleanth Brooks, "Implications of an Organic Theory of Poetry," in *Literature and Belief*, ed. M. H. Abrams (New York: Columbia Univ. Press, 1958), p. 68.

[32]Stevens and Musial, p. 24.

[33]C. S. Lewis, *English Literature in the Sixteenth Century Excluding Drama* (Oxford: Oxford Univ. Press, 1954), p. 331.

[34]All quotations from *The Scarlet Letter* have been taken from *The Scarlet Letter and Other Tales of the Puritans*, ed. Harry Levin (Boston: Houghton Mifflin, 1960).

[35]Joseph Summers, *The Muses's Method: An Introduction to Paradise Lost* (New York: W. W. Norton, 1962), p. 30.

[36]Darrel Abel, "Hawthorne's Hester," *College English*, 13 (1952), 304.

[37]Randall Stewart, *American Literature and Christian Doctrine* (Baton Rouge: Louisiana State Univ. Press, 1958), p. 88.

[38]Amos Wilder, *Modern Poetry and the Christian Tradition* (New York: Charles Scribner's Sons, 1952), p. 30.

[39]Joseph Schwartz, "Nathaniel Hawthorne, 1804-1864: God and Man in New England," in *American Classics Reconsidered: A Christian Appraisal*, ed. Harold C. Gardiner (New York: Charles Scribner's Sons, 1958), pp. 126-27.

Chapter 5: A Christian Approach to Literary Criticism

[1]Matthew Arnold, "The Function of Criticism at the Present Time," in *Criticism: The Major Texts*, ed. Walter Jackson Bate (New York: Harcourt, Brace and World, 1952), p. 452.

²Cleanth Brooks, "Forward" to *Critiques and Essays in Criticism, 1920-1948*, ed. Robert W. Stallman (New York: Ronald Press, 1949), p. xx.

³T. S. Eliot, *On Poets and Poetry* (New York: Farrar, Straus and Cudahy, 1957), p. 130.

⁴Morris Weitz, *Hamlet and the Philosophy of Literary Criticism* (1964; rpt. Cleveland: World Publishing Company, 1966).

⁵I do not deny that Christian criticism is sometimes too given to evaluation or judgment, but in general scholars who dislike Christian criticism have been entirely too paranoid, labeling as judgment what is actually a description of a work's adherence or lack of adherence to Christian belief. Even more objectionable is the way in which many critics attack the methodology of Christian criticism when it is clear that they merely disagree with the conclusion or interpretation to which a given religious critic has come.

⁶Leo Kirschbaum, *The Plays of Christopher Marlowe* (Cleveland: World Publishing Company, 1962), p. 103.

⁷Kirschbaum, p. 103.

⁸T. S. Eliot "Religion and Literature," in *The New Orpheus*, ed. Nathan A. Scott, Jr. (New York: Sheed and Ward, 1964), p. 223.

⁹Irving Ribner, *Patterns in Shakespearian Tragedy* (London: Methuen, 1960), p. 155.

¹⁰Walter Clyde Curry, *Shakespeare's Philosophical Patterns* (Baton Rouge: Louisiana Univ. Press, 1937), p. 92.

¹¹Roland M. Frye, *Shakespeare and Christian Doctrine* (Princeton: Princeton Univ. Press, 1963), pp. 254-55.

¹²Herbert R. Coursen, Jr., *Christian Ritual and the World of Shakespeare's Tragedies* (Lewisburg: Bucknell Univ. Press, 1976), pp. 314-73.

¹³Peter Milward, *Shakespeare's Religious Background* (Bloomington: Indiana Univ. Press, 1973), pp. 102-03.

¹⁴Jane H. Jack, "Macbeth, King James, and the Bible," *ELH*, 22 (1955), 179.

¹⁵Richmond Noble, *Shakespeare's Biblical Knowledge and Use of the Book of Common Prayer* (London: Society for Promoting Christian Knowledge, 1935), p. 233.

¹⁶Roy Walker, *The Time Is Free* (London: Andrew Dakers, 1949), p. 179.

¹⁷Coursen, pp. 318, 328.

¹⁸Paul N. Siegel, *Shakespearean Tragedy and the Elizabethan Compromise* (New York: New York Univ. Press, 1957), p. 144.

¹⁹Harold C. Goddard, *The Meaning of Shakespeare* (Chicago: Univ. of Chicago Press, 1951), pp. 514-15.

²⁰Roy W. Battenhouse, *Shakespearean Tragedy: Its Art and Its Christian Premises* (Bloomington: Indiana Univ. Press, 1969), p. 72.

²¹J. A. Bryant, Jr., *Hippolyta's View: Some Christian Aspects of Shakespeare's Plays* (Lexington: Univ. of Kentucky Press, 1961), pp. 163, 165.

²²Jack, pp. 173-93.

²³Harold S. Wilson, *On the Design of Shakespearian Tragedy* (Toronto: Univ. of Toronto Press, 1957), p. 52.

²⁴George H. Morrison, *Christ in Shakespeare* (London: James Clarke,

1928), p. 68.

[25]Virgil K. Whitaker, *Shakespeare's Use of Learning* (San Marino: Huntington Library, 1953), p. 299.

[26]Helen Gardner, *Religion and Literature* (New York: Oxford Univ. Press, 1971), p. 86.

[27]M. D. H. Parker, *The Slave of Life: A Study of Shakespeare and the Idea of Justice* (London: Chatto and Windus, 1955), p. 162.

[28]G. R. Elliott, *Dramatic Providence in Macbeth* (Princeton: Princeton Univ. Press, 1958), pp. x, 7.

[29]Milward, pp. 102-03.

[30]Roland Frye, *Shakespeare and Christian Doctrine*, p. 7. Ivor Morris, *Shakespeare's God: The Role of Religion in the Tragedies* (London: George Allen and Unwin, 1972), is guilty of this same troublesome use of the term "secular" in dismissing Christian criticism of Shakespearean tragedy.

[31]Frye, *Shakespeare and Christian Doctrine*, p. 255.

[32]R. P. Blackmur, "Religion and the Intellectuals," *Partisan Review*, 17 (1950), 227.

[33]This is the figure of S. L. Bethell, "Shakespeare's Imagery: The Diabolic Images in *Othello*," *Shakespeare Survey*, 5 (1952), 68.

[34]These phrases are, respectively, by Harold S. Wilson (p. 212); Roy Battenhouse (p. 301); Virgil K. Whitaker, *The Mirror up to Nature* (San Marino: Huntington Library, 1965), p. 273; Walter Clyde Curry (passim) and Irving Ribner (p. 9).

[35]Battenhouse, *Shakespearean Tragedy: Its Art and Its Christian Premises*, p. 138.

[36]One source that documents this commonplace of intellectual history is Herschel Baker, *The Image of Man: A Study of the Idea of Human Dignity in Classical Antiquity, the Middle Ages, and the Renaissance* (1947; rpt. New York: Harper and Row, 1961).

[37]Alexander Pope, *An Essay on Man*, Epistle III, 217-18.

[38]John Calvin, *Institutes of the Christian Religion*, ed. John T. McNeill (Philadelphia: Westminster Press, 1960), I, 258.

[39]All quotations from the play have been taken from the new Arden Edition of William Shakespeare, *Macbeth*, 9th ed., ed. Kenneth Muir (New York: Random House, 1962).

[40]Kenneth Muir, "Introduction" to the Arden Edition of *Macbeth*, p. lii.

[41]Whitaker, p. 265.

[42]Dorothy L. Sayers, "Introduction" to *The Comedy of Dante Alighieri: Hell* (Baltimore: Penguin, 1949), p. 11.

[43]Roland Frye, "Introduction" to *The Bible: Selections from the King James Version for Study as Literature* (Boston: Houghton Mifflin, 1965), p. xxv.

[44]Roland Frye, *Shakespeare and Christian Doctrine*, p. 8.

[45]Siegel, p. 87.

[46]Wilson, p. 70.

[47]G. Wilson Knight, *The Wheel of Fire* (1930; rpt. Cleveland: World Publishing Company, 1957), p. 140.

[48]Wilson, p. 74.

[49]Eliot, "Religion and Literature," p. 223.

[50]Allen Tate, *Reason in Madness* (New York: G. P. Putnam's Sons, 1941), p. 154.

[51]Donald A. Stauffer, "Introduction" to *The Intent of the Critic* (Princeton: Princeton Univ. Press, 1941), p. 29.

[52]S. L. Bethell, *Essays on Literary Criticism and the English Tradition* (London: Dennis Dobson, 1948), pp. 24-25.

[53]Douglas Bush, "Tradition and Experience," in *Literature and Belief*, ed. M. H. Abrams (New York: Columbia Univ. Press, 1958), pp. 31-52. The volume in which this essay appears is probably the "standard" source on the problem of literature and belief.

[54]Ibid., pp. 40-41.

[55]Ibid., p. 49.

[56]Ibid., p. 52.

[57]C. S. Lewis, *A Preface to Paradise Lost* (Oxford: Oxford Univ. Press, 1942), pp. 63-64.

[58]Ibid., p. 63.

[59]I. A. Richards's theories are contained in three books: *Principles of Literary Criticism* (New York: Harcourt Brace, 1925); *Science and Poetry* (New York: W. W. Norton, 1926); *Practical Criticism* (New York: Harcourt Brace, 1929).

[60]Richards, *Science and Poetry*, p. 72.

[61]A. C. Bradley, *Oxford Lectures on Poetry* (London: Oxford Univ. Press, 1909), p. 5.

[62]Nathan Scott, "Vision in the Poetic Act," in *Literature and Belief*, ed. Abrams, p. 129.

[63]C. S. Lewis, *An Experiment in Criticism* (Cambridge: Cambridge Univ. Press, 1965), pp. 136-37.

[64]Lewis, *A Preface to Paradise Lost*, p. 64.

[65]Lewis, *An Experiment in Criticism*, p. 138.

[66]Samuel Johnson, "Life of Gray," in *Criticism: The Major Texts*, ed. Bate, p. 239.

[67]W. H. Auden, "Criticism in a Mass Society," in *The Intent of the Critic*, ed. Stauffer, p. 140.

[68]Yvor Winters, *In Defense of Reason* (New York: Swallow Press, 1947), p. 476.

[69]John Crowe Ransom, *The New Criticism* (Norfolk: New Directions, 1941), p. 208.

[70]Lewis, *An Experiment in Criticism*, p. 82.

[71]Eliot, "Religion and Literature," p. 223.

[72]John Dryden, "Preface to Fables, Ancient and Modern," in *Criticism: The Major Texts*, ed. Bate, p. 167.

Chapter 6: What Is Christian Literature?

[1]I realize that the term "Christian literature" raises troublesome associations for some people, and I myself feel the awkwardness of the phrase in many of the contexts in which it is used. But I know of no other term by which to identify literature that conforms to the Christian view of reality, as distinct from literature that does not. Whatever one thinks of the term, the issues that it is designed

to cover are real and important.

2W. H. Auden's statement appears in "Postscript: Christianity and Art," in *The New Orpheus*, ed. Nathan A. Scott, Jr. (New York: Sheed and Ward, 1964), p. 76.

3Chad Walsh, "A Hope for Literature," in *The Climate of Faith in Modern Literature*, ed. Nathan A. Scott, Jr. (New York: Seabury Press, 1964), p. 232.

4Roy W. Battenhouse, "The Relation of Theology to Literary Criticism," in *Religion and Modern Literature*, ed. G. B. Tennyson and Edward E. Ericson, Jr. (Grand Rapids: William B. Eerdmans, 1975), p. 91.

5Flannery O'Connor, *Mystery and Manners*, ed. Sally and Robert Fitzgerald (New York: Farrar, Straus and Giroux, 1957), pp. 174, 196.

6Harold Bloom, *The Visionary Company* (Garden City: Doubleday, 1963), p. 148. One of the main thrusts of M. H. Abrams's book *Natural Supernaturalism* (New York: W. W. Norton, 1971) is to show the extent to which the writings of Wordsworth "transpose... the design, concepts, and images of Biblical history and prophecy" from their original meaning.

7Chad Walsh, *From Utopia to Nightmare* (New York: Harper and Row, 1962), p. 138.

8Aldous Huxley, *Brave New World* (New York; Harper and Row, 1932), p. 161.

9John Calvin, *Institutes of the Christian Religion*, ed. John T. McNeill (Philadelphia: Westminster Press, 1960), I, 273-75.

10Calvin, *Commentaries on the Epistles to Timothy, Titus, and Philemon*, trans. William Pringle (Grand Rapids: William B. Eerdmans, 1948), pp. 300-01.

11M. B. McNamee, "*Beowulf*—An Allegory of Salvation?" *Journal of English and Germanic Philology*, 59 (1960), 190-207; rpt. *An Anthology of Beowulf Criticism*, ed. Lewis E. Nicholson (Notre Dame: Univ. of Notre Dame Press, 1963), pp. 331-52.

12Gerald G. Walsh, *Medieval Humanism* (New York: Macmillan, 1942), pp. 45-46.

13For documentation, see, for example, Douglas Bush, *Mythology and the Renaissance Tradition in English Poetry*, rev. ed. (New York: W. W. Norton, 1963), pp. 5-22.

14F. A. Blackburn, "The Christian Coloring in the *Beowulf*," *PMLA*, 12 (1897), 205-25; rpt. *An Anthology of Beowulf Criticism*, ed. Nicholson, pp. 1-21.

15Cleanth Brooks, *The Hidden God* (New Haven: Yale Univ. Press, 1963), pp. 71-72.

16See especially O'Connor's essays entitled "Novelist and Believer" and "Catholic Novelists and Their Readers," in *Mystery and Manners*.

17Walsh, "A Hope for Literature," p. 232.

18O'Connor, *Mystery and Manners*, pp. 175, 27 respectively.

19Ibid., pp. 156-57.

20Ibid., p. 167.

21Ibid., p. 32.
22Eliot, "Religion and Literature," p. 226.
23Rod Jellema, "Poems Should Stay Across the Street from the Church," *Christianity Today*, 4 June 1976, p. 15.
24For a good discussion of the problems facing the Christian writer, see John Leax, "Unwelcoming the Christian Poet," *Christianity Today*, 12 Apr. 1974, pp. 16-18.

Chapter 7: Modern Literature and the Christian Reader
1Henry Zylstra, *Testament of Vision* (Grand Rapids: William B. Eerdmans, 1961), p. 5.
2T. S. Eliot, "Religion and Literature," in *The New Orpheus*, ed. Nathan A. Scott, Jr. (New York: Sheed and Ward, 1964), pp. 227-31.
3Ibid., pp. 233-34.
4Ibid., p. 228.
5Ibid., p. 233.
6Flannery O'Connor, *Mystery and Manners* (New York: Farrar, Straus and Giroux, 1957), p. 148.
7Eliot, p. 231.
8Edward C. Hobbs, "The Gospel in the So-Called Secular Drama," in *Christian Faith and the Contemporary Arts*, ed. Finley Eversole (Nashville: Abingdon Press, 1957), p. 147.
9Harold C. Gardiner, *Norms for the Novel*, rev. ed. (Garden City: Hanover House, 1960), p. 41.
10Irving and Cornelia Sussman, *How to Read a Dirty Book* (Chicago: Franciscan Herald Press, 1966), pp. 12-13.
11Harry Blamires, *The Christian Mind* (London: S.P.C.K., 1966), p. 45.
12Calvin Seerveld, *A Christian Critique of Art* (St. Catharines, Ontario: Association for Reformed Scientific Studies, 1963), p. 52.
13Roland M. Frye, *Perspective on Man: Literature and the Christian Tradition* (Philadelphia: Westminster Press, 1961), p. 64.
14Edmund Fuller, *Man in Modern Fiction* (New York: Vintage, 1949), p. 90.
15Ibid., pp. 84-85.
16Will Durant, "Man Is Wiser than Any Man," *Reader's Digest*, Nov. 1968, p. 68. '
17Louis A. Rongione, as quoted in Gardiner, *Norms for the Novel*, pp. 43-44.
18Frank Gaebelein, *A Varied Harvest* (Grand Rapids: William B. Eerdmans, 1967), p. 116.
19Harry Blamires, p. 98.
20Ibid., pp. 96, 100.
21William Wordsworth, "Tintern Abbey," line 140.
22Virginia Mollenkott, *Adamant and Stone Chips* (Waco: Word Books, 1967), p. 94.
23Ibid., p. 81.
24Roland Frye, *Perspective on Man*, p. 84.
25Hilda Graef, *Modern Gloom and Christian Hope* (Chicago: Henry Regnery Company, 1959), p. vii.
26Gaebelein, p. 106.

[27]Addison Leitch, "Art Is Long," *Christianity Today*, 10 Oct. 1969, p. 58.

[28]C. S. Lewis, *An Experiment in Criticism*, p. 68.

[29]C. S. Lewis, *Christian Reflections*, p. 16.

Chapter 8: The Bible and the Study of Literature

[1]Northrop Frye, *The Educated Imagination* (Bloomington: Indiana Univ. Press, 1964), pp. 110-11.

[2]William R. Mueller, *The Prophetic Voice in Modern Fiction* (New York: Association Press, 1959), p. 17.

[3]T. R. Henn, *The Bible as Literature* (New York: Oxford Univ. Press, 1970), p. 258.

[4]C. S. Lewis, *Reflections on the Psalms* (London: Geoffrey Bles, 1958), p. 3.

[5]Leland Ryken, *The Literature of the Bible* (Grand Rapids: Zondervan, 1974).

[6]I have argued this point at length in "Literary Criticism of the Bible: Some Fallacies," in *Literary Interpretations of Biblical Narratives*, ed. Kenneth R. R. Gros Louis (Nashville: Abingdon Press, 1974), pp. 24-40; and "Analyzing the Story of Abraham: Biblical Scholarship or Literary Criticism?" *Christianity and Literature*, Summer 1975, pp. 15-39. For a Bible-as-literature curriculum that is genuinely literary in approach, see the program of Literature of the Bible, Inc., Box 138, Zeeland, MI 49464.

[7]James H. Sims, *The Bible in Milton's Epics* (Gainesville: Univ. of Florida Press, 1962).

[8]John R. May, *Toward a New Earth: Apocalypse in the American Novel* (Notre Dame: Univ. of Notre Dame Press, 1972).

[9]Edmund Spenser, "Epithalamion;" quoted from *The Poem: An Anthology*, ed. S. B. Greenfield and A. K. Weatherhead (New York: Appleton-Century-Crofts, 1968), p. 51.

[10]*Biblical Images in Literature*, ed. Roland Bartel (Nashville: Abingdon Press, 1975).

[11]Amos Wilder, "Art and Theological Meaning," in *The New Orpheus*, ed. Nathan A. Scott, Jr. (New York: Sheed and Ward, 1964), pp. 407, 409.

[12]J. B. Phillips, *New Testament Christianity* (New York: Macmillan, 1956), pp. 48-49.

[13]Mueller, p. 25.

[14]Francis Thompson, "Books That Have Influenced Me," in *The Bible Read as Literature*, ed. Mary Esson Reid (Cleveland: Howard Allen, 1959), p. 177.

[15]Gerhard von Rad, *Old Testament Theology*, trans. D. M. G. Stalker (New York: Harper and Brothers, 1962), I, 420-21.

[16]Dorothy Sayers, *Christian Letters to a Post-Christian World*, ed. Roderick Jellema (Grand Rapids: William B. Eerdmans, 1969), p. 70.

[17]Ryken, *The Literature of the Bible*, pp. 95-106.

[18]Edwin M. Good, *Irony in the Old Testament* (Philadelphia: Westminster, 1965), pp. 56-80.

[19]Dan Otto Via, Jr., *The Parables: Their Literary and Existential Dimension* (Philadelphia: Fortress Press, 1967), pp. 93-144.

[20]Rolland N. Hein, "A Biblical View of the Novel," *Christianity Today*, 5 Jan. 1973, pp. 17-19.

[21]Northrop Frye, *Fables of Identity* (New York: Harcourt, Brace and World, 1963), p. 36.

[22]Northrop Frye, *Anatomy of Criticism*, p. 136.

[23]Ibid., p. 135.

[24]Arthur Koestler, *The God That Failed*, ed. Richard Crossman (New York: Harper and Brothers, 1949), p. 16.

[25]Nathan A. Scott, Jr., *Modern Literature and the Religious Frontier* (New York: Harper and Brothers, 1958), pp. 71-83.

[26]Marion A. Fairman, *Biblical Patterns in Modern Literature* (Cleveland: Dillon/Liederbach, 1972), p. 35.

[27]Honor Matthews, *The Primal Curse: The Myth of Cain and Abel in the Theatre* (New York: Schocken Books, 1967), p. 18.

[28]Roy Battenhouse, "Shakespearean Tragedy: A Christian Interpretation," in *The Tragic Vision and the Christian Faith*, ed. Nathan A. Scott, Jr. (New York: Association Press, 1957), pp. 85-86.

[29]Frye, *The Educated Imagination*, p. 111.

[30]Frye, *Anatomy of Criticism*, p. 140.

[31]Ibid., pp. 316, 325.

[32]Fairman, p. 34.

Chapter 9: Christianity and Literature

[1]Amos Wilder, *Modern Poetry and the Christian Tradition* (New York: Charles Scribner's Sons, 1952), p. 9. Sallie M. TeSelle, *Literature and the Christian Life* (New Haven: Yale Univ. Press, 1966), criticizes both Wilder and Nathan Scott for their "obscurity in the definition of religion" and for not taking seriously the differences between religion and art.

[2]Giles Gunn, "Introduction" to *Literature and Religion* (New York: Harper and Row, 1971), p. 13.

[3]C. S. Lewis, *English Literature in the Sixteenth Century Excluding Drama* (Oxford: Oxford Univ. Press, 1954), pp. 26, 28.

[4]J. Hillis Miller, "Literature and Religion," in *Religion and Modern Literature*, ed. G. B. Tennyson and Edward E. Ericson, Jr. (Grand Rapids: William B. Eerdmans, 1975), p. 34.

[5]Sallie TeSelle, p. 16.

[6]Charles Glicksberg, *Literature and Religion: A Study in Conflict* (Dallas: Southern Methodist Univ. Press, 1960), p. 227.

[7]Flannery O'Connor, *Mystery and Manners* (New York: Farrar, Straus and Giroux, 1957), p. 192.

[8]Alan Paton and Liston Pope, "The Novelist and Christ," *Saturday Review*, 4 Dec. 1954, p. 15. The statement was made about novelists, but it applies equally to literary critics.

[9]Joseph H. Summers, "Christian Literary Scholars," in *Religion and Modern Literature*, ed. Tennyson and Ericson, p. 109.

[10]Roland Frye, *Perspective on Man* (Philadelphia: Westminster Press, 1961), p. 84.

[11]John Killinger, *The Fragile Presence: Transcendence in Modern Literature* (Philadelphia: Fortress Press, 1973).

Index